Divinity in Things
Religion without myth

I wish to dedicate this book to my partners and my children, who have all given me much more than I have given them.

Divinity in Things
Religion without myth

Eric Ackroyd

sussex
ACADEMIC
PRESS

BRIGHTON • PORTLAND

2 4 6 8 10 9 7 5 3 1

First published 2009 in Great Britain by
SUSSEX ACADEMIC PRESS
PO Box 139
Eastbourne BN24 9BP

and in the United States of America by
SUSSEX ACADEMIC PRESS
920 NE 58th Ave   Suite 300
Portland, Oregon 97213–3786

British Library Cataloguing in Publication Data
A CIP catalogue record for this book is available from the British Library.

Library of Congress Cataloging-in-Publication Data
Ackroyd, Eric.
Divinity in things : religion without myth / Eric Ackroyd.
p. cm.
Includes bibliographical references and index.
ISBN 978-1-84519-333-1 (pbk. : alk. paper)
1. Religion. 2. God. 3. Theology. I. Title.
BL51.A37 2009
200—dc22
                                                                    2009000075

FSC is a non-profit international organization established to promote the responsible
management of the world's forests. Products carrying the FSC label are
independently certified to assure consumers that they come from
forests that are managed to meet the social, economic and
ecological needs of present and future generations.

Mixed Sources
Product group from well-managed
forests and other controlled sources
www.fsc.org Cert no. SGS-COC-2482
© 1996 Forest Stewardship Council

Typeset and designed by SAP, Brighton & Eastbourne.
Printed by TJ International, Padstow, Cornwall.
This book is printed on acid-free paper.

Contents

Prologue

In this book no claim to originality is made. Similarly, no claim is made to finality. I have ventured to say that the last word on truth will be pronounced, if at all, not by religion alone nor by science alone, but jointly by both. The ultimate truth will embrace both science and religion insofar as both are true. If this book posits a way for its realisation, that is all: one must not, and logically cannot, claim absolute certainty for any assumed truth until everything – but everything – is known.

This Hegelian view of truth takes full account of evolution. Truth itself evolves. A claimed truth rendered everlasting by some pretentious all-powerful authority could only be an everlasting lie. That is why Karl Popper cautioned the researching scientist not to be content with demonstrating the truth of an hypothesis, but to make every effort to disprove the hypothesis, as the royal road to further progress in science. Yesterday's orthodoxy, in religion as in science, must be prepared to hand over the baton gracefully to today's explorers. Great truths may come in a flash to an Einstein or a Hawking, as to a great painter or composer; but, no matter what the circumstances of the birth of an idea, the validity of the idea must never be taken altogether for granted.

If I have rejected or modified some conventional religious formulations, the motive for doing so has been a positive one. Any serious attempts to walk more closely with truth requires a willingness to relinquish any previously held beliefs that have actually obscured the truth. At the same time it makes me profoundly sad to contemplate the present state of the Christian Church, and particularly that branch of it – the Church of England – that was once a thinking person's church. Perhaps this book will enable some devotees of 'western' forms of religion to adopt a more relaxed, less dogmatic attitude and open themselves to the all-indwelling spirit that transcends everything that is particularist, exclusivist and therefore divisive. The most self-damning claim a religion can make is that it is uniquely true. 'Unique truth' is a contradiction in terms.

The true essence of Christianity (as of other religions) is an awareness of and a close personal relationship with God within oneself. Where does the Christian find God? In church or chapel? But church or chapel, and the liturgy, hymns and homily serve only as aids for the provision or reinforcement of the awareness of God within oneself.

Going within oneself is essential to spirituality. The awareness of God within oneself, however, is not the only component of true religion or spirituality. The other component is the awareness of God within all things – other people, all living creatures, and the whole fabric of the entire universe. This takes us into a further dimension of spirituality, a further reach of the mystical vision which sees the part within the whole and the whole within the part.

Perhaps the Vedanta Hindu will understand all this more fully than the common-or-garden Christian. But we are on the threshold of a new spiritual awakening in the Western world that will transcend the doctrinal and ethical dogmatism of this or that individual form of religion. The author of this book hopes that, though imperfect, his book will nevertheless enable some of its readers to cross this threshold, as well as strengthening (com-forting) those who have already crossed that threshold.

"I hazard the prophecy that that religion will conquer which will render clear to popular understanding some eternal greatness incarnate in the passage of temporal fact."

A.N. Whitehead, *Adventures of Ideas*
(Cambridge University Press, 1933), p. 40.

CHAPTER ONE

Is God Dead?

"Self-abandonment empowers God; but to abandon God himself is an aban-
donment which few human beings can take on board."

ANGELUS SILESIUS (1624–1677)

"Could it be possible? This old saint in the forest has not heard that God is dead!"

NIETZSCHE, *Thus Spake Zarathustra*, Prologue, 2

Religion would appear to be an age-old and universal phenomenon, existing in
all parts of the world and as far back as we can delve into human history and
prehistory. Now, however, particularly in the West but also to a lesser extent
in the East (that is, to the extent that its culture is becoming, at all social levels,
increasingly westernised), religious belief and practice are in decline; and,
whereas we know of no pre-religious phase of human development, it could
well be that we are now entering a post-religious phase. The refusal of Christian
fundamentalists to face up to the prospect of such a post-religious era may be
seen as a panic-stricken burying of one's head in the sand.

That prospect need not fill us with dismay. We may learn from anything
and everything that happens to us, and apparently negative and even catastrophic events are especially apt to bring us – if we let them – to new depths
of understanding, new values, new truths; so we may – and must – learn from
distressing events in the wider world, whether it be wars, global warming, or
disconcerting changes in our *mental* climate, including what may possibly be
seen as the end of religion. And, indeed, when we look carefully and see more
precisely what it is that is declining, and the reasons for its decline, we may
begin to acknowledge that this apparent catastrophe is really not such a bad
thing after all.

"God is dead", said Friedrich Nietzsche (1844–1900). "The greatest event
of recent times – that 'God is dead', that the belief in the Christian God is no
longer tenable – is beginning to cast its first shadows over Europe" (Nietzsche,
1884). Nietzsche probably got the idea from the philosopher Schopenhauer
(1788–1860) (Schopenhauer, 1819) but he might also have got it from the
Jewish-born poet Heine (1797–1856), who had written of "the old Jehovah
[Yahweh, the God of the Judaeo-Christian tradition] preparing himself for
death"; and even before Heine, the English mystical poet and engraver William
Blake (1757–1827) had declared:

"Thou art a Man: God is no more;
Thy own humanity learn to adore,
For that is My spirit of life."

What Blake means here is that God is not outside but within the human being. He is not saying that God no longer exists; rather, that he exists within our own humanity.

Blake may not have had much time for the Judaeo-Christian joyless God of vengeance; but he did acknowledge the God who tells us to look for him in ourselves and in the energy of life.

The concern of Heine was to get rid of all of the old anthropomorphically conceived personal deities, whether Jewish, Christian or ancient Greek or Roman. Nietzsche, however, was particularly keen to announce the death of the Christian God. (As the son of a Protestant pastor, Nietzsche must have had some firsthand acquaintance with the Christians of his day). The main force of Nietzsche's impassioned polemic was directed, not against God as such, but against the life-negating, world-despising, self-denying ethics which the Christian Churches had built upon a warped understanding of God which presented him as the enemy of humankind and of everything that is healthy and life-enhancing. Significantly, Nietzsche spoke highly of Jesus ("only one Christian, and he was crucified"). For Nietzsche, Jesus exemplified what Nietzsche called the "superman", a man who created his own values from within himself, even at the cost of exposing the hypocrisy and narrow-minded legalism of the religious leaders and moral watchdogs of his day, thereby incurring his own death as a threat to the social, and particularly the priestly, order of his day.

The theme was taken up by the outstanding German-born American theologian Paul Tillich (1886–1967), whose thinking on the topic was popularised by the then Bishop of Woolwich, John Robinson (Tillich, 1951 and Robinson, 1963) and has been developed in different ways by the so-called 'death of God' theologians in the USA. One of the latter, William Hamilton, said that Christians would now have to make do with the moral teachings of Jesus, seen as a purely natural human being. Another, Thomas Altizer, claimed Blake as "the first Christian atheist" (Altizer and Hamilton, 1966), but it would have been better – more precise – if he had said, not 'atheist', but 'a-theist'. Blake clearly distinguished the God of theism (which he called "Satan" or "Nobodaddy", a jealous and tyrannical deity) from the Divinity within.

If Nietzsche's ideas influenced Paul Tillich, it was in connection with Tillich's understanding of the function of theology as that of giving answers to the questions raised by contemporary culture. He did not see Nietzsche as a theologian, but as a radical and piercingly intelligent thinker whose reactions to Christianity had to be taken seriously. It was in response to Nietzsche that Tillich began to point the way towards a "God beyond God", that is, a God beyond the inadequate anthropomorphic god image of popular (and creedal) Christianity. God, said Tillich, does not exist: anything that exists comes out of ('ex-ists' = 'stands or comes out of') God. God is 'Being', that from which all existing things derive their existence and without which nothing could exist.

Dietrich Bonhoeffer (1906–1945) spoke of "man's coming of age". By this he meant that, just as a time comes when a father must recede into the background and allow his son or daughter to develop as an independent, self-determining person; so humankind as a whole has reached a stage in its development when it must no longer look to some heavenly-Father figure for guidance, but discover and exercise its own authority, make its own values.

This, I believe, is a true understanding of the present human situation vis-à-vis religion. Tragically, Bonhoeffer did not live to develop his ideas further. (He was executed shortly before the end of the Second World War for his participation in a plot to assassinate Hitler). But I believe he might have said something along the lines of the thesis presented in this book: *that God is within us.*

Theism

What is dead is not God but a way of thinking about God, a way of thinking that has become known as 'theism'. And when I say that theism is dead I mean, not that it no longer exists (theistic religion is still the most popular form of religion throughout the world), but that it is no longer credible, no longer a viable option for any thinking person in the 21st century CE.; and by 'thinking person' I mean anyone who distinguishes merely wishful thinking from rational thinking and refuses to indulge in the former where it contradicts the latter.

There is a very general and commodious use of the word 'theism' in which it includes any sort of belief in God. The opposite of 'theism' in this portmanteau mode is 'atheism', which means not allowing that there is anything in reality corresponding to the word 'God'. But I shall use 'theism' in its more recently acquired sense, in which it refers to a particular notion of God; the antithesis of 'theism' in *this* sense is not 'atheism', but 'a-theism'. If some Christian theologians of the post-Tillich era have actually dubbed themselves 'atheists', it is because they have failed to distinguish atheism from a-theism.

What *is* theism? Eastern theism differs significantly from Western theism. Western theism may be summarised as the belief that, in addition to the things that make up what is called the physical universe, there is one more, which created the universe but is not a part of it; and that this extra, supernatural entity is a person.

What is Wrong with Theism?

What is wrong with theism is, crudely stated, that its god is not big enough for the job. We need to bear in mind that the perceived job specifications for God have changed significantly over the last 150 years or so. In line with revolutionary developments in our understanding of ourselves and the universe, we now require a profoundly different God-concept from that of theism; and it is the purpose of this book to present such a concept. As a first step towards fulfilling that purpose, let us see what the god of theism looks like from the standpoint of our present understanding of ourselves and the universe. Basically this means examining theism from two main perspectives, that of psychology and that of the natural sciences; but it will also involve social, moral and philosophical perspectives.

Theism & Psychology: God as a Person

First, consider theism from a psychological standpoint. Theism represents Divinity, or Ultimate Reality (the ultimate source and explanation of all existence) as . . . a person. But everybody knows that to be a person is to be limited. It is to be this and therefore not that, to be me and therefore not you; to have these characteristics and therefore not those; to be good at some things but not at other things; to be predominantly male or female but not both.

In short, to be a person is to be an individual, and individuality consists precisely in whatever makes us different from one another. In common usage, 'person' is a disjunctive, separative term. Indeed, if there were no qualitative differences between persons and they could be distinguished only by a number tattooed on their foreheads, would we not begin to wonder whether they could properly be called persons at all? Machines perhaps, but not persons.

We should not be surprised, then, if distinctiveness and division were strongly characteristic of Western theism, which treats God as a person. Jews, Christians and Muslims all believe that there is only one god. But do they believe in the same god? These so-called Western traditions share a common Semitic origin and their respective gods may, historically speaking, be traced back to the Old Testament Yahweh; and it might be argued that the differences between these gods are less fundamental than some of the things they have in common. However, the differences are certainly sufficient to warrant the conclusion that, if the god they believe in is one and the same, then at least two of these three theistic groups are seriously misrepresenting that god.

This is borne out by what they say. When we look at the ways they describe this one god, his nature and his will (particularly what he requires of human beings), it is sometimes exceedingly difficult to believe that they are speaking about the same person. Even if these descriptions have some salient features in common (for example, they all speak of a male creator-god who is other than the universe he made) we are still left with the difficulty of explaining how one and the same person could both approve of and disallow polygamy, or pork, or – even more perplexing – how he could have both been and not been incarnate in Jesus of Nazareth. Of course, if God is a person, he can change his mind (as persons do) or be inconsistent or arbitrary (as persons often are) and so lay down different rules for different nations or even for the same nation at different times. But that only underlines the inadequacy of the theistic god-concept and does nothing to soften the contradiction between the Christian belief that this personal deity was uniquely made flesh in Jesus and the Islamic belief that he was never, and never could be, incarnate.

Such contradictions may be attributed to partial human ignorance with regard to a god who, being transcendent, would seem by definition to surpass complete understanding. But it would be naïve to expect Christians and Muslims to accept this simple view and change their doctrines and their styles of worship accordingly. A few intellectual, and a few intuitively spiritual, Christians and Muslims may be liberal enough to accept it; but these would have to be people who have already gone beyond the theistic god-concept and are to that extent no longer typical Christians or Muslims: indeed, they will probably be asking themselves whether they should continue calling themselves Christians or Muslims.

Dogmatism

On the other hand, wherever divinity is thought of as an individual person, two mutually reinforcing processes are discernible. First, the believing community projects its own distinctive character, interests and values on to its god. ("God made man in his own image, and man returned the compliment"). The second process is simply the reverse of the first: the group's distinctiveness having been projected on to its god, the group now has divine sanction for its rules and its values; all its institutions become sacred and therefore untouchable, absolute and unchangeable.

Where a society's laws and customs are acknowledged as man-made there is the possibility of changing them in response to new situations or new scientific or psychological insights and new moral sensitivities; but where they are seen as god-given they are rendered sacrosanct and well nigh immune to change. And what applies to rules and customs tends to apply also to the group's theological doctrines: these, too, become sacrosanct and adamantly resistant to change.

Divisiveness & Dogmatism

In Western theism divisiveness and dogmatism go together. If Jews, Christians and Muslims had looked upon their gods as different masks worn by a one and only Godhead that stands behind and beyond those masks (as is the case in Hinduism) the histories of these religious groups would have been considerably different from what they have been. The Jews would not have been so jealous of their status as the exclusive chosen people of the one and only true god, would not have waged 'holy war' ('kherem') against the Canaanites and other Semitic peoples who chose to remain rooted in the primeval reverence of

Nature; and perhaps they would not have brought upon themselves the terrible nemesis of the Holocaust dealt them by Hitler's Nazis in the name of the Rosenberg myth of another 'chosen people', the 'pure Aryan race'.

Similarly, Christians would not have launched their 'holy' crusades, which were ostensibly intended to win back the Holy Land (which was holy for Jews, Christians and Muslims) from the Muslims but provided opportunities for impoverished sovereigns and noblemen to procure fertile or otherwise lucrative land as well as booty to pay off their debts, not to mention the rank and file soldiers' rape and pillage of Jewish as well as Muslim communities. The title of First Holocaust, says A. J. Coates (*The Ethics of War*, 1997), might be awarded to the first Christian Crusade (which began in 1095 CE). Whether the *number* of Jews slaughtered in the Christian Crusades was anything like the five million or more murdered by Hitler and his Nazis is questionable, to say the least. Perhaps the title of *First* Holocaust should be given to the Turkish killings of approximately one and a half million Armenians in the infamous First World War (Hobsbawm, 1994).

Nor would Christians have persecuted those who expressed opinions that differed from what happened to be the orthodox doctrine at the time. However, it has to be said that some sections of the Christian Church have, possibly in response to humanist criticism for example, shown themselves capable of adopting a more liberal attitude in some areas of belief and behaviour; and it is such signs as this that encourage me to trust that this book may support such people and anyone else who acknowledges that true religion must be a personal quest for truth, not a ready-made substitute for that quest.

The same cannot be said of Islam, where influences flow in the opposite direction. Islam is essentially a theocracy in which the Qur'an virtually determines a nation's socio-political and moral ethos. (Exceptions are few.) Hence the clash between fundamentalist Islam and the secular and materialist Western political regimes. President George W. Bush's wily but rather childish attempts to construct a Christian façade by presenting the war against Iraq as a "crusade" against "evil" and being televised with born-again Christians must not be allowed to obscure the real motivation – the maintenance of US economic world dominance. Incidentally, Muslims commonly refer to Western people as "the crusaders". One remembers singing, as a boy, the hymn,

> "Onward, Christian soldiers, marching as to war,
> With the cross of Jesus going on before.
> Christ, the Royal Master, leads against the foe,
> Forward into battle, see, His banners go . . . "

This hymn, with its unmistakable references to the Crusades, was written well before the First World War and survived not only the wholesale slaughter of young men in that bloody holocaust, but also the massacre of civilians as well as soldiers in the Second World War and was still amongst the most popular hymns in 1950.

Such war-like language might be dismissed as harmless imagery. What is not harmless, spiritually and psychologically speaking, is the notion of an enemy that has to be exterminated. Even if we rightly identify the real foe as within the self, and see 'Christian warfare' as the conquering of wrong thoughts, feelings and attitudes, we should learn from modern depth psychology that this 'enemy' is not something to be suppressed or destroyed; that it appears as enemy only because fear has kept us from making its acquaintance; and that, when seen in the light of reason, it is something valuable for our personal growth. If only nations could see other nations in the same light!

If 'person' is psychologically a distinguishing and therefore a potentially divisive notion when applied to God, it may also be said to be a limiting, restrictive notion. Moreover, to be a person may mean being more or less variable, sometimes behaving well, sometimes behaving badly; sometimes rationally, sometimes foolishly. This is because persons are almost invariably divided internally, as well as being divided from other people and other things. The exception is the person who has discovered, and become united with, the divinity *within*.

Ludwig Feuerbach (1804–72) in his book, *The Essence of Christianity*, tells us that traditional Christianity has projected the human ideal on to a God who exists outside the physical universe; and that, by ascribing all possible perfection to a personal deity, we leave ourselves bereft of value and, consequently, of self-esteem. All glory to God; no glory to Man, just total depravity (à la Calvin).

Compatibility

There is a kind of individuality that is not divisive but constitutes that variety which is "the spice of life", "the rich tapestry of life". This makes life interesting and constantly opens our minds to new possibilities for our own personal development, new values and a consequent change of attitude. I have already said that people tend to be attracted to persons who are in some significant way different from themselves; and certainly some of the closest and strongest relationships are between persons who are, not outrageously different, but significantly different to complement each other and contribute to each other's self-fulfilment. The truth is that the human being achieves fulfilment and completeness by transcending what is purely individual, purely self-ish.

Where personal differences are too big, however, then either prolonged unhappiness or else a split must surely follow. The degree of difference that is tolerable for one person may not be tolerable for another: it depends on how opinionated one is. Where a partner can see only one side of an issue and will not even listen to opinions that differ from their own, there is not much hope for the relationship. In the case of a personal deity, then, we would expect that, the more *dogmatic* the deity (or his worshippers), the more *divisive* he (and his worshippers) will be; or conversely, the more dogmatic the worshippers, the more dogmatic and divisive the god will appear to be.

The fact that humankind consists of individuals, each one unique, no two having quite the same combination of genetic inheritance and environmental influence, makes possible a practically infinite variety. The greater the variety in a species, the greater its chances of adapting to changing circumstances and therefore avoiding extinction; and to the extent that *Homo sapiens* may be seen as the spearhead of cosmic evolution and therefore may be said to hold the fate of the cosmos in its hands, we may say that variety is the key to cosmic fulfilment. (The last statement may be true even if the human race fails to *fulfil* its potential.)

Hence the value of those warnings given by such people as Jean-Jacques Rousseau, George Bernard Shaw and George Orwell, of the all too real possibility – and consequences – of a style of government that would put the masses on to parade grounds (or into classrooms) and drill them and degrade them into a uniform state of ant-like conformity to the will of a ruling class that is mesmerised by power-lust.

Individuality is precious, then, not just for the species as such, or the cosmos as such, but also for the more ephemeral individual. Another instance of this is that we may enjoy the fruits of creativity, whether it be in the realms of technology or science, or literature, drama, poetry, painting, sculpture or music; or, indeed, the fruits of one another's *self*-creativity, what we have made of ourselves, given this or that starting-point and taking this or that route to self-fulfilment. I am not an avid reader of biographies or autobiographies, but each and every one of those I have read has in some way enriched me or stirred me to transcend my present self.

The Divided Self

The self that has been presented by modern depth psychology is a divided self. Freud distinguished three elements or forces in the human psyche: "id", "ego" and "superego", roughly corresponding to instinct, conscious self and conscience. The conscious self must adjudicate between the demands of instinct and conscience.

Jung made several distinctions. The "persona" is distinguished from the "shadow". The persona (originally used of the mask worn by a Greek actor and still used in the 'dramatis personae' – the list of characters in a play) is the rôle we play out (at least in the first half of life) as our chosen way of life, of making a living and making an impact on the world around us. The "Shadow" is that part of our psyche that has not yet been given expression in our conscious life and which, if too long neglected, may cause trouble in the psyche. It therefore must be brought into our conscious life and allowed an appropriate kind of expression. If we do this, the Shadow will cease to be dark and threatening and will instead become a positive force bringing fullness and balance to our psyche. One element in the Shadow is the "soul-image". In a man this is his "anima", the feminine element that must be allowed conscious expression if he is to achieve personal wholeness. In the woman it is "animus", the masculine element in every woman's psyche; again, it must be given appropriate expression in her life if she is to achieve her full and balanced self. Failure to integrate the contents of the unconscious will have damaging effects on the person and possibly on those around him or her. For example, the man whose anima has been kept under lock and key will tend to become a macho male, violent and destructive. The effect of this is well illustrated in the schizophrenic Jekyll–Hyde character. The corporate effect of it is warfare between nations instead of employing reason and tolerance and mutual respect to come to some amicable solution of the problem.

Thus we see that, in the light of depth psychology, 'individual' (= 'indivisible') has become something of a misnomer. It may be compared with the word 'atomic', which means 'unsplittable' but is still applied to atoms even though we know that they have internal components and can be split.

A large-scale example of the split personality is the god of Western theism whose prototype was the Hebrew Yahweh. There were several Yahwehs in the Middle East, but whereas the others were fertility, nature gods, each with a feminine counterpart, the Hebrew Yahweh was divorced from his consort and was entirely masculine. He was a volcano and thunder god who became a warrior[1] – decidedly masculine! – deity who entered a covenant with his tribe or tribal group, the Israelites, a covenant in which, in exchange for their obedience, he promised to give them victory in battle against any would-be aggressors.

Whereas nature-deities were generally benevolent and predictable, Yahweh was characteristically fierce and formidable, punishing his chosen people whenever they allowed themselves to be seduced by a nature-goddess (whom, remember, their ancestors had revered as Mother) by letting them be taken into exile and enslaved by their enemies.

The traditional Christian (and, later the Islamic) all-male god retained something of the fearsome, punitive character of Yahweh, albeit combined with a loving-Daddy element, the latter stemming largely from the example and imputed teaching of Jesus. In a word, the Christian heavenly Father and the Islamic Allah (from the same root as Yahweh, namely, 'yah'), are typically schizophrenic. The Christian god is now angry and jealous, now merciful and forgiving; sacrificing his Son to satisfy the thirst for justice, as a prerequisite for pardoning human disobedience and lack of respect. And does not the doctrine of the Trinity – three persons in one God – immediately suggest a multipersonal being and thus provide a basis for the shiftings between reasonable and irrationally emotional, exemplary and outrageously unethical and inhumane, behaviour?

Yahweh's split personality is underlined in Handel's *Messiah*. In part II, no. 38, a soprano sings, "How beautiful are the feet of them that preach the gospel of peace and bring glad tidings of good things." But the peace is shattered in no. 43, where a tenor declares, "Thou shalt break them with a rod of iron, Thou shalt dash them in pieces like a potter's vessel" – followed by the 'Hallelujah' chorus ('praise to Yah', an abbreviated form of 'Yahweh').

Theism & Cosmology:
A Personal Creator of the Cosmos?

In the earliest Old Testament account of creation, what God (the Hebrew Yahweh) creates is not the universe as we know it today and not even planet Earth, but a garden in Eden, somewhere in Mesopotamia. A second account, centuries later than the first, embraces Earth and Sun and Moon and Stars, but the Earth was flat and square, resting on four pillars. (We are not told what the pillars are resting on.)

When creation could be compared with a potter moulding clay and turning it on his wheel and so producing a nicely shaped pot (the clay being already there – and the wheel!), it may have been credible to think and speak of the creator as a person. If one reads any (readable) book on physics – and there are many to choose from – and is introduced to a universe so vast that our own solar system is, in comparison, a mere speck of dust; so vast that it can be measured, if at all, only by adding hundreds of zeros to a digit, whilst containing constituents so small that they can be measured only by putting hundreds of zeros in front of a digit; one is bound to question – or just to leave out of the question – the possibility that this universe (and any other universes there may be, as yet unknown) was created by a person (whether in six days or not!). (I love the 'six days': it makes one realise that this is a delightful fantasy, not intended to be taken literally.)

Moreover, already a long 'six days' (roughly, 15 billion years) have passed since Hoyle's Big Bang took place, and the creative process initiated by that stupendous explosion of energy still continues; it may be that this big bang was only one of many, with every expansion being followed by a collapse, followed by an explosion, and so on ad infinitum (Andrei Linde's theory referred to by Ferris, 1997). (Hindu philosophy contains such a hypothesis.) The (present) universe is still expanding, and the sound waves of the originative explosion are still detectable. (Is this 'the music of the spheres'?). And creativity has not ceased. The cosmic energy is still active in a still evolving world; it did not leave the world, as the traditional creator-god of theism is said to have done, but is still immanent everywhere and in everything. In other words, we live in a self-creative universe.

The theistic god is static. He has to be, traditional theology says, because he is perfect and any change would therefore be a movement away from perfection towards imperfection. This means the god of theism has no potential. The actual creative power, however – the cosmic energy – is, as you would expect it to be, dynamic. As the mathematical physicist and philosopher Alfred North Whitehead (1861–1947) tells us (Whitehead, 1930), an evolving universe requires a dynamic concept of perfection according to which a thing or person is at any given time as good as it can be expected to be at that time, but is also at any given time capable of becoming better. This applies to ourselves: we are self-transcendent beings, in the sense that we are not doomed to stay forever at our present stage of personal growth, but are able – if we so will – to grow beyond what we are at present. Even taking our genetic conditioning into account. It applies also to the whole cosmos. The pre-Socratic Greek philosopher Heraclitus (c. 544–483 BCE) perceived that everything was in flux and one never stepped twice into the same river. We know that our own bodies are continuously changing, old cells being replaced by new ones, so that even at a fairly advanced age a large proportion of our bodies is quite new.

CHAPTER TWO

The Western Split I

Transcendent Deity, Desacralised Nature

In the history of religion the sky has been a symbol of transcendence. That is why the chief male deity of nature-based religion was identified or associated with the sky and with high places – a mountain or a man-built mound or ziggurat. But this was the physical sky, part of the physical universe; the sky-god, along with the other deities, belonged to the natural world and functioned within it.

However, these sky-gods tended to become more and more elevated, beyond the physical sky and totally remote from all things earthly; consequently they became irrelevant to human needs and concerns. It is as if these gods, in their ascent, had run out of oxygen and could therefore no longer function in any useful capacity on or near planet Earth. They became 'dei otiosi', dispensable.

Such was the fate of those sky-gods that were not firmly anchored by an Earth-Mother consort. And as they vanished into thin air, so did their priests disappear, together with their rituals.

This was a common occurrence in the traditional religions of Africa. In Nigeria the supreme god Olórun ('owner of the sky') became disowned on earth: he has no temples or priests, and even before he had finished making the universe he lost interest in it and left it to an inferior deity to finish the job (which, of course, explains why the world may not be altogether to our liking!).

When a member of the Herero people in South-Western Africa was asked why they offered no sacrifices to their supreme god, Ndyambi, he replied, "Why should we sacrifice to him? We do not need to fear him, for he does not do us any harm, as do the spirits of our dead." The deities that did have relevance were the gods and goddesses manifest in the processes of nature.

Having used the word 'transcendence', one must distinguish two kinds of transcendence. We have just been considering the *supernatural* transcendence of God. But we can also speak of the *cognitive* transcendence of God, meaning that God is beyond – or transcends – our (complete) *knowledge* or understanding.

Philosopher Bertrand Russell declared that an ultimate explanation, which explains everything else, is and must be itself inexplicable. If it were explicable, it would have to be in terms of something else – which would mean that not it, but the something else, would have to be regarded as the ultimate. Similarly, we may say that God – or, as I would prefer to call it, *divinity* – is for believers the ultimate reality from which all else derives not only its existence but also its (ultimate) meaning, but cannot itself be fully comprehended.

The supernatural kind of transcendence typically attributed to the God of Western theism speaks of God as 'out there' or 'up there', meaning that he is not in the natural world. But this is the imputed transcendence of the God who is now dead or dying from a lack of credibility.

If religion is to survive in the West, it will have to return to the divinity that is *within*.

If God is merely 'beyond' or 'totally other', as such eminent Christian theologians as the 16th century Jean Calvin and the 20th century Karl Barth would have us believe, there is logically nothing that can be said about him/her/it. But that did not prevent Barth, in his multi-volume *Church Dogmatics*, from telling us just about everything one could wish to know about God.

One trusts one shall never be numbered among those theologians "who construct elaborate mansions and show us round with the air of God's own estate agents" (Shri Radhakrishnan, 1937). Actually, nothing can be said about a deity that transcends the universe, except that nothing can be *known* about such a thing: to transcend the universe is ipso facto to transcend knowledge.

The gods and goddesses of primal nature-based religion were immanent. They were the forces of nature: wind and storm, volcanic eruption and earthquake, thunder and lightning, the sun whose motion caused day and night and the seasons of the year, the moon whose motion governed ocean tides and the menstrual (= 'monthly') cycle. Divinity was the energy of the cosmos showing itself in fertility, in life in its many vegetable and animal forms, providing food for the gatherers and hunters to take home for their families.

'Primitive' peoples were never secular in the modern sense of the word. They had a deep-seated feeling for the sacredness of nature. Whether in hunting or, later, in farming, nothing was done without divine authority.

These early ancestors of ours worshipped – worth-shipped, respected – nature, and not only knew themselves to be parts of nature but also *lived* as parts of nature, consciously rejoicing in nature's symbiosis. They breathed in the oxygen given to the air by trees and culled their fruits and the indigenous livestock; they also exhaled the carbon dioxide needed by the trees, mourned the death of a hunted animal, and at death they returned their own bodies to Mother Earth who had given them birth.

They enjoyed the delights of sexual union, which was also a participation in the life of the natural world. In some parts of Europe a farmer and his wife might copulate in their fields to reinforce the fertility of the soil and promote the growth of their crops. Not far away, another farmer might sow his crop seeds from a prostitute's slipper, with the same intention – to increase the yield at harvest time.

Primitive people did not objectify their environment. Rather, they *participated* in it and their language was subject to what Lévy-Bruhl called the "law of participation" (Lévy-Bruhl, 1952), by which he meant that it – their language – did not contain the subject–object dichotomy which pervades our modern language and thought. For primal peoples, to perceive or know something was to participate in it and become united with it. (Compare the Old Testament use of 'know' as meaning 'have sexual intercourse with'.)

The Human Estrangement from Nature

"The world is too much with us; late and soon,
Getting and spending, we lay waste our powers:
Little we see in Nature that is ours;
We have given our hearts away, a sordid boon!
The Sea that bares her bosom to the moon;
The winds that will be howling at all hours,
And are up-gathered now like sleeping flowers;
For this, for everything, we are out of tune;
It moves us not . . . "

WILLIAM WORDSWORTH, *"The world is too much with us"*

When Wordsworth said "the world is too much with us" he was not, of course, referring to the (divine) world of nature, but to the world built by man for the glory of Mammon.

Today many of us who live in the West, and an ever increasing number of people in other parts of the world, are estranged from nature. This phenomenon is commonly traced back to the industrial revolution, which began towards the end of the 18th century, and caused thousands of poor people who could no longer find employment on the land to migrate to the burgeoning townships of the northern counties of England. There the mill owners built for them tiny hovels side-by-side and back-to-back in spitting distance from what Blake called the "dark Satanic mills", which blocked out the sunlight and belched black smoke from their chimneys which – together with smoke from the coal-fires of the crowded hovels – produced a noxious 'smog', a fog of smoke that hung over much of the town, though not the residences of the mill owners and the 'better class' of people.

The working poor people in those towns saw little of the natural world – not even a clear sky. Once a year, Sunday schools might organise the transport of their pupils on horse-drawn carts into the nearest patch of countryside, where their young eyes might feast on trees and streams or moorland strewn with glacial rocks and purple heather, and their young bellies on potted meat sandwiches.

Now the smog has disappeared, and probably the Sunday school outings. Most families have a car, so that access to countryside or seaside is relatively easy; others may have a nearby public park where they may lie on the grass or sit on a bench and gaze into the fathomless sky, listen to birdsong and perhaps watch ducks and swans and the ubiquitous Canada geese, and even sail model boats on a pond in a gentle breeze. All are now able to find a place where they can fill their lungs with fresh air and feel joyful in nature's presence.

The sad truth is that the Western human being no longer feels himself a part of nature. We may attribute this estrangement to the influence of science, insofar as science approaches the natural world with a view to understanding it and thereby controlling it and making it serve us. But the estrangement goes back further than the rise of the scientific outlook; indeed it has been said that it was Christianity that made modern science itself possible. It has been suggested that the desacralising of nature was a major factor in the rise of modern science in the West 500 years or so before it took root in those eastern parts of the world where there has been a continuously sustained belief in the presence of divinity in nature (e.g. Cox, 1965). The reasoning behind this suggestion is that the Christian's removal of the divine presence from the natural world swept away the taboos that had prevented humankind from meddling with, or even trying to understand, the working of nature.

The truth is that our primal ancestors *did* understand the workings of nature, the influence of the Sun and moon, the regularity of the seasons, the weather portents – good or bad – written in the sky. But this understanding was inter-fused with emotion: earth was their beloved and worshipped Mother, the originator of all life.

Notably, it is this aspect of nature that has been neglected in Western ethical institutionalised religion, which has presented only the rational aspect of nature, that of law and order. (Before those transcendent sky-gods disappeared altogether, they functioned as the maintainers of law in cosmos and in human society.)

Such an assertion may be hard to swallow in the face of the Western Church's persecution and excommunication of eminent astronomers and physicists (including Leonardo da Vinci and, later, Galileo and Copernicus) and the burning or banning of their books and teachings. To this day many evangelical Christians have seen science as a threat to their bible-centred version of Christianity. This is particularly the case in those parts of the USA where evangelicals strongly opposed the teaching of Darwinian evolutionary theory in schools unless it was accompanied by the doctrine of creationism, namely the belief that God created each biological species separately, as seems to be implied by one of the Old Testament stories of creation (which also tells how all this and more was done in six days!).

It should be added that there are other present-day Christians who regard the Old Testament creation stories as simply that – stories, or myths, closely resembling the Babylonian creation mythology. But it cannot be said that the Church's hierarchy has given whole-hearted and consistent support or encouragement for scientific progress. More convincing is the widely held view that it was the humanist Renaissance, not Christianity, that gave rise to modern science.

Be that as it may, the estrangement of human beings from (the rest of) nature goes back long before Christianity came on the scene. It started with the

Hebrew Yahweh. There were several Yahwehs in the Middle East, but the Old Testament Yahweh was the only one without a partner. *The Hebrew Yahweh's divorce is the earliest impulse towards the separation of God from nature.* If Yahweh took upon himself the role of farmer-god when the Israelites occupied parts of Palestine and adopted a settled way of life, living off the land, he was merely an absentee landlord; and if the people would have been happy to adopt the authentic farming-deities – those of the Canaanite–Phoenician population – their religious leaders were prompt and determined in their insistence that the Israelites should worship Yahweh, and him alone. (Here it should be noted that fertility cults often contained what might easily be seen as – and might in fact easily degenerate into – vulgar sexual orgies.)

The sphere where Yahweh might be seen at work was human history, and particularly the history of his Chosen People. Of course, Yahweh created the universe, but only as a potter creates pots. Just as the potter does not indwell his pots (except figuratively), so Yahweh does not dwell within the universe. He is the prototype Western god; the traditional Christian God and Islamic Allah are likewise transcendent. The universe is altogether outside this Western god and he is totally outside it.

Now we must look at the transcendent Yahweh's legacy in Christendom with specific regard to the desacralising of nature.

Does not the absolute transcendence of the western god suffice to explain this desacralisation? Does not God's absence from nature amount in itself to a secularisation or profanation[1] of nature? Yes, so it would seem; but it still leaves open the possibility that people might regard the natural world as untouchable – simply because God made it, no matter where this God lives. Nowadays, however, in the light of a fairly secure scientific account of natural evolution – not only in the biosphere (as in Darwin) but also in the lithosphere and all the chemical and electro-magnetic activity that preceded and prepared the way for the arrival of life – we must acknowledge that creation is a continuing process that takes place *within* nature, not a series of interventions in nature by some deity outside the natural order.

Since it appears that nature is itself creative, one might conclude that nature is self-sufficient and discard the notion of God, as superfluous to requirements. But then we should still have to account for the (apparent) intelligence of nature and what we may call its 'rightness' – a term I use to embrace rationality and goodness.

And what about the beauty of nature, and its awesomeness? The scientist is aware of such qualities, but for the purposes of scientific study they are either irrelevant or only peripheral. (Beauty, at least in the form of symmetry, features in the mathematics that play a crucial role in nuclear physics and astrophysics.) A religious – joyful, appreciative, marvelling, respectful and reverential – attitude to the world of nature is the response of the *total* human being and therefore emotional as well as intellectual.

This is the essence of religion. It is an attitude towards the universe, towards nature. It does not depend upon or require a supernatural deity. Sociologist Peter

Berger's definition of religion is apt: "Religion is the human enterprise by which a sacred *cosmos* is established" (Berger's italics). Berger takes a sociological view; but if we take 'cosmos' in the commonly accepted sense of 'physical universe', we may gladly accept his definition.

What is most hostile to the conception of divinity in nature is the determined and divisive desacralisation that had its beginnings in the Western world with the Israelite defamation of nature–religion referred to earlier. The religious leaders of Israel forbade the worship of any other gods than Yahweh. Yahweh, they reminded the people again and again, was "a jealous God" not to be trifled with. In this vein is the account (I Kings 18: 19–40) of the contest between the Israelite prophet Elijah and the prophets of the Phoenician–Canaanite god Ba'al Melkart and his consort, at a time when Phoenician–Canaanite culture was threatening to engulf Israel, the invading newcomer. Other attempts to belittle, decry and downgrade the fertility deities abound. The alteration of 'Ba'al-zebul' ('lord of the high place', i.e. the god who dwells in heaven) to 'Ba'al-zebub' ('lord of the flies') is a well-known example. Another – and very early – example may be found in the Yahwist's story of Babel:[2] the Akkadian Bab-el (as in what we know as Babylon) means 'gate of God'; but the Yahwist cunningly uses the similar word 'Babel' to mean 'confusion' (from the root 'balel' = 'to confuse'). Thus, what was originally considered a holy place was reduced to a profane place whose inhabitants Yahweh punished by rendering them incapable of understanding one another, and therefore incapable of conspiring against him.

The snake, popularly believed to be immortal on account of its ability to slough its old skin and replace it with another, was an emblem of fertility associated with the Earth Goddess. It is interesting to note that a bronze serpent was carried by the Israelites in the 'wilderness' (= a place uninhabited or sparsely inhabited by human beings) and eventually found a resting place in the Jerusalem temple. Obviously this was a relic – still much treasured – of their own recent and, it would appear, not entirely abandoned involvement in nature–religion. However, as we see from the biblical story of Adam and Eve, the serpent became a symbolic personification of Satan.

Significantly, William Blake (1757–1827), who revelled in Old Testament myths and symbols, declared nature (from which he excluded human beings) to be "the work of the Devil". The typical Puritan (but not Blake!) did not exempt the human 'natural' bits – namely, sexuality – from this stricture.

The Western Churches Profanation of Nature

As well as inheriting Israelite-Jewish examples of demonising the gods and goddesses of nature, the Western Church added its own confections.

The antlered Celtic Cernunnos, immortalised – one trusts – by the Gundestrup cauldron, became the Devil. Horns had long been associated with fertility gods and goddesses. Diana of Ephesus was depicted as wearing a headpiece whose symbolism was probably intentionally ambiguous, resembling both a pair of horns and a crescent moon, which symbolised respectively either the male and the female deities of fertility, or a female deity who produces food for humankind from both beast and vegetation.

The Western Church was determined to pour scorn on the worship of nature, even in its most benevolent aspects. Any deity with horns – including the seductive Greek fertility god Pan – was to be seen as the Devil.

Much the same applies to the Western Church's adoption and blessing of Celtic 'crosses', which were upright stones and represented the male phallus. Here the Church's motive was probably to seduce people gently away from their paganism, but at the same time demonstrate – again, fairly gently, or should we say cunningly? – that the old practices must give way to the new, or that the new religion was (only) a transformation and fulfilment of the old.

The same questions arise concerning the presence of the Celtic Green Man and Sheela na-gig sculptures in or on churches. Well-known examples are the Green Man heads surrounded by foliage, in the chapter houses of York Minster and Southwell Minster and in the cloisters of Norwich Cathedral (Anderson, 1998). The Sheela na-gig, which appears mostly in Ireland, depicts a woman in a crouching position and holding open her gaping vagina. She is the Celtic fertility goddess, who gives birth to all living things and at death receives them into her womb again for re-birth. One example may be seen on a corbel in the church of Ss. Mary and David, Kilpeck, in Herefordshire. The very fact that such effigies are found in churches means that the Church did not object to them; but do they signify the Church's acknowledgement of the sacredness of nature, or simply a concession to the common people who certainly did recognise the divinity of nature?

One of the fiercest, most violent examples of the Western Church's condemnation of nature-worship was its prolonged witch-hunting, reaching a zenith in the 13th century but continuing into the 18th and 19th centuries officially or unofficially – that is to say, with ecclesiastical authorisation or simply by ignorant and brutal bunches of rustics in search of amusement. The burning alive, hanging or drowning of these innocent priestesses of Mother Nature is one of the cruellest among the Western Church's many cruel crimes against humanity. Some of these women reacted to the Church's hostility and ignorance by mocking the Church's (magical) Sacrament of eating the body and drinking the blood of the dead Jesus, in what became known as the Black Mass. But that was a provoked reaction, not a normal practice among witches.

Perhaps one ought to make a distinction between these European witches and those of, say, Africa. The latter seem to be generally represented in a bad light, as sorcerers who, for a suitable reward, will cast a magic spell upon or poison the food or drink of your selected victim. European witches are known to have had knowledge of the medicinal properties of herbs and other plants and to have produced beneficial potions for the sick or those 'possessed by demons', and no doubt they had the know-how to produce lethal potions; but modern scholars seem to agree that, at least, they have been much more sinned against than sinning. Like Jews, witches have been made scapegoats to carry the blame for the plagues, famine or floods, failure of crops, stillborn babies or any other calamity that befell a community or family. One wonders if this is not also the case in Africa.

Science and Desacralisation

Over the last century or so the Christian Churches have become more and more aware of the need to care for the natural world. It would seem that, having driven the heathen gods and spirits out of nature, they could now happily resume their role as stewards of God's creation. Unfortunately, some sections of the Christian Church have seen it as part of their stewardship to inveigh against science. This has been especially notable in extremist evangelical protests against Darwin's theory of the evolution of species by natural selection, which was seen as a denial of God's supremacy over nature. Nevertheless, most thinking people in the Christian Churches have found a way of living with science whilst retaining their belief in a Supreme God whose workmanship is evident in the physical universe: whatever science's model of the universe may be, God can be superimposed upon it by anyone who wishes to do so.

We have noted that the rise of modern science has been attributed to the Church's desacralising of nature. But science itself has been seen as an agent, not only of the desacralisation, but also of the consequent abuse, of the natural world. As far as the desacralising of nature is concerned, it is easy to see how this could follow in the wake of a purely objective appraisal of nature. Objectivity demands that the observer should separate himself from whatever he is observing. This means that, to study and understand nature in this way, one must divorce oneself from it. This is the dichotomy that has caused us to regard ourselves as outside and above the natural world – rather like the god of theism.

From the pioneering days of modern Western science, from Galileo and his contemporary, the philosopher René Descartes, to Isaac Newton in the 17th century, the natural world came to be regarded as a lifeless, mindless machine that could be understood purely in terms of measurable objects and measurable forces. Significantly, this measurable machinery was bereft of things that many of us regard as having great significance – such things as colour and smell and taste, beauty and wonder and awe, consciousness and intelligence.

However, as physicist Fritjof Capra has told us, our Western culture, including science, is at a critical turning point (Capra, 1983). Over the last hundred years various branches of science – physics and biology in particular – have made it clear that we human beings are very much a part of nature, interdependent with all other parts of the cosmos and invested with many huge talents and a correspondingly huge responsibility.

A crucial notion here is that of control. Is it science's aim to control the universe, or simply to understand it? A rough but serviceable answer may be given in terms of a distinction between pure science and applied science (or technology). Pure science includes physics (including astrophysics and subatomic physics) and some aspects of chemistry and biology (including marine biology). Applied sciences (or technologies) include the various branches of engineering (civil, constructional, mechanical and aeronautical engineering, and biochemical, biological or genetic engineering).

It is only applications of science in various technologies that may properly be said to be (directly) concerned with controlling nature. Such attempts to control nature are more often than not directed towards improving or safe-guarding human well-being. Whether nuclear weaponry is more likely to improve the human lot than to annihilate humanity is open to question. I know there are some people who are quite sure that the latter effect would be the greatest service we could render to the earth and, indeed, the cosmos. But no kind of war would be needed if only egalitarianism were to take the place of unlimited competitiveness and greed. What if a bit of genetic engineering could generate the moral transformation of humanity that such a fundamental change of heart requires?

After all that, it is appropriate to comment briefly on the contribution made by science to what may properly be called a re-sacralising of nature. Some theo-retical and researching scientists have had what might be called a mystical feeling about nature, or at least a feeling of wonder or awe or reverence; and such feelings are typically a consequence of their scientific investigations rather than a theistic faith carried over from their pre-scientific years. This is hardly surprising. Who is in a better position than the scientists to experience the wonders – the miracle – of nature?

It is true that, in science as elsewhere, familiarity may erode a sense of wonder and awe; but there is nothing illogical in the view that science does not in itself diminish wonder and awe. Certainly, Einstein and Niels Bohr did not think so. Both described themselves as mystics and would have heartily agreed with Teilhard de Chardin's assertion: "Neither in its impetus nor in its achieve-ments can science go to its limits without becoming tinged with mysticism" (Teilhard de Chardin, 1959).

Even those of us who, though not scientists ourselves, try to keep more or less abreast of scientific theorising by reading some of the many books and jour-nals that provide simplified accounts of recent findings, cannot help catching something of that same feeling of wonder and awe – and beauty.

The same applies to those of us who watch some of the many wonder-packed nature films to be seen on UK television. Outstanding have been those given to us by David Attenborough and his team of photographers; more modest and homely, but also filling us with wonder and joy in the presence of nature, are those of Bill Oddie; and there are – and will continue to be – other television programmes that give an insight into the wonders of nature, from the astronomical to the subatomical.

Ralph Waldo Emerson (1803–1882), who placed individual consciousness on a higher level than historical creeds and dogmas, bibles and churches, once said, "I like the silent church before the service begins, better than any preaching." I cannot resist making a comparison between the quiet interior of a magnificent cathedral church and the even more magnificent 'cathedral' of the universe; in both we may feel the presence of divinity. Sadly, however, some of the preaching heard even in a cathedral nowadays might destroy that feeling. Also sadly, some people who live in the countryside or whose employment keeps them in constant touch with the natural world – farmers as well as scientists – may become immune to the beauty and wonders of the sky and sun and rain and trees and wild-life, or the amazing mechanisms within cells and genes, or continental shift and volcanoes and earthquakes, or whatever. Can familiarity make us all immune to the indwelling divinity?

It has been said that the farmer in the Western world has literally lost touch with the soil ever since the horse gave way to the tractor for pulling the previously hand-held plough; whilst the scientist must deliberately distance himself from nature by adopting a purely objective, unemotional attitude towards it. Unfortunately, we have to add that some farmers – those who have kept their egg-laying poultry in batteries where the poultry have little or no room to move and might even lose the use of their legs, are an example – appear to have dealt in a similar way with their own natural emotions, suppressing them so strictly as to cause them to atrophy. Others, largely out of ignorance, have been contributors, e.g. by indiscriminate use of fertilisers and pesticides, to air and water pollution and the degrading of the very soil they depend upon for their living.

One does not expect everyone to follow the example of the Buddhist who offered himself to a tigress to feed her starving offspring, or even that of the Jains who sweep the ground before them lest they inadvertently tread on minute forms of life and filter the water they drink so as not to swallow microscopic organisms. One asks only that we show proper respect for other sentient beings as having the same divinity within themselves as we have.

The Abuse of Nature

It is but a short step from the desacralising to the abuse of the natural world. Science has shortened that step by providing the chemical and biological knowledge that has put into the hands of farmers and others (via a commercially orientated biochemical industry) the tools by which they hoped to increase their production, but which have contributed to the devastation of our planet. Besides the massive and lasting impact of the Chernobyl disaster, one must consider the destructive capacity of those nuclear leaks and accidents that occur in connection with the military uses of nuclear weapons, and, in the long term, the destructive potential of inadequately contained nuclear waste, and we are already looking at the possible destruction of all life on our (beloved?) Mother Earth.

Abusing our planet is abusing the Mother from whose womb all life originates. We are not made elsewhere and deposited on planet Earth, like a plague of locusts, to devour and destroy everything that comes within our reach. But, sadly, that seems to be what is happening: the rape of Mother Earth, the desacralisation that began with Yahweh and was later (unconscioulsy?) confirmed by the Western Church.

Thanks to apparently random (but not uncaused) events within and outside our solar system, the earth received the means of life. The biosphere, the narrow zone that supports life on the earth (water, lower layers of the atmosphere, and parts of the earth's crust), took vast ages to form and seems to have been the result of an awe-inspiring combination of events, including a massive collision that altered the chemical properties of the earth's surface and volcanic eruptions that provided the oxygen needed for human beings and other animals of similar or larger size. That was 2,450 million years ago, long before human beings came on to the scene, but probably preparing the way for the first tiny single-celled creatures, namely, bacteria, which are probably still the most prolific form of life today.

In the first (but chronologically much later) of the two accounts of creation in the book of Genesis (1–2: 4a), Adam was created first, before the flora and fauna; Eve was created last of all – as an afterthought, so to speak – as a fitting companion for Adam. In the much later account the human being (man and woman together) came last in the order of creation and constituted the crown and consummation of all creation. Adam was trusted with the naming of all the other animals. At that time, it was believed that to know the name of something was to have power over it. Thus, Adam was given power over all other forms of life. Add to this the notion of humankind as made "in the image of God" (Genesis 1: 27), and we have the beginnings of the dualism not only of God and Nature, but also of humankind and (the rest of) nature, that is to say, human beings are seen to be on a higher level than other animals, having authority over them, and to that extent detached from nature. Of course the human species may be seen as the culmination of cosmic evolution. On the other hand, it is not impossible that some future species will be superior in every respect – or even just in one, but significant respect. Indeed, such a superior species may already exist elsewhere in the universe. It is also possible that *Homo sapiens* may create by technology such a new and superior species; and, if so, the natural offspring of *Homo sapiens* might eventually become extinct, unable to compete with the new species, unless the new species decided to keep them as farm animals for food or other uses.

Nevertheless, so long as we are 'top dogs' on earth, we are – again, largely by the grace of science but ultimately by the all-pervading cosmic energy – able to influence the future of our planet and even our solar system, or beyond. Scientists and engineers are already planning to send Innovative Interstellar Explorer to the outer edge of our solar system – a mere 10 billion miles away, 550 times the distance between Earth and the Sun! – in order to examine a cloud of mostly hydrogen and helium through which our solar system will be travelling for the next 10,000–20,000 years; and possibly to gain knowledge of cosmic rays that may be influencing the rate of biological mutations on Earth (Anderson, 2007). Perhaps it will not be long before interstellar probes pave the way for utilising extra-terrestrial sources of energy (Tipler, 1994).

All this is thrilling: how magnificent is human intelligence, which is part of the cosmic intelligence that I call 'divinity', but also how scary the implications!

If only we could sustain throughout our life the child's spontaneous untaught wonder at all things, we would not need to seek consolation or contentment or joy or peace or fulfilment in theistic myth and ritual; we would live in a constant state of awareness of the interrelatedness of all things and our own place and rôle on a life-giving planet, within a wondrous and awesome universe – a truly religious and truly moral life of universal love and joy coupled with a glad acceptance of our responsibility to the great whole of which we are part.

Body and Soul

A corollary of the split between God and nature is the dualistic view of spirit and matter, body and soul. "Keeping body and soul together" is an admirable policy: where it is constantly practised there will be no need for psychotherapists and very little need for doctors. 'A healthy mind in a healthy body' was a classical maxim to the same effect. But these are good *pagan* utterances. The split between God and nature in the post-pagan, post-nature-worshipping world was to bring about, particularly in Christianity, a negative evaluation of the animal aspect of the human being.

When selecting his disciples, Jesus chose either unmarried men, or married men (such as Peter) who were willing to leave wife and family in order to live, like Jesus himself, a celibate life. All Jesus' followers were also expected to relinquish the ordinary comfort of domestic life and their customary means of earning a livelihood; instead, they were to live as mendicant monks live, dependent on the charity of the people they encountered.

Albert Schweitzer (1875–1965), who was a theologian as well as physician and musician, put forward a strong case for understanding Jesus' strongly ascetic and world-renouncing ethical teaching as bound up with a conviction that the end of the world was imminent (Schweitzer, 1906). This meant that Jesus and his disciples must prepare people spiritually for the coming day of judgment. The synoptic gospels of the New Testament give ample support to Schweitzer's thesis. The "Kingdom of God" (more accurately, the 'Kingship' or 'reign' of God) may be seen as the main burden of Jesus' message in those gospels; such was the early Church's reverence for those books, that Jesus' mistakenness ("And I tell you this: there are some of those standing here who will not taste death before they have seen the Kingdom of God" (I Kings 9: 27)) was allowed to pass uncensored.

Let us forgive Jesus his error. After all, there was at that time a wave of messianism across the Middle Eastern world, throwing up several putative messiahs. Nonetheless that error must be taken into account if we ask ourselves how much of Jesus' moral teachings has relevance today.

Schweitzer described Jesus' teachings as a 'Notethik', an 'emergency ethic', applicable (only) to a time of extreme crisis. We live in a similar critical situation today, namely, the threat of a global cataclysm wrought, not by God, but by human beings, either with a sprinkling of nuclear bombs or with a rapidly accumulating destruction of the means of life by pollution.

The analogy is a fair one; but going around barefoot, repenting in sackcloth and ashes and living a celibate life would not seem to be the most effective means of dealing with the present-day crisis. Most people would be more apt to look for a solution, not from clergy, but from statesmen, scientists and technologists, with persuasion from non-commercial media.

This is not to say the contemporary world is effectively immunised against all things spiritual or ethical. There are plentiful signs that the world will gladly welcome spirituality and ethics that are based on a recognition of our position of responsibility in and to the awe-inspiring universe and demand that we should renounce, not the joys of sex or other physical pleasures, but any disrespectful attitude towards the natural world that provides these joys.

Bodies can sometimes be a grievous burden, especially in old age, and even from birth, perhaps resulting in premature death – which is in some cases tragic, in others a blessed relief. But this is not to say that our bodies are evil (as Manichaeans and Jansenists and other puritanical souls have averred). Even if diseased or maimed, bodies are products of natural processes in a universe where randomness plays a large part. We just have to realise that what at a physical level is randomness (as in Darwin's "random mutations", which make new species possible) takes in the human being the form of freedom – freedom of will, freedom to choose not only what to have for lunch but also how to live one's life and what sort of person one is going to be – in other words, the possibility of self-creativity. A fine example of such self-creativity achieved to a high degree in a crippled body is Stephen Hawking, who, though seriously disabled by a motor-neuron disease, has become one of the world's greatest mathematical physicists, comparable with Newton and Einstein. Most of us, for most of our sojourn on planet Earth, have good reasons to be indebted to our bodies: first of all, of course, for life itself, but in particular for the exquisite pleasures of sexual congress, and also for the pleasures of eating and drinking, of beholding sky and sea, hills and valleys, trees and flowers and animals of all shapes and sizes, some flying, others running or creeping or swimming; hearing the songs and chirping of birds and the music – soothing and uplifting, challenging, tragic or sublime – composed and performed by specially talented members of our own species. These are just a small sample of the delights made possible for us by having a body. To these must be added the pleasures of reading, thinking, conversing with others, learning the wonders of the universe we live in and even making new discoveries ourselves and sharing them with our fellow human beings, or creating works of art for others' enjoyment and spiritual benefit.

Not only are all those pleasures and delights offered by our bodies, but the body is itself a miniature – but still unfathomed – universe, one that we must not ignore or neglect. Knowing ourselves, our deepest needs and higher aspirations, as well as any blockages we are harbouring – doubt, fears, feelings of guilt or inadequacy that may lead to slothfulness or depression and disable us from realising our positive creative potential – is at least as important as knowledge of the universe of space and time outside us. These two universes, microcosm and macrocosm, need each other, are interconnected and interdependent; both of them demand our attention and care, our reverence and our love and gratitude.

A Christian minister in Australia helped many people – including myself, indirectly – to give up smoking by putting them in mind of the words of Paul! " . . . know ye not that your body is a temple of the Holy Spirit which is in you . . . " (I Corinthians 3:16). Smoking, drug and alcohol abuse, over-eating or following a malnutritious diet, giving oneself insufficient exercise or fresh air, or allowing oneself to be driven frantic by unceasing busy-ness – aptly termed workaholism – and not countering it with periods of stillness and silence, are some of the ways we damage ourselves by losing touch with our body and the divinity within it.

We desperately need to heal the Western split between God and universe and between spirit and body. The human race has suffered enough from the life-denying and body-despising effects of the belief that the world is godless and the body a sink of corruption. Certainly, there are good reasons for withdrawing (if only from time to time) from the getting-and-spending world of greed and conflict: there is a spiritual dimension of human life and we need to immerse ourselves in the divinity that pervades the universe and permeates our soul, or spirit, our unconscious and – it is to be hoped – our conscious mind. To be fully human is to be aware of and responsive to that indwelling divinity which Hindus refer to as "the inner guru". Some of us may feel that this requires an occasional withdrawal, whether in privacy, in a meditation group, or in a monastery. But a determined and full-time denial of the body's natural enjoyments must be seen as a pathological phenomenon which, in religious terms, is describable as a consequence of not having found and related to the divinity – the intelligence and wisdom and energy of the cosmos – that is immanent in one's physical (but also spiritual) self.

The dualism of body and spirit stems from a dualism of nature and divinity. Once we perceive the divinity *within* nature and see nature itself as divine, all feeling of antagonism between body and spirit, physical and spiritual urgings, will be seen as an inner prompting to remedy any imbalance there may be in our expression and enjoyment of these two contrasting, but mutually supportive, dynamic components of our humanity. The Buddha's way – called the Middle Way – is to be commended: keeping watch over our *mental* states, not punishing our innocent body.

The Western world is still passing through an age of extreme individualism in which to be a person is to be an individual, and the more individual – the more different and separate from, competitive and antagonistic with others – the better.

One wonders which came first, the sense of ourselves as individuals, or our sense of gods as individuals? It would seem that individualised representations of the divine preceded any significant degree of human individualisation: tribal gods were individuals, but the *members* of the tribe were just that – functioning parts of a social organism.

Today, as always, there are personal depths of experience in which we feel at one with 'the whole', the social group or nation or civilisation or species; with bees and birds, hills and valleys, all kinds of flora and fauna, sea and sky, sun and moon and multitudinous stars; with the whole world of nature, the total cosmos in all its unimaginable vastness and complexity.

We also have other experiences, more intimate perhaps, but with the same power to take us out of ourselves, so that we leave our self behind and transcend our separateness. Such pre-eminently is the experience of human love and sexual love in particular.

The loss of love and of reverence for our fellow human beings (of all nationalities and skin colours) and our fellow animals and all physical components of the universe is a direct result of that false exaltation of divinity to a sphere that is professed to be infinitely superior to the world of nature. Indeed, the loss of reverence for nature *is* our loss of divinity: the only place we can find God is *within* ourselves and *within* the natural world.

Divinity is a quality and a function of the cosmos. Reverence for the earth is reverence for God, that is, the divinity in all things. An age-long reverence for Mother Earth is not easily extinguished. Fritjof Capra believes that this reverence was rekindled when astronauts passed on to us their feelings when they looked at planet Earth from outer space: "Their perception of the planet in all its shining beauty – a blue and white globe floating in the deep darkness of space – moved them deeply and, as many of them have since declared, was a profound spiritual experience that forever changed their relationship to the earth. The magnificent photographs of the 'Whole Earth' which these astronauts brought back became a powerful symbol for the ecology movement and may well be the most significant result of the whole space program" (Capra, 1983).

Perhaps a word may be added on what may be called the desacralising of the Church. By this I do not mean the various denominations' efforts in modern times to draw people's attention to the social injustices and the ever-widening gap between rich and poor. Evangelical Christians have been commendably active in social work, including the care of drug addicts and the provision of board and lodging for the homeless, thus demonstrating that their Puritanism does not prevent them from showing compassion to life's casualties. Christian monks and nuns have, of course, cared over the centuries for all kinds of people in need, nursing the sick and giving comfort and counsel as well as physical sustenance. That sort of secular concern should be seen as a valid extension of the teaching and example of Jesus.

But the Church was infected in pre-modern times by a different, internal and noxious form of secularisation. I refer to what happened in the 4th century CE when Christianity gained the favour of the Roman emperor Constantine. The bishops of Rome, later to be called popes, modelled themselves on the emperor, who had given them palatial accommodation to match their new-found status as religious head of the empire. They wore the imperial purple and assumed the autocratic style of the emperors, thus taking the first step towards the papal claim to supreme authority over kings and princes – the very same secular world-power that Jesus, when offered it by Satan, firmly rejected.

The imperial purple is still worn by bishops but, happily, the present churches' social concern is a welcome contrast to that papal brand of secularism that was the very antithesis of what Jesus stood for and exemplified. One might say that the Church has taken to heart Marx's moral protest against 'pie in the sky' and has become aware of the need for a social gospel that will seek to redress the inequalities and ruthless greed that disfigure the human world. Tragically, the widespread dismissal of the Church's mythology is likely to detract from people's respect for any social agenda the Church may offer.

CHAPTER THREE

The Western Split II
God's Otherness, Humanity's Degradation

Nietzsche, renowned for his proclamation of the death of God as "the good news", was not unaware of or undisturbed by the possibility that God's death might have a terrible backlash on the human being. Nietzsche's principal endeavour was to lift humankind out of slavery to God into the noble liberty of "the free spirit"; but he came to see quite clearly the possibility that getting rid of God might itself rob human beings of their rightful dignity – by leaving them in a purely deterministic, machine-like and meaningless universe.

Perhaps Nietzsche had been too optimistic in his rating of humanity's ability to lift itself up by its own shoelaces from servile submission to God or Church or Bible to the joyful freedom of self-determination and self-creation.

Nietzsche was both right and wrong. He was right so far as Western theistic belief was concerned. The Church itself tended to take a rather low view of humanity: unable to remove the weight of its sinfulness – only God could do that. Calvin referred to the "total depravity" of humankind, which meant that it could not work out its own salvation. Some Christian priests and ministers have even attempted to use Jesus' crucifixion as a demonstration of the collective guilt of humankind. This stratagem, by which people have been filled with deep guilt and self-execration, has served to reinforce the Churches' hold on humanity. In this way masochism became "an important motif of religious consciousness" (Berger, 1969). Personally I do not believe in a jealous god; but I fear the Church may have been sometimes over-jealous – and over-zealous on his behalf.

Nietzsche was wrong only in so far as he seemed to concede too much. He should not have wavered in his conviction that the human being was *in principle* a free agent, able to make choices independently of others, and to live according to his freely chosen beliefs and values, even if in practice this freedom was more or less compromised by ignorance and lack of education, or by governmental or ecclesiastical pressure to conform to established external authority. Being true to one's humanity means rejoicing in one's human freedom and creativity, *not* burying one's talents but using and developing them. One knows from experience the masochistic effects of an early diet of piety, prayer and discipline such as was offered by *The Imitation of Christ* (attributed to the 14th century Thomas à Kempis) or even the 17th century John Bunyan's *Pilgrim's Progress* insofar as it represents a journey *to* God rather than a journey *in* or *with* God. In fact, in this respect Bunyan typifies the

Church's general orientation to a transcendent out-of-this-world god, with the result that the natural world is bereft of divinity and is seen as simply a place we must be saved from.

Nietzsche's Zarathustra says that God died out of pity for humankind who, comparing themselves with God's infinite perfection, must inevitably see themselves as worthless. "It is a beautiful gift, that of disappearance: which of the parents among us is capable of it? By comparison, sacrificing even only begotten sons is easy." Here, I suggest, we have a much grander, more moral and more logical truth than the traditional Christian notion of human sinfulness requiring God to send his Son to sacrifice himself in order to make amends (to God!) for us (Higgins & Solomon, 1988). But I am afraid that what we see here is just one of many instances of Nietzsche's love of satire.

A true religion, I suggest, is one that sees, experiences and responds to the divinity that is *in* all things. This must include acknowledging and uniting with the divinity within oneself; and this, in turn, means that the religious pilgrimage has to be seen as a journey *within* the all-embracing and all-pervading divinity. To where? To wherever an ever-widening and ever deepening realisation of that oneness takes us. A useful analogy is the relationship between two lovers, which begins as mere togetherness but develops into a oneness. One may also assert that in both cases – the relation with divinity and that of lovers – there is a modulation from one kind of love to another, i.e., from the erotic kind, which is a desire to possess its object, to what might be called a mystical or atmospheric kind, where love is the medium – or atmosphere – in which the relationship exists. This medium or atmosphere may be seen as divinity itself (Buber, 1923).

There is another way in which *science* may contribute to the belittlement of the human being. What I am referring to now is not the science of the Newtonian mechanical model, but contemporary science, which tells us of the Big Bang and a universe that has been expanding for 13.8 billion years or more and is still expanding, its size so vast as to defy all imagining. The planet we live on is infinitesimally small in comparison with the galaxy to which it belongs, and this galaxy is only one of billions; indeed, there may even be other universes of which we know nothing.

"What is man, that Thou art mindful of him?" asked the Psalmist (Psalm 8:4), whose perceived world was miniscule compared with ours. Physically, the human being is puny even when compared with some other animals – lions or whales, for example. But mentally and spiritually this otherwise unremarkable being is surely one of the greatest known wonders of the world; and – most important – this fragile human being is probably the only living thing that can *consciously* participate in and use the divine energy and intelligence that pervade the universe. We may say, perhaps poetically, that it is in the human being and in the human race that divinity can – and does – manifest itself fully. We must add, of course, that it is only the human being that can choose *not* to allow the indwelling divinity to express itself – except perhaps in involuntary features such as physical beauty. But this freedom of will is a mark of the dignity of the human being.

Nietzsche was certainly right in expressing anger at the traditional Christian notion of a god outside the universe, a notion that demonised both nature and, as a part of it, humanity. The German philosopher Ludwig Feuerbach (1804–1872) was equally percipient. His projection theory, which was the predecessor of Freud's projection theory, stated that, in creating God in their own image, Christians were projecting on to God what was in fact their own human excellence (whether realised or potential), thus leaving themselves bereft of their own innate value. What they gave to God they took away from themselves, that is, from their own ideal but possible selves. The Church's continual insistence on the antithesis of God (perfect) and humanity (sinful and depraved) would seem to bear out Feuerbach's thesis[1] (Feuerbach, 1841).

The absolute otherness of God has been laboriously expounded in recent times by the German Swiss theologian Karl Barth, who nevertheless – and probably unwittingly – contradicts this otherness in his massive many-volumed *Church Dogmatics*,[2] where he describes the nature and will of God so exhaustively and in such fine detail as would suggest that he had easy and total access to God's mind. If only Barth had learned to know himself as well as he claims to know God, he would have realised that God and humanity, though different, cannot be entirely incompatible or antithetical; and he might even have felt compelled to confess that God is within us.

Perhaps we should not judge Barth severely. His pessimistic view of humanity and human reason doubtless owed much to his having lived (1886–1968) at the time of two appalling wars and the Nazi Holocaust. But could not the human creativity   and the astronomical amount of money – that went into the construction of weapons capable of wiping out the whole of the earth's biosphere be applied to improving the human situation on this planet, removing the impotence of the suffering poor and the blinkered selfishness and greed of the prosperous? True, this would require a change of will and heart. But just imagine what a difference would be made in the world if everyone became aware of the divinity in things, the divinity in every human being and in all life. Right action follows from right values, and right values from right seeing, a right vision of, and a right attitude towards, the cosmos. What is certain is that a low view of humanity and human faculties will get us nowhere but to hell on earth. (Earth, incidentally, may be the only place where hell or heaven can exist.)

It may be argued that the cosmic dualism of Western religion, accused – rightly – of devaluing the natural world and the natural human being, may nevertheless, by its efforts to save the spiritual self from 'the world', be seen as promoting fuller recognition and further development of our unique spiritual capacities, such as unselfish contentment and unselfish compassion. There is indeed such a thing as unworldly wisdom – a pearl of great price.

Morally and intellectually our nature as human beings is a self-creative nature. If a creator-god had built into my mind knowledge and complete understanding of everything, so that I was incapable of error, I would have been an inferior kind of being to what I actually am, with my ample capacity for error.

Being able to make mistakes is a mark of true freedom, which in turn is a prerequisite of any self-creative process. To keep this dignified status unblemished by wilful or unheeded lapses into error, one needs to keep in touch with what a Hindu might call one's inner guru, which I call the indwelling divinity. Creativity, whether in science or philosophy or in the realm of ethics, cannot ever be mere compliance with what others have said or done. Nor, on the other hand can it – without disastrous consequences – be achieved by an unfettered and uninstructed ego.

Pride and Humility

There is good sense in the dictum that we should maintain a proper balance between pride and humility. "May the words of my lips and the meditations of our hearts be now and always acceptable in thy sight, *O Lord, our strength and our redeemer*," said the clergyman before embarking on his Sunday sermon. Although I no longer accept the traditional Christian belief in redemption by proxy, that is, by the death of God's Son offered as compensation to God the Father for human sinfulness, I do acknowledge that, as well as rejoicing in the divine energy and intelligence and rightness that are immanent in the world of nature and therefore in me, I must be constantly on guard lest I mistake my ego for that divinity that is accessible to me in my true and total self.

I have inveighed somewhat against the cult of self-denial. To remove any appearance of self-contradiction, let me distinguish clearly between ego and self. By 'ego' I mean, not my whole self (I trust!), but that purely selfish component of myself which is completely subjective in its judgments and totally centred on what is often called 'self' but is only the ego; not the entire self, but only the selfish self. The word 'self', by contrast, I shall use to refer to what one might call the whole self: all that is meant by such word-combinations as 'heart and soul' and 'body and soul', 'heart and mind' (ideas, values, desires, emotions) but also potentially including an awareness of divinity, by which I mean whatever is the ultimate reality that is manifest in the energy, intelligence, beauty and rightness of the universe.

Ego must be transcended, but as a means of opening up the full self, where truth and beauty and goodness are to be found, all the wonder of life and existence; in other words, the ultimate reality and meaning of all things – which I call divinity. The selfish ego is the individual self set over against other individuals and separated from divinity. If ego were allowed to dominate the whole self, then the awakening of the divinity in oneself might become an impossibility.

But how does one justify a capital letter for 'Self' whilst retaining the lower case for 'divinity'? I do not think we can. What is referred to as 'Self' must be distinguished from 'self' as that self's fullest realisation. But one can do this more accurately, I think, by replacing 'self' with 'the selfish self' and replacing 'Self' with 'the indwelling divinity'.

As for divinity, I see no absolute need for giving this word a capital 'D': unlike personified deities, divinity does not take umbrage.

While on the subject of capital letters, one must consider the word 'nature'. First, let us distinguish nature from the multitude of natural forms created by it, be they stars or star-fish, microbes or mountains. Then it should be clear that nature is identical to divinity. Do we, then, give 'nature' a capital letter, in order to bestow on nature an emotional valuation and promote human respect for it? Or do we achieve these ends better by identifying nature with divinity? I opt for the latter.

Does this amount to the dreaded heresy of pantheism? Personally, this is not a matter of great concern; after all, I have already aligned myself with paganism. Philosophically, however, my divinity hypothesis may narrowly avoid pantheism insofar as it is not possible to *know* whether there is or is not a God outside the physical universe. This being the case, one must weigh the respective advantages (credibility, and ethical and spiritual benefits) of super-naturalist theism on the one hand and immanent divinity on the other – which is precisely what this book aims to do, in divinity's favour.

Sacrifice

After that slight digression, let us return to the question of how to distinguish acceptable from unacceptable forms of denial or sacrifice. The criterion is easily stated: does the denial or sacrifice in question facilitate spiritual growth? Sacrifice is good only if what is achieved thereby exceeds in value, spiritually speaking, that which is sacrificed. The value may be measured in terms of benefits to other people or benefits to oneself, or both. But any benefits to oneself must be spiritual: the sacrifice must enable further development of the total self, the attainment of a fuller union with the divinity within. Thus, although the criterion is straightforward and universally applicable, only the individual person – and perhaps a few close associates – can know if and when the criterion is met. In a few cases, where the person's creativity is so outstanding as to make his or her name a household word – an Einstein or a Beethoven, for instance – and detailed biographies are published, any relationship between sacrifice and achievement will become public property impressing many, and even inspiring some to follow suit, if only on a more modest scale.

'Fallen' Humanity

As found in the book of Genesis and therefore in Judaism and Christianity, the myth of the 'Fall' is confined to the human race: Adam's sin – tasting the fruit of the tree of knowledge – and the guilt of it were inherited by all human beings, like some loathsome disease, with the consequence that "there is no health in us", as Christian liturgy has it: nothing we can do can take away this inherited 'original' sin.

It is interesting to note that this myth was not adopted by Islam. In the Qur'an Adam is said to have repented of his sin and Allah forgave him forthwith. There was therefore no inheritance of Adam's sin, and consequently no need for a saviour to redeem humanity from it.

If one is firmly committed to a theistic notion of God as a person, the Islamic account is more acceptable than the morally repugnant Jewish–Christian version. But all theism leads to so many absurdities, logical as well as moral, that any thinking person must reject it. The fact that the myth of the Fall and inherited sin, coupled with the ideas of a proud and jealous deity and a humanity that can obtain forgiveness only by membership of the Christian Church, has given the Church immense power over millions of human beings, will reinforce the outsider's scepticism.

The Cosmic Fall: From Spirit to Matter

There is another, more philosophical version of the Fall motif, in which the whole of god's creation 'fell' from the perfection it had shared with its creator when it was still only an idea in his mind. Just by becoming separate from its creator, creation 'fell' from the realm of spirit to the level of matter. This is a sophisticated replacement for the widespread myth of an interfering, incompetent or mischievous, inferior deity who prevented the creation from embodying the whole perfection of the supreme creator-god.

Nowadays, with the benefit of science, we are able to accept what might otherwise be seen as deficiencies or defects in the natural world. We now know that the universe, including ourselves and the whole human race, is not something static, fixed and finished, but something that is dynamic, in constant process and not yet complete (per-fected).

We also know that what we refer to as spiritual – mind, thoughts, values, intentions – is a function of matter, namely the brain and its components. In the words of Bertrand Russell, "No matter, never mind". But this should not be seen as a downgrading of spiritual reality to something other than and less than itself. Rather, it means that, although the material and the spiritual may be – and must be, for some purposes – distinguished, they are not separable.

That the brain, a piece of matter, is *conscious* should be seen as no more mysterious (or no less mysterious, according to one's viewpoint), than that a lump of matter – the human body – is *alive*. In both cases what we observe at surface level – consciousness, life – owes its existence to the activity, at deeper levels, of molecules, atoms and sub-atomic particles. These deeper-level entities or activities are still parts of the piece of matter under consideration – the human brain or body. This does not mean, however, that only matter – *mere* matter – exists. Perhaps we should say either that spirit is not so spiritual after all, or else that matter is not so material after all! But what we are dealing with is *one reality, not two*; and both aspects of this one reality must be recognised and valued.

The Jesuit priest and palaeontologist Teilhard de Chardin maintained that there is no such thing as 'mere' matter. He saw consciousness as existing in a thing in proportion to the complexity of that thing and, since there was no known completely simple entity in the cosmos, he concluded that there must be some degree of consciousness, or potentiality for consciousness, in all things. We are all familiar with the fact that an 'atom' (from the Greek word meaning 'indivisible') is now known to be a more or less complex structure of dynamic particles. Even if there were an infinitely small particle of matter, it would almost certainly function as part of a complex entity.

The philosopher A. N. Whitehead (1861–1947) also believed that all living things had some degree or other of awareness or sensitivity. For the lower levels of awareness he coined the word "prehension", which he may intend as a modified form of 'comprehension' or 'apprehension', or as a metaphorical use of the Latin 'prehendere', = 'to grasp' (Whitehead, 1978).

For one who believes that there is divinity in all things, the Teilhard–Whitehead thesis that there is no such thing as mere matter will not come as a great surprise, since it is already implicit in the indwelling-divinity hypothesis.

A purely materialistic way of looking at nature may have considerable utility value for one whose main concern is with controlling nature; but a scientist whose prime concern is with understanding nature may also – not as pure scientist but as total human being   find herself filled with wonder and awe which, like the quest for truth, are spiritual passions. And I suggest that spirit, along with energy, may be subsumed under divinity and that all spiritual reality – beauty, truth and goodness, thought and imagination and love – are manifestations of divinity.

Anyone who feels that immanent divinity is a second-rate substitute for the 'real thing' (meaning a deity outside the universe – that is, nowhere) should consider: first, that 'immanent' means that the universe is inseparable from divinity, so that we do not need to go outside that universe – perform the impossible – to find God; secondly, although we never fully comprehend this immanent divinity, we can at least experience it within the universe and within ourselves; and thirdly, since all divinity and all spirituality are contained within the universe, we have no good reason for wanting to go outside the universe.

One trusts that the spirit–matter dualism is fast approaching its end. The life of its subsidiary, the mind–body dualism, is within our own hands. This is apparent particularly in sexual relations. A merely physical sexual relationship must be declared sub-human insofar as it does not involve the whole human being. No human being is a mere object, and none should be treated as such – that is, as mere matter, mere body. If two people who truly love each other decide that it would be therapeutic – or just great fun – to engage in 'all-in' sex, each thinking only of his or her own gratification, the effect might indeed be a liberation from irrational neurotic inhibitions, a liberation consequent upon a developing trust in the other's love. But true lovers would soon become dissatisfied or disgusted with any impersonal – less than fully human – sexual engagement.

In any case, it is never the body that should be blamed for our moral shortcomings. The body is never wrong. The body – our unconscious – always knows best. What is wrong is the thought or emotion that takes control of our body in any act that may be classified as morally wrong.

It is not only in the sphere of sex that we may find the misplaced objectification of human beings. When I was a boy, employers advertised for "hands" in their mills or factories or other manual work. Not persons, just hands.

In all such cases the fundamental consideration is the acknowledgement of and respect for the divinity within the body, within the person, whether the body or person is one's own or that of another human being. Properly understood, a man's wonderment at a woman's body is not only enhanced by but actually comprises reverence for the divinity within that body; not only that, but ideally the wonderment would embrace divinity within all matter.

We must bid a final goodbye to the notion of the body as the prison-house or tomb of the soul. Instead, we must learn again to rejoice in the *marriage* of body and soul. How sad it is that the Christian church felt obliged to invent a mythological virgin birth of Jesus – to bypass the assumed sullying effects of conception by sexual intercourse. How terribly sad that it failed to take seriously the age-old belief in the divinity in nature, and therefore in the act of sexual intercourse.

The Hebrew view, which persists among Jews today, was an altogether healthier one: "The body is the soul in its outward form". 'Keeping body and soul together' really is a key to health and happiness. You might ask yourself: is it only your body that sleeps, or you, or both? If you, the conscious self did not sleep, you would eventually cease to exist, simultaneously with the cessation of your bodily processes – breathing and blood-flow and all the rest. Do dreams arise from your unconscious to your (temporally wakened) mind? But the unconscious is your body's awareness, and the dream is a signal to your brain, which is the site of those mechanisms that receive and process (make sense of and respond to) the dream. Where in all this can one separate mind from matter, self from body?

CHAPTER FOUR

The Western Split III

Gender Discrimination, its Origins and its Consequences

James Lovelock introduced the notion of planet Earth as an organism consisting of innumerable interdependent constituents, some living, some inorganic. He gave it the name Gaia. "When I first introduced Gaia, I had vague hopes that it might be denounced from the pulpit and thus made acceptable to my scientific colleagues. As it was, Gaia was embraced by the theologians and by a wide range of New Age writers and thinkers but denounced by biologists."[1] That was in the 1970s. But as early as the 17th century the astronomer Johannes Kepler had suggested that the earth resembled an enormous living animal;[2] and even 'devil's chaplain' Richard Dawkins notes that Lovelock's hypothesis has been reformulated by a much respected biologist, W. D. Hamilton, to make it compatible with Darwin's theory of evolution.[3]

I see no good reason for withholding organic status from the cosmos, if by 'organism' we mean a whole whose parts interact in such a way as to maintain (or, indeed transform) both it and themselves. Plato (c. 427–c. 347 BCE) in his Timaeus (called by its English translator, F. N. Cornford, 'Plato's Cosmology') speaks of the universe as "a living creature of which all other creatures, severally and in their families, are parts."[4]

'Gaia' (='Mother Earth') might suggest a failure to recognise the importance of polarity at all structural levels in the universe. Such polarity is creative. On a most elementary level we experience – and our life depends upon – the alternation of inhalation and exhalation, exertion and relaxation, wakefulness and sleep – and, we must add, life and death. From science we learn about the negative–positive polarity on which the flow of electrical energy depends (and which Sigmund Freud adopted as the model for the flow of psychic energy).

In ancient mythology, nature's creativity was ascribed to a primal pair, a coupling of opposites, earth-mother and sky-father.

The Zohar (the seminal book of the Jewish Kabbala) tells us: "The title 'human being' can be given only to man and woman bound together as one being";[5] and indeed in one of the two accounts of human beginnings given in the biblical Book of Genesis (the one that appears first in the text but is chronologically much later than the other) male and female appeared as a composite whole.[6] Is this to be seen as representing humankind as made in the image of an androgynous Creator? If so, we have long ago relinquished that image of

God and that image of humankind. We need to recover, not the mythology-taken-literally that constitutes the basis of Western religion, but the everlasting truth: that the union of opposites (but without forfeiting their interplay) lies at the heart of everything, including what we call God or divinity. Everything derives from energy and, as will be shown later in the book, God was first 'seen' in energy. In the East the primal coupling still survives, as in the Hindu Shiva-Shakti, the Tibetan Buddhist Yab-Yum, and the Chinese Yang-Yin.

Whether or not we retain the ancient androgynous masculine–feminine imagery, we should not succumb to the alluring oversimplification inherent in Western monotheistic systems. Science shows us that there is no absolutely simple thing anywhere in the known cosmos. Depth psychology shows us – as does introspection – that there is no such thing as a simple self.

Whereas Freud tended – in his earlier years, at any rate – to trace nearly all psychological disorders to a sexual base, his one-time follower Gustav Jung asks us to entertain the possibility that our human sex-life may itself reflect something beyond itself – namely, the internal and spiritual integration of consciousness and the unconscious. In doing so, Jung recalls the ancient mystical view of sexuality and reproduction as a human participation in the ubiquitous creativity of nature – a view more easily shared by woman (for whom these things are integral internal processes) than by men (for whom they are – like the male sexual organs – an external appendage).

The male–female conjunction needs to be understood and achieved on two levels, the biological and the mental–spiritual level. Before enlarging on this, I feel obliged to justify the use of the word 'level' in this particular context. Earlier,[7] the point was made that there can be no spiritual activity or spiritual reality without a material base. But, although there can be – for example – no thinking without a brain, one cannot assume that wherever there is matter (e.g. brain) there must be spirit (e.g. thinking). Nowhere is this more clearly the case than in human sexual relationships. Spiritual love is a totally invisible and intangible entity, whereas mere physical gratification entails a reduction of the other person from the status of subject to that of object, a *mere* thing. Not all biological male–female conjunction is (also) spiritual; this is due to the fact that there is variation (between individuals or within the same individual) in human levels of spirituality. In other words, not all human beings are fully human, and perhaps only a few are fully human all the time.

Some of us have developed muscles more than brains (both physical things!); some of us have developed brain, but only for intellectual or, shall we say, financial achievement. Spiritual development entails something more: the discovery of divinity – and thereby, one's true and total self.

Jung

Jung throws much light on this holistic development of the human being. He calls this process "individuation", which is a somewhat misleading title, sugges-

tive of an over-egocentric or individualistic enterprise; but what he means by
it is self-realisation, or full and balanced personal development and integration.
This can be achieved by exploring your unconscious, either by meditation or
– what amounts to the same thing – by paying attention to your unconscious
when it 'speaks' to you in your dreams.

Whereas for Freud the unconscious was principally a bin for receiving the
conscious mind's rejects, Jung took a much more positive view of the unconscious, as containing the wisdom, the direction and the energy you require for
a completely fulfilling life – but only if you let it. The rational mind may reject
the unconscious, as a mere figment of the imagination. It is the conscious mind
that can explore the unconscious, not in its rational mode, but in the mode of
pure awareness (what the Buddhist calls 'mindfulness'). Reason conceives –
imagines and speculates; pure consciousness perceives reality directly. Reason
knows about things; pure awareness knows the things themselves experien-
tially, and is thereby able to penetrate the appearance of things to the
underlying mystery and wonder.

An important aspect of what Jung calls "individuation", or self-integration
– 'pulling oneself together' – is the integration of masculine and feminine within
ourselves. Says Jung, we all – psychologically speaking – contain, in varying
proportions, both masculine and feminine aspects. The feminine aspects of a
male psyche Jung calls the 'anima'; it comprises, for example, gentleness,
tenderness, patience, receptiveness, closeness to nature, readiness to forgive,
and so on. The male side of a female psyche, called the 'animus', consists in
assertiveness, the will to control and take charge, fighting spirit and aggressiveness, and so on.

Says Jung, the activation of our soul image (anima or animus) is the unmis-
takeable sign that the second half of life – psychologically or spiritually, rather
than chronologically speaking – has begun. It is the turning point from playing
an arbitrary rôle in life to discovering and expressing more and more fully our
true self.

Unfortunately, for many centuries, and particularly in the Western world,
it has been considered a virtue – 'the done thing' – for men to suppress their
femininity; and until very recently women have been socially conditioned to
think it unbecoming to show their masculinity. Man's fear and neglect of his
own femininity have had dire consequences. Not only has he repressed the
feminine in himself; but also, being frightened of women – who are 'the feminine' par excellence – he has suppressed them.

A further consequence of this suppression of femininity in a world domi-
nated by men is war. Wars are the result of the lopsided development of men
whose self-pride and aggressiveness have not been tempered with patience and
a feeling for harmony and reconciliation, a reluctance to give way to reason if
one will not benefit in some tangible way, preferably immediately, by doing so.

When you have made the acquaintance – on respectful terms – with your
'soul image' (another name for anima or animus), it will lead your conscious
ego safely into the unconscious and safely out again. When Theseus needed

to penetrate the labyrinth in Crete in order to slay the Minotaur, the beauti-ful Ariadne, with her thread, enabled Theseus to fulfil his mission. Understood in Jungian terms, the labyrinth is a symbol of the unconscious, the monster is the threatening aspect of whatever in the unconscious has been neglected and has therefore 'gone wild'; the slaying of the monster means taming that wild and frightening force and bringing it – welcoming it – into our conscious life.

We should not wish to destroy or 'defeat' any part of our psyche. If we show respect for the 'trouble-maker' and converse with it, we shall discover that it was right and necessary to draw our attention to it, in order to achieve a more balanced and therefore fuller self. Similarly, a loving relationship with a person of the opposite sex (or with someone whose sexuality complements our own) can be of strong assistance in our quest for personal wholeness or healing. Conversely such a relationship may be enormously enhanced by progress made by one or both partners towards total integration. Thus an energising reci-procity develops between the physical and the spiritual, leading ultimately to a deep and constant bonding not only of the two partners with each other, but also of both with the indwelling divinity, the inner source of wisdom and universal love.

I hope I have stressed sufficiently the element of dualism. On the other hand, I hope I have not overstressed it at the expense of oneness. The feeling of oneness is the essence of the religious outlook; but the feeling of oneness, whether with lover or friend, with your dog or with nature at large, or with the divinity immanent in all these, always requires an other. 'Oneness' is not the same thing as strict numerical identity. As will be seen later, when we shall turn our attention to the Christian doctrine of Incarnation, oneness preserves the freedom of the individuals who unite. Divinity and nature can plausibly be seen as identical. But divinity and the individual human being are not exactly iden-tical, since here the relationship – and therefore the degree of oneness – entails spirituality, and therefore will and freedom, all of a much higher order than is to be found in any other products of the evolutionary process. The individual person may – and should – converse with and thereby become 'at one' with divinity; but union is not quite the same as identity.

Masculine, Feminine, or Neuter? The Feminine Principle in Western Religion

Masculinity has presided over Western religion, from Yahweh to the present day. But almost certainly the first gods were female and God was female for the first 200,000 years of human life on earth. Moyra Doorly[8] tells us that male dominance began round about 2,400 BCE, with the Indo-Aryans, or Indo-Europeans. There is archaeological evidence of a matriarchal agricultural society in Anatolia (the Asian part of Turkey) in 7,000 BCE, in which deceased women were buried but men's bones were thrown into a charnel house, there were no violent deaths, and vegetarianism prevailed: the goddess was predominant until the Hittites appeared there in about 2,000 BCE.

One of the earliest icons was the triangle. Like our present-day triangular road-signs, it gave a warning, but not of anything so mundane as an approaching bend or steep hill, but of the holy, the sacred and therefore taboo; the downward pointing triangle was chosen because it was an abstract but clear representation of the Goddess or, more specifically, her vagina. Thus Glotz tells us that from the Euphrates to the Adriatic the first supreme deity was represented by the figure of a woman with prominent breasts and buttocks and a "triangle traced on the pubis".[9] What is generally regarded as the earliest figurine depicting the Mother Goddess – the so-called Venus of Willendorf, in Austria – is dated 25,000–20,000 BCE. But earlier figures were made of wood and have therefore been lost. The fact that such images were found (and, not in cult sites but in homes) suggests a matriarchal civilisation. We tend to associate fertility goddesses with agriculture, but there were also goddesses presiding over the fertility of animals in the Palaeolithic hunting stage of human evolution, before the beginnings of agriculture.

Matriarchy gave way to the primal pair: sky (masculine) and earth (feminine) – except in Egypt, where the sky was feminine and earth masculine. This long-lived universal arrangement remained unchallenged until the prototype totally masculine Western god, Yahweh, come onto the scene and became firmly established. Elsewhere, wherever indigenous traditional (nature-based, creed-less) forms of religion continued to thrive – in Africa and Polynesia, Borneo and Indonesia and (until recently) among the North American Indians, the Maoris of New Zealand, the aboriginal Australians, the Celts of Ireland, Wales, Cornwall and Brittany, and many more – the Earth Mother held her own alongside the Sky Father. In Hinduism there is an unbroken line of tradition from the earliest forms of nature-worship, incorporating the Sanskrit yoni-lingam (an early abstract representation of the primal pair) along with the ancient icon that shows a plant emerging from the goddess's genitals, and the later anthropomorphic representations of the primal pair (Shiva-Shakti and equivalents).

We have seen how matriarchy had given way to patriarchy in the Hebrew-Israelite world with the advent of a totally masculine Yahweh. In the so called 'Priestly' account of creation, however, much later than the Yahweist account, God created the primal human being as twofold, "male and female . . . and called their name Adam".[10] 'Adam' means '(of) the earth or soil' and 'Eve' means 'life'. Earlier,[11] the first woman is described as "the mother of all living things". Thus the primal human couple is a replica of the divine primal pair found in the world-wide cult of nature.

Where, then, is the feminine element in Christianity? When the Protestant Christian utters the Lord's Prayer ("Our Father who art in heaven, . . .") does he ever ask himself what has happened to 'our Mother'? After all, common-sense insists that where there is a father there must also be a mother.

Just as the 'Venus' of Lausell has been declared the earliest extant representation of the Mother Goddess,[12] so it might be argued that in Christendom the Virgin Mary has become the latest representation of that goddess. But in Christendom – and, we may say, in the whole of Western religion – it is only Roman Catholics, Eastern Orthodox and Anglo-Catholics who seriously pay allegiance to the feminine principle. Not only do they speak of 'Mother Church', but they have well and truly deified the Virgin Mary. This applies just as much to the Eastern churches as to the Roman Church, but it is the Roman Church that has formalised the exalted status of the Virgin, in papal and conciliar pronouncements, beginning in the fifth century, with Cyril, bishop of Alexandria.

Cyril was not the first to bestow on the Virgin the title 'Mother of God' – it had already been used informally, but Cyril chose to make a dogma of it. Another bishop, Nestorius of Constantinople, showed reluctance to use that title and suggested that 'Mother of (the) Christ' was more fitting. At this point Cyril, bishop of Rome (not yet 'pope', but regarded as the senior bishop) was called in to act as an adjudicator, and he convened a synod, which declared itself in favour of 'Mother of God'; and that title has survived.[13]

This may perplex anyone who naïvely supposes that a mother must chronologically precede her offspring! But Christian dogma – should I say ecclesiastical dogma? – shows how words can work magic, for those who believe them. Here, a few tricks can be performed. One is that Jesus, who was Mary's son, was also God : ergo, Mary is the Mother of God. How that same woman can be the mother of the god who is eternal and created the universe is a little more difficult to explain. Nevertheless, where there's a will, they say; and a Mother of God met the needs of Christians who did not wish to be totally up-rooted from their traditional paganism, which was probably deeply imbedded in their unconscious – as it is, I believe, in ours. Dante (1265–1321) has no hesitation in addressing the Virgin as "daughter of thine own Son"![14]

Latourette suggests that this adulation of Mary should be seen within the context of a prevailing medieval belief in spirits, good and bad: the more angels and saints you had on your side, the safer you felt from the devil and his minions; and the Virgin Mary was to be seen as a formidable addition to the heavenly host, so formidable that we must see in it a "semi-conscious appreciation of the imbalance of the masculine and the hunger for the ideal which womanhood could supply."[15] At a more conscious level, perhaps there was a realisation that forgiveness was more likely to come from a woman than from a man – which may also be one of the reasons, in addition to deep-rooted paganism, for the popularity of Lady chapels.

Says Dante:

> "Lady, thou art so great, and so availest, that whoso would have grace, and has not recourse to thee, would have his desire to fly without wings. Thy benignity not only succours him who asks, but oftentimes freely foreruns the asking."[16]

In this context it is interesting to note how, in Chinese Mahayana Buddhism the bodhisattva Avalokiteshvara ('Lord who looks down from heaven'), whose face, so to speak, was turned in compassion to earth and its inhabitants, was eventually represented in Chinese iconography with feminine physical features, under the name of Kuan-Yin.[17]

The sculptured Virgin emerging from foliage in the Lady chapel of Ely Cathedral is a clear example of the way the Church used imagery to reach and teach the illiterate, who were also likely to be emotionally attached to the Earth goddess. This does not imply that the Church, or any section of it, was paying homage to the Earth goddess. Mary is a virgin, and represents not an endorsement but a transformation of the Earth goddess. In the Middle Ages virginity, not fertility, was the Christian ideal, for men as well as women, for secular clergy as well as for monks and nuns. The worship of the Virgin is not a sexual cult! It is as far removed from nature as any Protestant Puritanism.

At all events, a significant cult of the Virgin became established in the 12th and 13th centuries, and some of the most magnificent cathedral churches newly built during that period – Chartres, Paris, Rouen and Rheims – were dedicated to her.

Nor is it surprising that in the 19th century, amidst a revivalist surge of devotional piety which gave rise to the cult of the Sacred Heart of Jesus, the prestige of the Virgin soared to new heights in the Roman Catholic Church. In 1854 she was declared to be of "immaculate conception", which meant she was miraculously conceived in the same way as Jesus, the God-man, was conceived in her own womb.

To crown all, in 1950 Pius XII announced her "bodily assumption". Thus, it may be said, Mary followed – if belatedly – in the footsteps of her son and shared in his glorification.

Worthy of mention is a striking (Renaissance or Baroque?) painting showing a flash of lightning penetrating the cave in which the Virgin Mary is lying. The cave is a familiar symbol of the Earth-Mother's womb. Lightning represents the Sky-God's semen entering the womb. Thus we have a vivid depiction of the creative union of the Male and Female principles: the Taoist Yin-Yang, Hindu Shiva-Shakti, Tibetan Yab-Yum and – in more secular present-day terms the interpenetration of the intelligence and energy of the universe. In contrast, Yahweh's thunderbolts were lethal and were hurled against the Chosen People's enemies.

A painting by Bernardino Butinoni (active 1475–1510), probably intended, along with other small paintings, for an altarpiece in Lombardy, depicts the child Jesus conversing with doctors of the law in the temple. Jesus is seated atop a spiral platform. The spiral is a universal symbol of fertility – perhaps because it represents a whirlwind, which brings rain – so here again we have a representation of the creative union of the Masculine and Feminine principles in a Christian setting.[18]

However, one must see things in proportion. From being worshipped from time immemorial as the source of life, the Feminine had become, in the biblical figure of Eve, a source of evil and consequently made subservient to man.[19] Catholic and Orthodox exaltation of the Virgin may be seen as a concession to those Christians – mostly women? – whose hearts still kept a warm place for Mother Earth and a grievance against a church that had besmeared her. But it was a limited concession: for the ecclesiastical hierarchy Mary's glorification was an adjunct to the deification of her son Jesus; it was not a glorification of Woman – not, for example, the ritualised worship that the spiritually mature tantric Hindu offers to his wife!

The Roman Church and the Orthodox have no women priests, and Roman Catholic priests are not allowed to marry and are expected to live a life of total celibacy. In some Protestant churches there are a few women priests or ministers, and one or two feminine bishops. There are also some female rabbis. In Islam the leader of worship – the imam – is male; women are allowed to conduct services only for other women and children (rather similar to the deaconesses of the early Church). Sufi women take part in ritual on equal terms with men; but generally the patriarchal system, which has recently begun to crumble in Christendom, still persists in most Muslim countries, even within the family unit[20] - whereas in Judaism the mother has traditionally been the head of the household.

Perhaps mention should be made of the primeval symbolism perpetuated in the Christian practice of baptism, by which people – nowadays usually babes in arms – enter the womb of Mother Church. Water, of course, represents cleansing; but baptism in water symbolises (spiritual) death and rebirth. Behind this lies the pagan Earth Mother: from the waters of her womb comes life, and at death all things return to that womb, for rebirth. Baptism is a significant pagan legacy in Christianity, where it may – for those possessed of understanding – be a healthy reminder of the divine presence in the natural world.

The Union of Male and Female

So far, so good. But we need to go further. First, we need to reinstate the anima or animus within our own psyche, in order to achieve the balance that is the golden key to open the doors of health and self-fulfilment; secondly, within societies, particularly in the world of Islam but also in Jewry and Christendom and also in international relations, as an essential prerequisite – an absolute sine qua non – of balance, which in its turn entails fairness and justice, objectivity and reliance upon the power of reason, frankness and respect, in preference to cant and duplicity or a hot-headed wielding of weapons that only destroy, and accomplish nothing except a further degradation of the humanity of those who physically survive.

Says Robert Graves (1895–1985) in *The White Goddess* (1948):

There can be no escape from the present more than usually miserable

> state of the world . . . until the repressed desire of the Western races,
> which is for some form of Goddess worship . . . finds satisfaction at last.[21]

Robert Graves, like William Blake and Friedrich Nietzsche, saw the Christian God as the prototypical Father, the great prohibitor. The art historian Kenneth Clark points to the civilising influence of women in the 12th and 13th centuries, and also in 18th century France, where it was women who were responsible for the institution of the salon, where small gatherings listened to readings from contemporary literature and to 'live' music from a string quartet, or a solo voice with piano accompaniment. Civilisation, says Clark, depends absolutely on maintaining a proper balance of the masculine and feminine principles.[22]

But there must be balance, not a total swing to the opposite pole. One thinks of Margaret Thatcher who, having fought her way – manfully – to the top, proceeded to extol the 'virtues' of aggressiveness and greed, which she saw – rightly? – as the keystones of the 'free market' capitalism which she championed, and in 1982 insisted, against both ministerial and military advice, on plunging her nation into a pointless war to regain possession of islands that were of no use to the UK – a war costly in human life out of all proportion to any foreseeable benefits.[23]

What Freud and Masson termed "the oceanic feeling" describes the similar but opposite tendency in the male who cannot free himself from mother and may subsequently resign himself to a homosexual existence, perhaps after a liaison with a woman which proved disastrous because he could only love his mother.

In particular, Masson gave examples of religious men who projected a mother fixation on to a goddess. Rāmakrishna is a striking example: he became priest of a Kālī temple, where he spent much of his time meditating on the goddess or singing hymns to her as Mother, sometimes passing into a trance-like state of fusion (or confusion) with Kālī. His family married him off to a young girl, but to no avail: the marriage was never consummated, though the girl willingly stayed with him.

In psychic symbolism sea, or ocean, represents Mother, whether it be one's natural mother or the Mother Goddess ('mer' – 'mère'); Masson points to the frequent occurrence of the 'ocean' metaphor in the Hindu Upanishads, where it is used to throw light on the nature of 'brahman', the Hindu equivalent of 'divinity' in the way I use this word. Sometimes the ocean metaphor is used in a way that suggests that brahman – divinity – is the only reality, and that human beings have no independent, separate reality – only an illusory reality (māyā), which one must disown and 'drown' oneself in the oceanic brahman, the one and only reality. But this sort of relation to god or goddess is to be avoided by any man who does not wish to relinquish his valuable and creative masculine psychic components in an otherwise praiseworthy attempt to express his femininity.

Secondly, enabled by a healing and wholesome – whole-making – oneness of the feminine and masculine components of our being, we need to enter the ultimate stage of the human quest for truth: namely, the dynamic heart of that oneness of opposites that is found everywhere in nature but only imperfectly established in the human realm. For this see CHAPTER FIVE, *Energy and Divinity*.

The Oedipus Complex

Freud's Oedipus complex is based on the story of a man who murdered his father and married his mother. This complex, says Freud, arises from a young boy's incestuous desire for his mother and consequent envy and resentment of his father, whom the boy sees as a rival. Usually this complex resolves itself before puberty; but if it does not, the boy's fixation on his mother may prevent him from enjoying sexual relations with any woman, especially if guilt feelings have become attached to his recollections of his early incestuous desires, with the result that, as a grown-up, his attitude and approach to sex are poisoned and his actual sexual relations sullied and spoilt. The lesson Freud draws from all this is that we must liberate ourselves from parental dominance, including psychological fixations that prevent us from becoming properly independent and truly free to be ourselves and enjoy ourselves; each generation must win its freedom to move on from the previous generation's shibboleths and set ways of thinking, feeling and behaving, in order that humankind may constantly progress towards fuller truth and greater understanding (which will in turn increase the stature of the individual).

Without any desire to deny or diminish the validity and fruitfulness of Freud's – and other theories, particularly the 'Oceanic-feeling' variant[24] – I would draw your attention to Nicholas Berdyaev's understanding of the Oedipus complex.[25] For this Russian Christian (Orthodox but unorthodox) philosopher, Oedipus' struggle against his father's domination, and his desired union with his mother, symbolise a rebellion against a society and a culture that subordinate the feminine to the masculine.

For Berdyaev 'the masculine' comprises reason; market-place values and competitiveness; power. 'The feminine' comprises intuition; oneness with Nature, the primary source of life; creativity and communion with Nature, the source of our human creativity. (He also speculates that humankind was originally an androgynous form of life, and that the 'fall' of humankind consists in its subsequent division into two sexes.)[26]

Interestingly, in the *Gospel according to Thomas* (found in 1945 in the Gnostic library situated where the city of Nag Hammadi now stands) Jesus says, first, that only a woman who has become man can be saved, and "When you make the man and the woman a single one, so that the man is not the man and the woman not the woman . . . then you will enter [the Kingdom of God]."

For the Hindu all natural things are sacred: sun and moon and earth, air and water, all animals (not just the cow), trees and vegetation of all kinds. Even sex.

(The fact that I feel the need to insert 'even' is indicative of the difference between East and West.) The most common piece of religious iconography in India, the yoni-lingam, representing the female and male sex organs in conjunction, would most likely be considered obscene (and blasphemous?) in the West; but for the Hindu it represents the divine creative energy of the universe. Special forms of puja (offering or worship) and yoga feature in connection with this sexual symbolism. For example, Kundalini yoga concentrates attention on the spinal column ('sushumna', which may mean the spinal cord as we know it, or a 'subtle' or imagined equivalent). Kundalini is sometimes envisaged as a serpent, the cosmic snake, representing the cosmic energy (feminine). The purpose of the practice is to raise this energy through all the chakras – energy centres – from the perineum to the crown of the skull, where it meets and fuses with the divine cosmic intelligence (masculine); then to bring the intelligence down to 'awaken' the 'sleeping' energy; and so on, until a creative fusion of the two divine elements – feminine and masculine, or physical and spiritual – is achieved and established in oneself.

Here we should perhaps pause a while and remind ourselves of the wealth of 'erotica' in Hindu and Buddhist cave temples, and also of androgynous representations of divinity. Ardhanarishvara is perhaps the most complete symbol of the union of Shiva and his consort Shakti. This hermaphrodite is feminine on the left side of the torso and masculine on the right. Genitals are not shown. In the Western world one of the best-known androgynes is Hermes. Significantly, his staff is adorned with two snakes mating: the male grasps the female and their bodies intertwine[77] – a Greek Shiva-Shakti or Yab-Yum.

When homosexual musicians go the rounds asking for alms, some Hindus may ignore them, but traditionally they have been respected, perhaps reverenced – or superstitiously feared – as a survival of a primal stage of evolution prior to the separation of masculine and feminine.

To that primal stage we shall now return – for a new beginning.

CHAPTER FIVE

Energy and Divinity

" . . . . And I have felt
. . . .
A motion and a spirit, that impels
All thinking things, all objects of all thought,
And rolls through all things."

WILLIAM WORDSWORTH, '*Lines composed a few mile above*
Tintern Abbey, ll 93, 100–102

"The divine is understood either in terms of social images –
master, tsar, father, or in terms of dynamic images – power,
life, light, spirit, truth, fire. Only the second
interpretation is worthy of God and worthy of man."

NICHOLAS BERDYAEV[1]

It used to be thought that the earliest form of religion was a belief in spirits (animism), which developed into polytheism. Then came monotheism via monolatry (worship of one deity but accepting that there were other gods or goddesses). In this neat scheme, it was supposed that a later form was superior to any earlier one. Then came recognition of the prime status of Mother Earth and the worship of her as the earliest form of religion.

However, in recent times scholars have pointed to evidence of a form of religion that preceded all these and was centred on what is generally referred to by the word 'māna'.[2] This is a Melanesian–Polynesian word, but there are equivalent terms in other languages in other parts of the world. The Yoruba of Nigeria use the word 'ase'; the Arabian equivalent is 'baraka'; some North American Indians use 'orenda', others 'wakanda'; and the concept represented by 'māna' and its equivalents is almost world-wide. Melanesia itself covers quite a large area, including the north and north-east of Australia as well as Papua New Guinea, the Solomon Islands and the Fiji Islands; Polynesia ('many islands') extends from Hawaii in the north to New Zealand in the south and Easter Island in the east. Add the Indian and Inuit regions of North America, several locations in Africa and Europe, as well as India and China, and we see that māna is an almost world-wide concept.

'Māna' (and its equivalents) is a dynamistic term. It refers primarily, not to a particular object or objects, but to the power or energy in them; all energy is conceived as coming from an ultimate divine source. This means that any manifestation of māna is treated with great respect and reverence or, in some cases, with awe and dread.

Unlike gods and goddesses, māna is neuter. Gods and goddesses have māna, but it is by no means limited to them. Human beings are said to have it if they are specially gifted: the shaman or medicine-man, the renowned warrior or hunter, the accomplished potter or weaver. In other words, great – extraordinary – wisdom or physical strength or manual skill. A king or chief was honoured or revered for his māna; but if and when this māna – his power and charisma – waned, he was deposed, and sometimes disposed of by ritual murder or given the means to commit suicide. Similarly, a shaman, referred to as 'holy' ('wakan') by the Lakota and treated with reverence, could be punished by the tribal marshals if he was found to be cheating and deceiving people.

In this connection one cannot help thinking of the concept of 'thesaurus', a 'treasury' of divine power or energy ('grace') from which the pope might (for a price or for services rendered) bestow upon individuals a sufficiency of grace to ensure a safe place in heaven. This would seem to be a corruption of the notion of māna/divine energy; and it may be appropriate to describe the recent decline of papal authority as a loss of māna.

In the Rig Veda 'brahman' denoted the *power* of rituals, including the chanted mantras, the sound of which was believed to actualise the truth they expressed.[3] In later Vedas the priests were called brahmanas (='having to do with brahman') because they were supposed to partake of brahman.[4] Much (perhaps a millennium) later, 'brahman'[5] was the title given to the all-pervading ultimate reality, the universal Self, the realisation of which in one's own self was now (from the time of the Upanishads) the supreme goal of human life.

The sixteen gods of the Oglala (a Sioux tribe) were all what we would call natural phenomena: sun, sky, earth, moon, wind, thunder and so on. One of them was Rock, regarded as the primal material source of all things and invoked by the Oglala more than any other god. The belief that stones have special power or energy is worldwide. Cairns, heaps or piles of stones, as well as great rocks, were regarded as providing powerful protection both for the living and for the dead (hence tombstones, which in the modern Western world are mere tokens of respect for the dead or of the wealth of the provider).

It was not the Greek god Hermes who gave his name to 'hermai' (upright stone pillars); rather, he acquired his name from *them*. Later, a male head was placed atop these herms, to represent a god (Apollo, for instance).[6] Originally, the pillars were abstract representations of energy in general, not merely of masculine fertilising energy. Ironically, it is this more primitive, abstract representation of divinity that can sit comfortably side by side with present-day physics.

In modern times Western observers have been presented with various accounts of māna. One Maori said māna was a completely supernatural force; another said it belonged both to gods and to human beings, but that the māna of the gods was much stronger. A Fiji Islander said a thing had māna if it worked; if it did not work, it had no māna. Perhaps the last speaker had swallowed a slice of Western pragmatism and was at pains to assure the Western anthropologist that his (the Fiji Islander's) people's beliefs were not the mumbo-jumbo of ignorant savages. On the other hand, it has to be recognised that primeval religion was an attitude towards nature, *a way of looking at and making sense of the forces – the energy – of the natural world.*

The concept of power or energy is strongly present in all nature-based religion, which means that, just as the concept of energy is universal, so the religion that is based upon it has its roots in a universal holistic experience. Such religion is commonly referred to as polytheistic, because of its 'many gods'; but these deities are (personifications of) natural forces. What was awesome about the Greek sun-god Helios was the tremendous power or energy in the sun. It was only later – in the time of Homer – that the Greek gods were represented as intervening in human affairs with anger or loving support, avenging injustices or succumbing to the delicious lure of a beautiful woman; and it was this crude anthropomorphic degrading of the gods that led to the agnosticism (often laced with wit) of Aristophanes and other Greek dramatists, not to mention Plato's replacement of such gods with his spiritual triumvirate of goodness, truth and beauty.

It may be argued that an anthropomorphic choice of epithets helps us to envisage the Ultimate. But such argument does not convince. If we admit that such a Creator God exists, did not this God also create trees and beetles and rhinoceroses? If so, must we say that that God is tree-like, beetle-like *and* rhinoceros-like? If the reply is that the Creator must necessarily exceed (in power or complexity or whatever) his creations, then why should we stop at the human level; and can we be sure that the human species is really the ultimate achievement of the creative process? Suprapersonal? Yes, but what does that mean? More emotional and egocentric and perhaps morally less sensitive than human beings (like Yahweh, who came off badly in his treatment of Job)? Surely not. Not one individual among many, but the One that is within all things, the immanent creative energy of the cosmos. As the Brihādaranyaka Upanishad says, brahman is "the vital force" (compare Bergson's 'élan vital').

Fetishism

Fetishism is sometimes carelessly referred to as simply the worship of things (an axe or a shield, or a pile of stones); and from Sigmund Freud onwards the word has come to signify merely a sexual perversion in which, for instance, a man is sexually excited by a piece of fur or a lady's shoe. Consequently, one might think that the words 'fetish' and 'fetishism' should be dropped from religious discourse as altogether too misleading. Properly understood, however, the concept of fetishism has great significance for anyone who is disenchanted with the Western anthropomorphic notions of God. In the context of pre-anthropomorphic religion, the fetish is something – anything – in which one or more human beings have 'seen' – intuited, experienced – God/divinity/divine power; in a (Melanesian-Polynesian) word, 'māna'. For students of religion this phenomenon is known as an 'hierophany', a manifestation of divinity. Says Eliade, "Indeed, we cannot be sure that there is *anything* . . . that has not at some time in history been transformed into a hierophany."[7] Seen against this background fetishism is identical with reverence for māna; in both, divinity – as (cosmic) energy – is within things, not outside them. Fatefully, as Gustave Glotz tells us, "Anthropomorphism took the fetish inhabited by the divine spirit and turned it into the image of deity."[8] Prior to anthropomorphism, that indwelling divine spirit is universal, omnipresent and omnipotent, the Ultimate Reality, before which the entire multitude of anthropoid deities looks like a cheeky impertinence. Sadly, just as the Hebrew Yahwism had displaced nature-worship, so the ensuing anthropomorphic theisms of the Western world disastrously caused this primary notion of divinity to fade almost into oblivion.

Glotz points out that half-human, half-animal figures (he instances the man–bull Minotaur, the man–stag Minelaphos and the man–boar Minokapros) may represent a bridging phase between the reverence of the divinity manifest in the animal world and the later man-centred, anthropo-morphic religion that followed it.[9] One may also suggest that such half-human, half-animal images bear the mark of an age in which the human being saw himself as belonging, together with all (other) animals, to one vast biosphere filled with and manifesting the one divine energy. Even if this suggestion were shown to be mere speculation, it must still be seen as depicting a religious 'blik' that is particularly appropriate for the presently burgeoning 'new' ('Aquarian', or 'Green' or 'Gaian', 'Neopagan', or just 'spiritual'?) era that still awaits an adequate rational formulation. Such a formulation or rationale will not create a brand new religion but, rather, revive and re-clothe the religion that came naturally (through nature) to our early ancestors and still comes naturally to those who, like children, gaze open-eyed and innocently upon the miracle of a dewdrop or the stupendous miracle of the whole universe pulsating with what physicists may eventually uncover as *the ultimate ground of every form of energy, which truly religious people will see as the awesome One manifest in the mind-boggling many.*

The conviction that all things are ultimately inseparable from the One was represented in much of the bas relief (as distinct from round) sculpture of early times. In Indian art this kind of sculpture is known as the 'visionary' style. The very fact that ancient wall-paintings have no frame expresses the perceived ulti-mate groundedness of all things in the One.

Yes, physics may be in the vanguard of further genuine religious discovery! It would certainly appear likely that both the scientific and the religious search for the Ultimate – that in terms of which everything else may properly be under-stood – will merge in one hypothesis; and that hypothesis, though differently expressed by the two groups of truth-seekers, will focus on an energetic, dynamic reality. "Atoms consist of particles, and these particles are not made of any material stuff. When we observe them we never see any substance; what we observe are dynamic patterns continually changing into one another – the continuous dance of energy."[10] Is this not what the Shiva natarāja ('lord of the dance') icon is telling us? In Einstein's words, " . . . the field [of energy] is the only reality." "The apparently concrete matter of experience dissolves away into vibrating patterns of quantum energy."[11]

The Shiva 'lord of the dance' icon. The outer rign of flames represents the continuous flow of cosmic energy, of which Shiva is the divine source and sustainer.

Whether we stay with quantum theory or adopt a 'super-string' theory (which seeks to unite space, time and matter), we ultimately arrive at fundamental energetic vibrations of subatomic particles or of (notional) sub-microscopic loops of invisible 'string'. In either case we can see that ultimately matter is energy, the creative cosmic energy which, I suggest, is spirit, or divinity – the God that, unlike the theistic anthropoid deity, is a fully qualified creator.

The notion of energy is represented in a variety of religious traditions across the world by the word 'spirit' or 'Spirit'. Among the Nuer cattle herders of the Southern Sudan 'spirit' ('kwoth') is particularly associated with celestial phenomena such as rain and lightning and thunder but is not *identified* with any of these. Kwoth is 'the Spirit of the Universe', truly spiritual and therefore both invisible and ubiquitous, but also revealed through physical phenomena. Kwoth is the creative Spirit that "thought" the world into existence.

Likewise the Sioux Indian 'wakan', which means 'spirit' or 'mystery', is used of the tribal healer's 'medicine', or rather the spirit or power *in* the medicine (which might be roots or leaves, or the well-known vapour bath), as also in such dynamic events as birth and death. It is also experienced personally in solitary meditation, where it is described as 'mysterious feeling' or 'consciousness of the divine'. Anyone who wishes to boost his store of wakan (and thereby his status in the tribe) must, after sitting in the 'sweat-tent' ('encépee') or vapour bath, spend some time in meditation in some unfrequented part of the local landscape. It should be noted that what is referred to here is not spirits (plural) but what the Lakota Sioux called 'Wakan Tanka' ('Great Spirit'), which means the spiritual essence of all spirits. If in this book we keep the distinction between the individual human spirit and the ubiquitous cosmic Spirit, this is not to be taken to mean that there is a *qualitative* difference between the energy (or spirit, or divinity) in an individual human being and the energy (or spirit, or divinity) in the rest of the universe. The spirit of the individual is not ubiquitous, but the essence – the defining quality – of spirit or Spirit is everywhere the same.

In the Old Testament (*Genesis* ch. 1, verse 2) the English Authorised and Revised Versions have "*the Spirit* of God moved upon the face of the waters". In the Hebrew text we have "*ruach* Elohim" ("the *breath* of God").[12] The Hebrew word 'ruach' is an almost exact equivalent of the Greek 'pneuma' (as in pneumatic tyres or drills). Both words refer to any kind of moving air – breath, wind, etc. – and hence (since such phenomena are dynamic) to energy. There was a Stoic doctrine of an all-pervading pneuma, a breath – or energy – diffused throughout the universe.

The Old Testament reflects the more ancient Babylonian story of creation and uses the same imagery: God "breathes" upon the primeval ocean, the "formless" deep – 'formless' because water has no shape of its own – and it is God's breath (i.e. divine creative energy) that, so to speak, knocks it into shape. In other words, from chaos the divine energy produces an ordered manifold universe.

(Incidentally, how different is this creative divine energy from that of the later Israelite Yahweh who displays his energy in acts of anger and destruction! But this anthropomorphic Yahweh was not the universal creator mentioned in the Old Testament Priestly account of creation, only a local tribal deity.)

Interestingly, kwoth, the Nuer creative Spirit, is said to have given life to all things by his breath. We may also note the correspondence between the Sioux emphasis on the human spirit's meditative communion with the Great Spirit and the words of the author of the Fourth Gospel: "God is Spirit, and they that worship him must worship in spirit and truth".[13]

Prāna

A Sanskrit cognate of 'ruach' and 'pneuma' is 'prāna'. Like māna, prāna is universal energy, or the 'life force' (Bergson's 'élan vital'), but it can be encountered most intimately in one's own bodily processes, and especially in one's breath. Prānayāna is the practice of regulating the breath, and is incorporated into yoga. It develops one's awareness of the body and its bio-motor dynamics and the ability to control the flow of energy to unblock clogged-up neural circuits and revitalise the whole metabolism, thus energising both mind and body. That flow of energy is a manifestation of nothing less than the cosmic prāna, which is not only the earliest human notion of God, but also the one that would seem to be the most appropriate for the modern Western world, where energy in one form or another holds centre stage in several areas of human endeavour, notably physics and politics, and in engineering and aerodynamics, as well as in acupuncture and shiatsu. One might say humankind has never been closer to divinity, albeit unwittingly.

Even the uneducated Indian villager knows that the ultimate reality is not the image in the temple or in the family shrine. Typically, the image of the much loved (Earth) Goddess is thrown into the local river when her festival is over. (Compare the Buddhist adage, "If you meet the Buddha, kill the Buddha": what is visible or tangible is not the ultimate reality). Personal ritual devotion (bhakti), including offerings (puja) to whichever deity is favoured by one's family or village – usually Vishnu, Shiva, or the Goddess, – is still the popular form of Hinduism. But the educated Hindu tends to favour 'the way of knowledge' ('jñāna'), which may include yoga, and is directed towards oneness or communion with the Ultimate, known as 'brāhman' (not to be confused with 'brāhmin', 'priest' or with Brāhma, now a minor deity despite attempts to depict him as one of a trinity of deities on the model of the Christian trinity). 'Brahman' is a neuter, genderless word used to refer to the Ultimate One that is without name or form, of which the gods are merely inadequate representations.

Hinduism maintains an unbroken continuity from ancient nature-religion. There has been no Eastern or Indian split corresponding to the Western God–nature split. In its nature-based beginnings Hinduism, in common with many other nature-religions (the Celtic and North American Indian, for instance), combined meditation with its animism and polytheism; and finally – and most remarkable – the primeval māna-energy notion developed, in the later Upanishads, as the *un-named* divinity, brahman, which may nevertheless be encountered intuitively in the many forms of energy, even those within one's body.

There have been many schools of thought in the Hindu tradition, but no creed. In other words, Hinduism is not dogmatic, it accepts that there are various ways to God/brahman/truth, like several rivers merging in the same ocean. In this respect Hinduism learned much from the Jain and Buddhist teaching of 'non-violence' ('ahimsa'), which engendered, among other things, a general respectful tolerance of other people's beliefs.

Here let me quote the Indian philosopher S. Radhakrishnan (1888–1975): "Hinduism is bound not by a creed but by a quest, not by a common belief but by a common search for truth. Every one is a Hindu who strives for truth by study and reflection, by purity of life and conduct, by devotion and consecration to high ideals, who believes that religion rests not on authority but on experience."[14] This, whatever name we give it, is true (and therefore universal) religion. For the Hindu there is ultimately only the One, which is within all things and without which nothing could exist. This One, also called 'brahman', is what I refer to as divinity or māna, energy.

Māna/brahman/energy/spirit is to be commended as a reliable starting point for any future universal religion. It lacks the rigidity and dubiousness of Western anthropomorphic and mythological concepts of God. It is an intuitive, immediate and totally appropriate response to experience that is both universal and truly spiritual – mystical, yet compatible with a strictly empirical understanding of things.

If only our Western forms of religion could detach themselves from the (rusting) iron grip of creeds and inviolable scriptures! When all is said and done, even our best images, "metal or mental",[15] are only analogues – what Bishop David Jenkins has called "pointers" to the ineffable Ultimate. Unfortunately Christianity, the most anthropomorphic of extant religions, seems to be very backward-looking and therefore incapable and unwilling to make any changes that are not merely superficial and inconsequential. The last thing that Jesus did before his ascension into heaven was to promise the apostles the power of the Spirit.[16] But institutions and invented orthodoxy have a way of quenching the Spirit, the *indwelling* divinity.

We may not customarily equate spirit with energy – e.g., when what we have in mind is the spiritual dimension within everyone, comprising all that we mean by 'mind' and 'consciousness': thought, feeling, sensitivity, values and principles. Nevertheless all these things are energetic processes or products of such processes. We generally reserve the title 'creative spirit' for a creative genius: a Leonardo or a Picasso, a Bach or a Mahler, a Newton or an Einstein. But all spirit is creative, and for that reason we need to pay attention to what we, as spiritual beings, are creating. In using the phrase 'spiritful being' I wished to draw attention to the inescapable fact that we are all 'spirited' things, energetic, dynamic; if not, we are not even vegetables. Energy is the ultimate reality, present in every process, every motion, every vibration, and therefore in all things, which on examination are seen to have an energetic core without which they could not exist. There is even energy latent in rocks – which is why the primitive holistic being held them in awe; we can all 'feel' the energy in a great mountain or a massive tree-trunk. Not a particular thing, but the energy within it and within all other things is, I believe, the truly worshipful ultimate reality. *Anyone who unlocks the mystery of energy will have unlocked the mystery of the divinity in all things. And let us hope that then the mutual disrespect of scientist and religious believer will cease.*

Generally speaking, Christianity has been concentrated by the Church on God the Son, the Saviour from sin. The idea of God as (Holy) Spirit, though officially acknowledged, has been seen as a threat to the Church's authority: if God is within all things (as Spirit/cosmic energy) and – especially if God as spirit is present within the human being – then each individual can become a Church to himself.

The big question is: Why has the Church not paid attention to the implications of its own teaching and adapted itself accordingly? To recognise the Holy Spirit is ipso facto to relinquish (or, at any rate, not to accept uncritically) any authority – any claim to truth – that does not clearly and indisputably arise from internal converse of spirit with Spirit. And the fact that there is no foolproof process for adjudicating on this question means that toleration – certainly not dogmatism! – is required.

Nevertheless, it may plausibly be argued that, since the fruits of the Spirit – of divine inspiration – are by definition good, positive, creative and dynamic, and since we may discern such fruits in those persons, groups and movements that in our own time are pointing towards a better, more reasonable, humane, equable, or more liberating (more prejudice-free and dogma-free) order of things in the personal, social, international, racial, global and cosmic dimensions of life, we may commit the divine energy at our disposal to support such trends, though maintaining our critical acumen (our contact with the indwelling divinity). After all, nothing is perfect in this world – yet. But let us travel hopefully and energetically as well as circumspectly. *The language of spirit and energy can, I believe, open doors between different religious traditions, and also help people who have rejected religion to realise or express their inborn spirituality unburdened by religious dogma.*

In the popular Shiva-Shakti cult, Shakti (=‘energy’ or ‘power’) is the cosmic energy, which is ubiquitously immanent – not merely in the biosphere but, as we now know, in the subatomic realm, in our own intelligence and in what we call ‘mind’ or ‘spirit’.

In non-dualist (advāita) Vedānta the ultimate, brahman, is the One in the many. There is multiplicity in abundance in the universe, but only at a superficial level; fundamentally there is not even duality, only the One.

Uniquely among world religions, Hinduism combines polytheism and monotheism (which we must call ‘monism’ in order to reflect the lack of anthropomorphism in the brahman concept). Which of these is truer to experience? One must say polytheism, since experience is manifold, the universe is manifold. Which is more rational? One must say monism, since understanding seeks oneness, or simplicity: in this respect science and (true) religion are on the same track.

In Tantric Hinduism we see another parallel with science, this time with regard to the wave–particle conundrum. Tantra sees energy as vibration and takes this to be the primary cosmogenic element that gives rise to all structures and all motion. If we could reach the reality beneath appearances, ostensibly static structures would be seen as vibrational patterns (which are illustrated in tantric paintings).[17] Not only that; but transcending the elements (tattvas) is the ‘bindu’, the ultimate ‘point’ beyond which no thing or energy can be condensed. “It is the repository of all manifestation in its complexity and variety and the basis of all vibration, movement and form”.[18]

Polarity

The Chinese Taoist system described in the *Book of Changes* (*I Ching*) is based on the notion of 'tao', 'the way' of nature, evident in the constant flow of energy that constitutes the cosmic process; but this process depends upon the inter-action of polar opposites, yin and yang, negative and positive, or 'female and male' poles. Here is the familiar t'ai-chi (energy) icon:

It is worth noting that the dark spot in the light sector and the light spot in the dark sector represent respectively the 'feminine' element in the 'masculine' sector and the 'masculine' element in the 'feminine' sector. This means that some admixture within each of the opposites is required for efficient dynamics.

In view of the fact that yang is represented as light and yin as dark, it is important to bear in mind that the dualism here is not a moral dualism of good and evil. "What is good is not yin or yang but the dynamic balance between the two; what is bad or harmful is imbalance."[19]

We may compare this with Jung's anima and animus, respectively the femi-ninity within the male psyche and the masculinity within the female psyche that need to be integrated in order to achieve balance, harmony and fullness in oneself; and with the Kundalini expression: 'What need have I of an outer woman? I have an inner woman within myself.' Speaking of psychic energy, but in a way that applies to all energy, Jung says, "Energy necessarily depends on the pre-existing polarity without which there could be no energy." Freud had already said as much, comparing the flow of the psychic energy with that of electric currents between negative and positive poles.

Jung speaks of māna figures, the Wise Old Man in the male psyche and the Great Mother in the female psyche. They symbolise the power and wisdom that lie in the deep parts of our psyche, our unconscious mind. Says Jung, they must be integrated into our conscious mind, so as to enrich us with a wisdom that is not accessible to intellect alone. Failure to do this may result in our being 'possessed' by the māna personality, so that we become megalomaniac. On the other hand, we must not project this source of wisdom, disowning it and seeing it as the property of someone else, for example, some national leader or some superman (or superwoman) figure from contemporary mythology. Remember Hitler!

In Hindu Tantra ('tan' = 'expand') the spiritual is not seen as conflicting with the sensory, but rather as the supreme ideal goal of all longing. One may compare Plato's conception of 'eros' ('desire') as that urge to possess all that is beautiful and good and true. Chakra-pūja (worship, or making offerings, in a circle) is a tantric ritual in which couples form a circle with the guru and his partner in the centre. Each man makes obeisance and gives flowers (the red hibiscus) and perfumes to his female partner as to the Goddess and shares food with her. The ritual ends in intercourse, but this is free from all emotional and sentimental impulses, and without ejaculation. (The guru allows only those who have reached a high level of spirituality to participate in the ritual.) The union achieved in the ritual may be understood as that of Shiva-Shakti, whose inherent nature is joy, or – what amounts to the same thing – as the self's achievement of conscious oneness with the One, brahman, beyond male–female duality. (In tantric tradition the Goddess is understood as 'the Void', in the sense of being beyond all imagery, 'beyond name and form'.)

The Chinese notion of polarity is clearly founded on the biological creative union of opposite sexes that we have encountered in the primal pair, Earth-Mother and Sky-Father; but the Taoist dynamic understanding of reality, of the cosmos and everything within it, can be expressed equally well – and perhaps more usefully and more adequately – in non-sexual terms. Polarity is a more commodious concept than sexuality. It embraces not only the polarity of gender that is readily observable in flora and fauna, but also the polarity that modern science has discovered in what are regarded as non-living (but dynamic) phenomena, the behavioural patterns of the negatively charged electrons surrounding the atomic nucleus and the positively charged protons within the nucleus. The essential – natural – necessity of polar opposites is displayed in all energetic phenomena: in the positive and negative charges in subatomic particles and, at a mesocosmic level, in the repulsion and attraction of electro-magnetism; in the binding, uniting forces of gravity and the strong nuclear force.

T'ai-chi is energy in all its forms throughout the universe, from the subatomic to the astronomical, from inhalation and exhalation of breath to the overall cosmic expansion and contraction, explosion and implosion – which incidentally is a notion found also in ancient Hindu tradition as well as among present-day scientific hypotheses.

Similarly, Hindu and Buddhist tantra regards vibration as a primary cosmo-genic element, giving rise to all motion and all structures. If we could penetrate the appearances of things to their reality, the ostensibly static structures would be seen to be vibrational patterns.[20] Vibrations are, of course, energy. Again, the Sanskrit 'bindu', the ultimate 'point'[21] beyond which no thing or energy can be further compressed or condensed, may be seen to resemble the modern physicists' view of the point whose explosion – the 'Big Bang' – is the still continuing expansion of the initially absolutely compacted cosmos.

Hindu Shrī Yantra (supreme aid to meditation) representing cosmic energy expanding from its original state of absolute compression ('bindu').

Campbell makes a distinction between the Hindu meditator seeking oneness with a reality beyond the universe (with eyes closed to the world) and the Far Eastern Taoist meditator seeking oneness with the way of nature (with eyes open).[22] There is truth in this distinction, but generalisations about such a complex phenomenon as Hinduism are inevitably somewhat precarious. It is interesting to note that in Buddhism, which is proclaimed as 'the Middle Way', meditation is typically practised with eyes *half*-closed. One must point out that the Vedānta Hindu sees brahman as pervading everything and as the essence of every thing. For example, in the *Chandogya Upanishad* (*the* Upanishad for brahman) a father tells his son that, just like salt in water, brahman cannot be pointed out as some individual thing, but pervades everything. "Here also, in this body, you do not perceive the True, my son; but there indeed it is. That which is the subtle essence, in it all that exists has its self . . . .. and you . . . . are it."[23] Sen enlarges on this: "The goal, according to the Upanishadic view, is the realisation of the Self. This realisation of the one and unique brahman pervading everything frees us from all shackles and we realise the Reality as *Saccitānanda* – being (*Sat*), Consciousness (*cit*) and Delight (*ānanda*). The fullness of this realisation transcends the desire for heavenly comfort."[24]

This does not seem to me to be an absolute denial of the world, but rather an enhancement of that world's value from the presumed fact that its essence is divine; not a search for an extra-cosmic reality, but a joyful feeling of oneness with the intuited indwelling divinity.

Basically, Western religions offer a relationship to God as *Father*, a child's relationship to a father. The distinguished New Testament scholar Matthew Black taught me that, where Jesus is said to have spoken of God as 'father', the Aramaic original was the word used by any child to address its own 'daddy'.

This is quite touching. But such anthropomorphism nowadays puts God on a par with Father Christmas.

If the concept of māna is the core of the earliest form of religion, most of the ensuing development of religion in the West must be seen as a decline. It is the concept of māna/energy that provides a significant link with modern physics; what comes later – the separation of divinity from nature – transforms institutionalised religion into an obscurantist, myth-bound opponent of science and reason. As a consequence, creativity is found in science and its technological offspring, whilst religion, lacking creative dynamism (i.e., lacking divinity!), becomes useless except as an occasional purveyor of truths generated in the secular world – for example, when a church prelate shows himself receptive to some moral insight publicised at the interface of politics and media, and gives it his blessing.

Relating to God as *Spirit*, on the other hand, is a much more acceptable, intelligible and feasible proposition. In the form of energy, spirit is everywhere and needs no special introduction. But it is within our own spirit – our own consciousness – that we are most immediately connected with the cosmic energy in spiritual form, the creative energy by which we are able to fashion ourselves and fulfil ourselves without external coercion. This God within us is God at our disposal.

One should pay tribute, not only to Berdyaev, but also to H. Wheeler Robinson, a Christian theologian who almost a hundred years ago expressed a preference for the notion of 'Spirit' rather than that of 'Fatherhood' or 'Sonship'. The latter, he said, "never escape from the perils of anthropomorphism", whereas "Spirit denotes a reality; it faithfully represents the human experience of being integrated into something larger than oneself and yet within oneself."[25]

Of the various words I have used to refer to the indwelling cosmic divinity – 'energy'. 'power', 'spirit' and so on – it occurs to me that two of them may require a safety precaution. 'Power' and 'force' are the words in question. 'Force' as used in science has my absolute blessing: it refers to dynamic expressions of energy. However, when used as the equivalent of 'compulsion' in such moral human contexts as 'being forced/compelled to do something against one's will,' 'force' does not readily express what I have in mind when speaking of divinity. But divinity, expressed as energy or force, must be understood as something that lies within the discretion of the individual person: in one's utilisation of the divinity, energy, force or power, it may become contaminated or radically deformed by egotistic motivation.

Chapter Six

Divinity Within

"Apprehend God in all things
For God is in all things,
Every single creature is full of God
And is a book about God.
Every creature is a word of God."
                    MEISTER ECKHART (*c.* 1260–1327)

Some readers may be taken aback by the suggestion that divinity is manifest in energy, and completely gob-smacked by the suggestion that energy and divinity may even be one and the same thing. If so, please notice that I have just used the word 'thing'. 'Thing' may not be the right word here: I do not want to suggest that divinity, or God, is a particular object. I use the word to demonstrate that I am not equating energy with a supernatural person, as if God were some Superman with bulging biceps. Rather, I am saying that God, or divinity, is *within* the cosmos, *within* nature and within all things. For this reason I am inclined towards abandoning the word 'God'; and perhaps I shall eventually do that. If I hang on to the word 'God' it is because I do not want to say that God does not exist, but only that the word 'God' must be given a new filling – new to us, but in fact very ancient. It is a 'universal' meaning, in both senses of the word: as the antithesis of 'particular' and as 'within the universe'.

Gods are particular entities. Even the single or so-called 'unique' god of a monotheistic religion may be seen as only one of several monotheistic deities; and if it may be said that these several deities simply represent different ways of 'seeing' the one God, these different characterisations are themselves sufficient to cause adherents of each religion to claim that they alone worship the true God and all other characterisations are false.

When all is said, all notions of God are just that: notions. Some notions, however, are more feasible than others.

Universality is what establishes or increases the credibility of a scientific theory; and if and when scientific explanation accounts for everything, it will be a 'TOE' or a 'GUT', a theory of everything, or a grand universal theory. It is universality that we should look for in religious concepts; if they fall short in this respect they should be discarded.

Energy

What is more universal than energy? No one doubts its existence: it is omnipresent. It is also the ultimate reality, that from which all things derive their existence and by which they exercise their various functions. This is probably the earliest concept of what we call God: the māna that preceded the gods and that, having claimed its sovereignty in science, must now resume its religious sovereignty.

The name Paul Davies gives to the projected ultimate energy source that will embrace electrical and magnetic, atomic weak and strong, and gravitational forms of energy is "Superforce".[1] This term matches the concept of "supersymmetry" and presumably creates no problem for physicists. But for one who equates energy with divinity (which means seeing energy as the *revered* ultimate source of a *revered* universe) 'force', and especially 'Superforce' – redolent of science-fiction and Batman – produce an undesirable image of a supernatural (and therefore fictional) Autocrat.

Werner Heisenberg (1901–76) fathered the uncertainty principle: that it is not possible to calculate simultaneously and accurately the position and momentum of subatomic particles. If I understand this rightly, it means that any physical properties ascribed to these particles are merely inferred.

It is interesting that Tantric Hinduism regards vibration as the primary cosmogenic element which gives rise to all structures and all movement. If we could penetrate the reality behind appearances, ostensibly static structures would be seen as vibrational patterns.[2]

Without straying too far from scientific correctness, one may picture energy, not as itself a thing, but as a great ocean or field out of which all things take form and develop. Things are not energy, and energy not things; but all things contain energy, and without energy nothing would or could exist. That is the relationship between God and things, God and the cosmos, God and me.

God understood as the creative force from which all things receive their existence (their 'coming out of') and all their faculties is, I think, most aptly referred to as 'divinity' (with or without a capital initial letter) because this word more readily suggests a kind of quality or function than does 'God', which immediately suggests a thing or person.

From Energy to Beauty

It is not only in energy but also in beauty that divinity may be 'seen' or intuited. This is Otto's "mysterium-fascinans".

One does not need to be particularly intelligent to experience for oneself the beauty of the natural world. It is almost inevitable that young lovers, on their first sight of each other's unclad body, will have a sense of overwhelming wonder which for long afterwards will flow into and inform their vision of the rest of nature – sky and clouds, flowers and trees and grass, water bubbling or gurgling, birds singing – as if they were seeing and hearing those things truly for the first time; and their feeling of wonder is their intuition of the ultimately incomprehensible mystery that is called Divinity or, less adequately, God. For Plato truth and beauty go together – a viewpoint shared by Keats and Wordsworth. Beauty, said Plato, was the object of love ('eros', the love that is attracted by and desires to possess its object); and all who sought *truth* were driven by eros. In the light of this one can understand those scientists who speak of the 'beauty' (sometimes 'symmetry', sometimes 'order') they observe in nature or in the formulas or hypotheses they construct to represent natural phenomena.

"Beauty is simply the spiritual making itself known sensuously", said Hegel. When beauty deserves the title of sublimity it is a veritable theophany, a clear manifestation of the divinity in things. Such sublimity may be encountered in art (I think particularly of music – Bach or Mahler, for instance, or late Beethoven) as well as in nature.

Sometimes energy and beauty appear together, giving the observer a feeling of awe and even naked fear mixed with open-eyed wonder and bliss. The flashes of lightning across a dark and misty sky and the gigantic rumbling of thunder make Plot-night fireworks look like damp squibs. Awe and fascination, energy and beauty: what a combination! In my young days I knew a man (Derek Hall, senior curate in a parish where I was the junior curate) who thrilled to the sound and sight of explosions or gusts of steam in sky or in factory. His thrill was an aesthetic and at the same time a truly religious response, which I did not properly understand at the time but do now.

Energy, being that from which all else derives, must be given pride of place among theophanies. How different from "gentle Jesus, meek and mild"! The raw theistic equivalent would be the volcano and thunder god Yahweh, who, being depicted in anthropoid terms, is a rather distasteful person, arrogant, autocratic, and revelling in punitive destruction. When we cast off the tyrannical shackles of that God-person we are able to see the *rightness* of nature's violence: its volcanic eruptions, its meteoric bombardments – not to mention the Big Bang – can now be seen in a positive light, as providing the right conditions for life on earth as we know it. Divinity then becomes truly awe-inspiring, Otto's "mysterium tremendum".

Now (March 2007) scientists are warning us that a huge asteroid is predicted to fall earthwards sometime in the very near future and that, if it collides with earth, the effect will be devastating, resulting in the end of the human species.

But from the viewpoint put forward in this book that would not be an absolute end. The cosmos would continue its business as usual, with a new age of evolution. Earth has suffered such calamities before; indeed, had there not been such intrusions from space, the epoch of chemical and biological evolution that eventually gave birth to humankind might never have got under weigh. What from a purely anthropomorphic point of view must be seen as cruelly devastating and rendering the universe altogether meaningless, will not cease to make sense – good sense – for those whose viewpoint is cosmic. *Rather, they will have trust in the rightness of things in a universe whose awe-inspiring energy (divinity) is continuously creative of something new and therefore occasionally destructive of what stood in the way of the new.*

Humankind may rise to the challenge of the expected asteroid. Scientists have already devised several strategies for deflecting the asteroid's fall away from our planet or for reducing its mass. If so, well and good: we may then begin to believe that our species deserves to survive. However, there is a dark side: our species is now the most destructive of life and of the means of life. We have grossly, selfishly and greedily competed with one another – person with person, nation with nation, ideology with ideology – in the rape of Mother Earth. We should therefore respect the (divine) intelligence of the universe if it engineers the decline or demise of humankind. Which comes first, humanity or the universe?

The Latin poet Statius (*c.* 45–96 CE) said that it was fear (not awe) that "first created gods in the world". But the gods he had in mind were anthropoids written large. If it was any particular fears or a generalised anxiety that caused humanity to invent these anthropomorphic gods with a view to doing a deal with them, offering them obedience and homage in return for security and consolation, the contract has not worked out as planned. The fears remain, but are now displaced on to the gods themselves! We see this still in Western monotheism, where God has been presented as an object of both love and fear and the individual is left to choose between the two, or else shift nervously from one to the other as the best means of winning the favour of this schizophrenic deity. Particularly in some forms of Christianity, Roman Catholic and Protestant, it is guilt-feelings and guilt-fed fears that have been the dynamic base – a sad distortion of divine energy. Hitler cashed in on xenophobia. To cash in on people's (misplaced) fear of God is no less hideous.

The cure for fear is courage: not handing ourselves over to some supreme external authority, be it god or pope or priest or – heaven forfend! – a Hitler or a Bush, but uncovering and re-energising our own authority, which is nothing other than the divinity within us. For the yogi this may mean working on the central chakra, the heart chakra, to release one's courage (coeur-age),[3] or on the third chakra, just above the navel, where the warrior's power is centred. Such sensuous focussing is not necessary, but may be an invaluable aid for facilitating the flow of the divine energy and power within us. All authority is within us, not outside us – in institutions or 'leaders' – unless we give them that authority; and we must never relinquish the truly supreme authority of the indwelling divinity, namely, our true self.

In more liberal forms of Christianity a happy optimism based on trust has replaced fear. Paul Tillich sums this up in his distinction between the believer and the unbeliever: When the Christian wakes up he smiles and says 'Good morning, God!'; when the unbeliever wakes up he groans: 'Good God, morning!'

To see the divinity in things is to transcend egocentric languishing in guilt and fear to a positive, energising delight in the glory, and trust in the rightness, of things.

Awe, yes! that, coupled with wonder, is something we do need. As our vision of the universe is enlarged and we become aware that our galaxy is only one of 100 billion galaxies and that planet Earth is only a youngster compared with the total age of the universe (which may be only one of several universes), we ourselves should grow *younger* and experience afresh the open-eyed wonder of a tiny toddler seeing his first snowfall or his first earthworm. That toddler feels awe, but not fear.

To realise that 60% of the matter in our bodies is hydrogen atoms that were once constituents of the Big Bang, and the other 40% are "recycled star dust"[4] and that all living and non-living things, from rocky mountains to rye grass and from trees to hippopotamuses, originated from something as small as a pinhead: that is truly religious awe, which takes us out of ourselves and more deeply into ourselves. The divinity that is the ultimate energy source of the cosmos is also within us. All is connected by energy, by which and from which all things exist. Our primal ancestors knew this. We must begin to re-learn their conscious oneness with the universe and their respect and gratitude for it and its all-sustaining energy/māna/divinity.

Was it the Scottish theologian John Baillie or the Danish Søren Kierkegaard – or both – who said that God is revealed only in what is not God, namely, in things that belong to the world of nature? At all events, I agree with this assertion, but believe it is more accurate to say that God is present in nature. This view is commonly known as 'pantheism' (literally, 'everything is God'). which, being associated with those pre-Christian pagans who were aware of divinity in things, became anathema in the Church. Berdyaev opted for 'panentheism' (literally, 'everything is in God'). This is not a position I would wish to contradict, even if there were any logical or empirical way of doing so. But if all things are in God, God must also be in all things: see diagram below. What must be avoided is the notion of one-to-one identity of human being and God/divinity. Union, yes; this is something we may all experience. But strict identity is a dangerous concept inasmuch as it opens the way to megalomania.

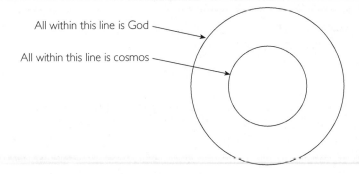

All within this line is God

All within this line is cosmos

My purpose is to propose a view of reality that, whilst not itself scientific, merges with science by daring to equate energy with divinity. In keeping with this project I shall concentrate on the immanence of divinity, which means those aspects of divinity that may be experienced in the universe.

Divinity is the energy of the cosmos, the energy from which it came into existence. We live by that energy, think by it, love by it. Whatever we do or fail to do, we are using or abusing the divine energy and intelligence of the cosmos. All this divinity we can experience, just by opening our doors of perception – our minds and our senses – to the universe and, most intimately, to planet Earth set within the solar system. This is all we need to know. Whether there is divinity – divine energy and intelligence – outside the universe, no one can know; or if there is someone who knows, she has not made herself known to me.

Intelligence in Nature

Our early ancestors seem to have believed that there is intelligence in nature; one may see evidence of such a belief in the sculptured head of the Celtic Green Man (who has prehistoric antecedents). This head, which appears in several Christian churches, is surrounded by foliage; and this image is a clear representation of intelligence in nature. The human head had great significance for Celtic and other head-hunters as a centre of spiritual power (māna)!

It is generally assumed that every kind of creativity requires intelligence as well as energy. This holds true for everything that is worthy of the name of art, whether in sculpture or music or architecture; or of technology, space rockets or computers or grand pianos. I believe it is true also of nature's self-creativity.

Is it anthropomorphism to see intelligence in nature? Or is it anthropocentric to think that human beings are the only intelligent species? In an evolving universe, is it not reasonable to suppose that intelligence may have had a long history before reaching its present peak in humankind?

There was a time when both scientists and theologians saw the universe as a piece of clockwork mechanism. The only difference between them was that the theologians in question maintained that it had a creator who was outside the universe and had simply set the mechanism in motion and then left it to unwind, so to speak. In both these scenarios the universe has energy within itself but lacks mind, or intelligence.

Indeed, Richard Dawkins refers to nature as a *blind* watchmaker.[5] If Dawkins were consistent, would he not have to say that the workings of his brain are blind? And if blind, how trustworthy are they? The same would have to apply to all brains, including that of Charles Darwin. If nature is 'blind' in Dawkins' sense, it would follow that there is no creative intelligence in nature, only the artificial intelligence of a machine. If that were the case, how could scientists manage to make sense of nature in mathematical (that is, logical) terms? I suppose the answer would be: because machines themselves (including the natural universe) are logical. In other words, the answer must be a simple repetition of the basic assumption: that nature (and therefore everything within it) is 'blind'.

Today we have extremist evangelical Christians who reject the Darwinian theory of evolution by natural selection and prefer to see the universe as a colossal computerised mechanism programmed by God. This might seem to be an advance on the fundamentalist view that God brought everything into being by separate acts of creation, or the view expressed by Pope Pius XII who, whilst accepting physical evolution, declared that "souls are directly created by God."[6] But the programming model would appear to be a regression to an outmoded scientific materialistic determinism, which may have lent some sort of credibility to Calvinistic pre-destinarianism but is now itself discredited.

Darwin spoke of natural selection from *random mutations*. Hardly a day goes by without providing fresh evidence of such mutations at a genetic level – a baby with six fingers instead of five, or with eyes of different colour. Today's quantum physicists see totally random behaviour at the subatomic level.

One should not suppose that such randomness means that the whole cosmic process is "a tale told by an idiot . . . signifying nothing". Nor should one suppose that the presence of *determinism* in the universe means that the universe is mindless. The bewildering behaviour of the cloud of particles outside the nucleus of an atom is random; yet one particle takes note of and adjusts itself to the motion of another, and random behaviour at the micro-level results in predictable behaviour at the macro-level; and does not predictability entail some degree of determinism? The predictable behaviour at the macro-level combines (especially in animals and particularly in human beings) with freedom of choice in the subject; and freely made choices may have a determining effect upon either the self or other persons or things. There are degrees of determinism, and there are degrees of freedom, sometimes varying in inverse proportion to each other; sometimes freedom produces determinism, and sometimes determinism produces freedom. Moreover, the fact that variety plays a positive role in evolution, by providing alternatives to those species or subspecies that are put at risk by catastrophic happenings, suggests that such a combination of determinism and freedom (or chance) might well be seen as an intelligent design worked out on an immeasurably superhuman scale. This combination of chance and necessity – random mutations and natural selection – within the processes of nature suggests, not that an external deity set a mindless machine in motion, but that the universe is itself creative, self-creative; that there is a sophisticated intelligence at work in nature, as well as tremendous energy.

This means that we have to abandon or at least modify the Newtonian physics which perceived everything as determined by pre-existing causes, themselves entirely determined by other causes . . . There is, it would seem, a kind of causation that is not deterministic in any strong sense of the word: just as atomic particles are seen to behave *as if* they had freedom of choice, so human beings display – and are aware of and can consciously employ –

freedom of choice. We can even choose to *relinquish* our freedom, either just drifting like a twig on water or else submitting ourselves to some external authority. The crucial significance of human freedom of will and its momentous consequences finds dramatic expression in the biblical myth of Adam and Eve and the apple. But, if the Genesis myth would have us believe that the awareness and exercise of our freedom are the devil's gift, we should rather see them as the work of the indwelling divinity, that is, the cosmic self-creativity that is commonly referred to as evolution.

For Moses, God was a lawgiver, but only at a modest tribal level. Later there were supreme transcendent Gods who represented cosmic law and order. Today, scientists still regard the universe as a domain of law and order and therefore penetrable by human reason, which finds in the universe something amenable to and therefore akin to human reason. *This may be seen as something very similar to our early ancestors' feeling of affinity with nature.*

It would seem that nature produces organisms – including the human being – that are more sophisticated, complex or versatile than anything produced by human chemists or engineers. Even if this were not true and it really was the case that human beings can 'outdo nature' (which in a sense is perfectly true), it must be acknowledged that human beings – even the cleverest – owe their existence and their intelligence to nature. If human beings create machines or organisms that are more intelligent than the human beings that created them, that human creativity is itself a product of the cosmic (self-) creativity – indeed, it is an *expression* of that cosmic creativity. Given the fact that human beings possess such intelligence and creativity, it is vitally important that a purely objective perspective should be supplemented – and, where necessary, held in check by – a subjective spiritual attitude of wonder and awe, gratitude and devotion towards nature, which is indeed our mother.

The universe is not a mindless machine. It has intelligence as well as energy. Intelligence, mind and consciousness are closely related and all are dependent upon energy. Mind overlaps with intelligence and consciousness; and in the human being all three are functions of the brain and the nervous system. There is consciousness in the body, which may become aware of a drop in temperature in a room when 'the mind' was otherwise occupied, perhaps in reading a book. Some neurologists speak of the mind, or brain, as present in just about every part of the body. Do individual cells in our bodies have no awareness of other parts with which they work together? Single-celled amoebae react to external stimuli; so why not the cells in our bodies?

States of mind – anxiety, fear, anger and also peacefulness and pleasure – may express themselves in and through the body: a smile reveals pleasure, and negative states of mind express themselves as physical tension in neck and shoulders. Thoughts and emotions, 'physical' pain and 'mental' anxiety are all energetic phenomena. Intelligence may be associated with mind and is a product or function of the brain, so long as the brain receives energy.

The word 'intelligence' is sometimes reserved for rationality and logicality in human beings, but is applied also to animals; and now we talk of 'artificial intelligence', in computers for example, which can make calculations at mind-boggling speed, employing a binary logic fashioned by highly intelligent human beings and enabling scientists to achieve solutions to problems in their lifetime that otherwise might have take several generations.

In view of *Homo sapiens'* extraordinarily developed intelligence – far beyond that of apes – it is quite understandable that the hypothesised supernatural creator of the universe should be depicted in human terms, with intelligence, and with emotions, too. In contrast to this anthropocentric theistic notion is the primeval ecological, even cosmological notion of māna/energy as the awesome *immanent* creative source of all things. Our primitive ancestors saw themselves as an integral part of nature and had not begun to think metaphysically. Even their own practical intelligence – their skills of hunting and weaving, martial arts and pottery – was the fruit of māna, the same energy as they saw in the sun's heat and the moon's light, in thunder and rainstorms, fertility and growth. These people were not to witness the tragic turn in the development of the human species when its intelligence became the great separator, making humanity the master and nature the slave.

Nevertheless we may look forward to a time when, the mechanical view of the universe having been abandoned once and for all, "The nature-spirits will return to us; nature will awaken to life again" and "the human being will control the hierarchy of nature-spirits, not by self-interested dissociation from them, but in a loving union with them".[7]

Teilhard de Chardin

Teilhard de Chardin (1881–1955), Jesuit priest and palaeontologist, argued that, since intelligence is a characteristic of creatures that have a certain level of complexity in their physical structure, we may assume that, since some degree of complexity is found even in the most elementary organisms, there may be some degree of intelligence or consciousness or awareness (Teilhard subsumes all these under the French word 'conscience') in everything. This thread of consciousness throughout the course of evolution is God. In other words, God/divinity is the intelligent self-creativity of the universe. At this point Teilhard's argument seems to break down. For it not to break down one needs some equation of God with energy; otherwise Teilhard's God is the (nowadays laughable) deus ex machina of some Greek drama.

Since Teilhard's death we have become familiar with the microcosmos contained in a miniscule atom. But his bold extrapolations from the known segment of evolution to previous and future segments did not enamour him with scientists. For them the very fact that Teilhard's hypothesis cannot possibly be disproved, even in principle, condemns it as nonsense.

Nor did the Vatican take kindly to his thesis: his books were placed on the index. The papal encyclical *Humani Generis*, mentioned above (page 66), had Teilhard in mind along with other disapproved thinkers. What the Vatican failed to perceive – or refused to accept – was that Teilhard's vision was of a universal Christ, *a cosmic incarnation of God*, a vision that grew out of (or grew into?) an anti-dualist vision of spirit-matter as the basic stuff of the universe. This vision (or visions) – incomparably grander and also more feasible and rational than the particularist, exclusivist and highly contentious myth of a god who spent about thirty years on earth as a human being – was rejected because it was a threat to papal and ecclesiastical authority. In other words, truth could not be allowed to usurp dogma.

I agree wholeheartedly with Teilhard in general terms: that there is some degree of consciousness even at the lower levels of life than the human. There is what Whitehead calls 'prehension' in trees and plants, some awareness of light and of neighbouring trees or plants. If plants and trees had no awareness of light and were therefore not phototropic, would they not die from a lack of photosynthesis? How do we know that a tree does not feel pain when we cut off one of its branches? In non-human animals there is a wide range of sense-perception, in some cases far exceeding our own: bats use echolocation to navigate in darkness, listening to echoes of their supersonic squeaks, dolphins excel in hunting sardines by a combination of intelligence and sonar beams, and many oceanic creatures employ electromagnetic navigation systems;[8] many animals of prey have powerful olfactory senses, as do parrots and warblers:[9] colour-awareness in birds is well documented especially in connection with mating rituals; and birds are now known to have greater powers of communication than was once thought – not only do their songs often exceed our auditory range, but they also contain sequences that are too rapid for our ears to catch. Pet birds are known to enjoy music and to have their favourite tunes;[10] and whales can communicate over several miles. Ants can transmit at least fifty different messages using body language and chemical substances (pheromones) that cause responses in others of its species. The female Atlas moth releases a pheromone to advertise her readiness for mating. It can be detected by a male of its species more than 8 kilometres/5 miles away. Crocodiles, elephants, and finback and blue whales use infra-sound for communicating to one another; insects (Earth's most numerous inhabitants apart from bacteria), bats, dolphins and shrews use ultra-sound. Stridulation (rubbing one body-part against another) is employed by ants, crickets and grasshoppers; and the honey-bee forager gives its followers information about the type, quality and location of food by vibrating its wings and performing a waggle-dance.[11] All physical features required for human speech as we know it today were already present by circa 150,000 years ago. *Australopithecus* (more than 4 million years ago) could communicate by gestures and vocally (by shrieks, sighs, etc.).[12]

An even more significant example is to be found within the atom itself. "In some mysterious way the electron encodes information about a comparatively vast structure in its neighbourhood and responds accordingly." "There is no hope of building a full explanation of matter from the constituent parts alone. Only the system *as a whole* gives concrete expression to microscopic reality."[13]

It is in such a holistic viewpoint (the antithesis of reductionism) that science will find its consummation; that consummation will constitute the ultimate merger of science and true religion.

Where one might differ from Teilhard is where his idealism causes him to adopt a possibly over-optimistic view of the future impact of human freedom and human creativity upon the temporal process. I am referring to Teilhard's presentation of God as the transcendent goal of evolution as well as being involved *in* evolution. From a belief in divinity in the universe we may infer the *rightness* of the universe, and therefore trust that natural evolution is going in a right direction. But part of that glorious design is the freedom of humanity to use the indwelling divine intelligence and energy in whatever way it chooses. This means (to resort to anthropomorphic language) that God/divinity is vulnerable, having put itself into the hands of human beings.

Of course, divinity must be assumed, being universal, to be more powerful and more intelligent that any human being. Nevertheless, freedom is freedom; and unless it is rescinded, we must acknowledge the possibility that human action may put a spanner in the works, thus preventing the glorious consummation in which God will be all in all – except in the sense (which for me suffices) that divinity already is and will ever be all in all, since divinity is within our very freedom. But the fact remains that, since the human species can to some extent affect the development of the universe, we cannot be certain about the future – good or bad, improvement or deterioration – of the cosmos or any part of it. Einstein said, "God does not play dice." I think he did when he gave such liberal portions of intelligence and creative energy to the human species.

> The earth is beautiful, joyous, cosmic, eternal.
> The world is the unhappy superstructure man has
> imposed on the earth.
>   BARRY LONG[14]

Rightness

For all that, I nevertheless pin my faith on nature and its indwelling divine energy and intelligence, and *rightness*. 'Rightness' comprises those qualities that make nature acceptable to us (as total human beings, not merely as scientists), so that we may assert with good reason that the world we live in is the best of all possible worlds. Intelligence and goodness are two of those qualities. A third is beauty. Plato spoke of beauty as the object of 'eros', love that desires to *possess* its object; and eros was the motivator of the philosopher's search for truth. For Plato (as later for Keats and Wordsworth) truth and beauty were inseparable. Truth, beauty and goodness: these were the Platonic trinity. Beauty plays an interesting and significant role in theoretical physics. "String theory is too beautiful a mathematical structure to be completely irrelevant to nature."[15]

Plato also said that the intrinsic goal of the human being was to become "like God as much as possible."[16] But this goal, one must add, can be achieved only if the human being deploys the indwelling divine energy and intelligence rightly, that is, with reverence for the whole and for every part of the whole. It is here that the Christian notion of the Kingship of God comes into its own: namely, in the personal, social and ecological dimensions – not as an eschatological event in some other world, but as the acknowledgement and reverence of the divinity that is nature itself.

Both Berdyaev and Teilhard de Chardin submit that, with the human being, evolution has become conscious of itself; and that it is this fact – and the implied tremendous responsibility – that gives meaning to human life. Both describe this responsibility as that of collaborating in the divine-cosmic process of creation and redemption. Again, both were strongly but not blindly or dogmatically opposed to Communism: for them what was the most characteristic and defining quality of the human being was freedom, freedom of will, freedom of thought and speech, freedom to create one's own self and to participate (or to withhold participation) in the transfiguration of the world. But Teilhard agrees with Marx that class struggle must be resolved, since it is a hindrance to human progress. (And what an unproductive waste of human – i.e. cosmic – energy!)

Is development of consciousness a good thing? Most of us would say, 'Yes'. Since it means greater capacity, for good or evil, it is imperative that it should be accompanied with a correspondingly greater feeling of responsibility; but this is part of the process of maturation. Today we seem to have reached a critical stage in that maturation process, a stage in which more and more power for destruction is controllable by heads of state and anonymous commercial conglomerates whose moral awareness appears to have diminished in inverse proportion to their ascending power. This, together with our self-centred stripping and raping of Mother Earth, may spell the end of the human race, either prestissimo as a result of nuclear and chemical warfare, or more protractedly as a consequence of our irreverent despoliation of our planet.

Not that this would be the end of the world! Nature-divinity 'knows best', so to speak (which, incidentally, is why it is often our 'unconscious' mind that knows best). It has been said that, not the survival, but the *arrival* of the fittest is the miracle. Without the random mutations there can be nothing new, no evolution. But nature also has its own intelligent way of disposing of species that have outlived their fitness for survival: natural selection. Indeed, Darwin's account of evolution seems to require a capacity in all living things to adapt to – and by implication, to be *aware* of – their environment. Lovelock's Gaia hypothesis presents the natural world as a self-regulating system having feedback mechanisms which enable it to maintain the survival of life. To believe in nature is to believe not only in its energy, but also in its intelligence – and, last but not least, its rightness.

Cosmic Rightness

Religion lifts the concept of goodness or rightness to a cosmic level, from social consciousness to universal consciousness. Rational religion is a response of human beings to the universe in which they find themselves. " . . . in a puri-fied religion, rationalised under the influence of the world-concept, you study [God's] goodness in order to be like him".[17] But Ruskin's romantic view of nature as subject to and displaying the moral law is difficult to accept. Morality applies only to human beings, as the only species that has the freedom and therefore responsibility to create its own spiritual self; though of course this includes right attitude and behaviour towards the rest of nature.

Otto's 'mysterium fascinans' includes the beauty we see in nature and math-ematical physicists see in the symmetries and harmonies of their theories (literally = 'visions'!). Here we see how the two concepts, beauty and rightness, overlap. If beauty is a vague concept, rightness is even vaguer; but I shall take it to mean 'being just as it ought to be' (which may embrace ethical approval), or 'in tune with the perceived total scheme of things.'

To speak of rightness as one of nature's properties that justify the appella-tion 'divinity' is to believe that nature can be trusted, so that anything that happens in the cosmos, when seen in a universal – but not an egocentric or even anthropocentric – perspective, will be seen as necessary in what may prop-erly be called "the best of all possible worlds."[18]

> ROBERT BROWNING: "God's in his heaven.
> All's right with the world!"[19]

> YURI GAGARIN: "I don't see any god up here."

Browning is not quite right: we can be truly sure that all is right with the world if we experience God's presence – divinity – *in the world*.

That most remarkable mystic Julian of Norwich declared: "It is necessary that sin should exist. But . . . all will be well, and every manner of thing will be well "[20] Had she undergone a stricter training in logic, Julian would have felt compelled to say that the *possibility* of sin was necessary. (But perhaps she was thinking that the coming of Christ as saviour would have been redundant if there had been no sin.)

On the other hand, Darwin, who had read theology at Cambridge and been deeply influenced by William Paley's view that everything in the natural world reflected God's perfection,[21] later felt obliged to remark in a letter: "What a book a Devil's Chaplain might write on the clumsy, wasteful, blundering law and horribly cruel works of nature!"

If only Darwin had linked his "random mutations" with human freedom of will . . . ! Human free will contains the possibility of good or evil. And this freedom is the apex of a triangle that has its base in widespread randomness at the subatomic level and rises through inanimate and animate, conscious and self-conscious creatures to *Homo sapiens*. Even if randomness at the subatomic level results in statistically predictable behaviour at the macroscopic human level, this does not preclude the possibility – borne out by our own experience – that we are free to choose between different courses of action (or inactivity). This freedom is at the root of responsibility: no freedom, no responsibility in law or in conscience. Such provision at a subatomic level for what at the human level is conscious freedom of choice is just one good reason for believing that there is not only intelligence but also a rightness in the universe.[22] Even Tennyson, who spoke of "Nature, red in tooth and claw," declared in the same poem:

> Oh yet we trust that somehow good
> Will be the final goal of ill."[23]

Movements of the plates in the earth's lithosphere, earthquakes and volcanic eruptions, ice ages, floods and droughts: all these might conceivably be justified by extending Darwin's theory of biological evolution made possible by random mutations, in the way that Teilhard extended it – backwards and forwards in time – so that nature's 'laws', or regularities or order (and therefore its intelligibility to human beings) is seen as the product of an underlying randomness, just as the quantum physicist makes predictions based on statistical probabilities. (If the creator of the universe were a person, this is where s/he could be said to be playing dice, since even s/he could not have foretold the outcome with any rationally justifiable confidence.)

We have seen how our early ancestors associated a flash of lightning or a thunderbolt with fertilisation. Today scientists tell us that life on earth may have resulted from the action of lightning upon chemicals contained in the primeval 'soup', giving birth to single-celled bacteria; that both algae and volcanic eruptions helped to produce an atmospheric mix favourable eventually for human life; and that volcanic activity itself may be due to asteroids colliding with the Earth.

But that is not the whole story. (Does anyone know the whole story?) Chemical building blocks needed for life came from outer space – and still come, brought by comets or just falling as dust. Everywhere things – including ourselves – survive by interaction with what is in our environment; and that environment must ultimately be seen as extending to the edges of the universe (if there are any), which is itself two or three times as old as our planet Earth, where life began a mere three or four billion years ago! (Perhaps we may consider: Time, or duration, as we ordinarily experience it may be conditioned by our mind or 'body clock'. In either case our sense of duration may differ from that of an ant or a butterfly. May we not speculate, then, that if the cosmos may be envisaged as a vast organism endowed with intelligence, its sense of time may differ vastly from our own – just as Hindu mythology pictures the duration of a universe as one exhalation in Vishnu?)

At all events it would appear that the beginnings of life are rooted in what looks like a random combination of random events. This, however, does not cause me to despair of meaning, a *good* meaning – in a word, 'rightness' – in the universe. The universal process is not "a tale told by an idiot, full of sound and fury, signifying nothing".[24] I cannot prove this, and it is possible that Macbeth is right, whether he is speaking of (a particular) human life or the cosmos. But what I see in nature – its beauty, its fruitful mix of chance and determinism, its awesome creative energy (which destroys only what hinders further creativity) – combines to convince me of the *rightness* of nature. I do not look for supernatural miracles to redeem the universe. *Nature itself is the miracle.*

Why then do we need a God? No intelligible sense can be made of a supernatural, extra-cosmic deity; but the immanent divinity – nature's own energy, intelligence and rightness – is 'something else', as they say. This immanent divinity is adventitiously revealed, or at least suggested, by the scientific account of nature's awesome wonders and law-abiding order. This divinity is transcendent in the sense that it is the ultimate, that from which all else derives, whereas we are just among its products. But the fact that this divinity is the omnipresent cosmic energy, intelligence and rightness, and therefore our own energy, intelligence or rightfulness, gives us a very special role within the universe and particularly on planet Earth and its environs: that of cooperating consciously with the divinity within ourselves to bring ourselves, and subsequently the rest of nature, close to fulfilment. Such are the meaning and dignity – and responsibility – bestowed on humanity by the indwelling divinity. There is no contradiction – indeed, no distance, – between divinity and humanity except the contradiction and distance we perversely (sometimes masochistically) invent. In essence there is no difference between divinity and humanity: we share the very same spirituality. But of course there is a difference of degree: divinity is universal; but I am not. Our primitive ancestors who saw divine energy and order in nature, displayed an allegiance to nature and a trust in its rightness. What made sense for them will also, I believe, make sense for future generations – if there *are* any! If not, that would not discredit my optimistic trust in the rightness of nature. Only what is perfect ('per-fect', i.e. consummate) deserves to last forever. (But what is per-fected is finished, and has no future!). That is why it is appropriate that human individuals should die; if they did not, there could be no further development in the human race. For the same reason it would be appropriate that our species should cease to exist if it were malfunctioning so excessively and incorrigibly as to be a costly irredeemable liability in the universe. May I suggest that divinity, not being a person (though perhaps suprapersonal), may be seen as impartial towards all things, animate or inanimate, great or small?

In short, *it is logically possible to be an optimist with regard to nature without being unrealistically optimistic about one's own or some other particular species.* That said, however, one hopes that humankind will come to its senses and, for its own sake as well as nature's, assume or (remembering our primitive forebears) *resume* a role of stewardship on earth and – with an eye on possible future technological advances – in the cosmos at large. Failing that, I trust that any succeeding 'superior' species will not perpetuate our errors. That is what I call faith in nature.

Back to Nature

The revelations of cosmic sacrality are in some sort
primordial revelations; they take place in the most
distant religious past of humanity, and the
innovations later introduced by history have not
had power to abolish them.
                MIRCEA ELIADE, *The Sacred and the Profane*, p. 138.

We shall not cease from exploration
And the end of all our exploring
Will be to arrive where we started
And know the place for the first time.
                T.S. ELIOT, Four Quartets, 'Little Gidding', ll. 234–242.

But as Hegel points out, when the same returns, it is not the same, because it has been enriched by experience of its antithesis. Any viable future religion will not be a mere revival of an old one, for it will emerge from a profound and unforgettable experience of atheism, having learned from it.

Émile Durkheim (1858–1917), one of the founding fathers of modern sociology, thought that one could uncover the essence of religion by going back to its origins, where one would find religion pure and simple, free from its various historical accretions.

Durkheim focussed on totemism, as did the anthropologist Claude Lévi-Strauss (1908–1990). Totemism, which was at one time an almost universal phenomenon, reflects a felt symbiosis with nature. Lévi-Strauss described it as basically a symbolic means of presenting the natural world and human society as interdependent components of an all-comprising organic whole. Ritual connected with the totem symbolised (or – magically? – brought about) the replenishing of the life-force – the bio-energy – within all members of the totemic group, human beings and animals.

In any case, if we are right in believing that, in its earliest manifestations, religion consisted in an attitude of reverence for the natural world (living off the land without degrading it), a feeling of oneness (a conscious symbiosis) with it, we can certainly say that religion's beginnings provide us with a perfect template for the religion of the future: awareness of and positive response to the cosmic energy and intelligence and rightness which, transposed by reverence and joyful gratitude and love, present themselves to us as a worshipful divinity in all things. *Now is the time for all anthropomorphic supernatural deities to be pensioned off, to allow humankind to renew its deep acquaintance with the divinity within.*

Primal nature-based religion had no creed, no scriptures – and therefore no dogmatism. What need could there be for a creed or scriptures where people's self-awareness was bound up intimately with a shared awareness of their existence as parts of a whole, a whole which in the first place was the known natural world, the ecological environment with its fauna and flora, and in the second place, the tribe or clan? At both levels there was a sense of belonging and contributing to something bigger than themselves, not forcefully dominating them, but rather bestowing upon them a sense of identity and purpose, in an inter-active and interdependent relationship characterised by gratitude and reverence. This is, I believe, what Wordsworth meant by "the primal sympathy": unity of the human consciousness with the divine in nature.

Comparison may be made with Chinese Taoism, insofar as Tao is 'the Way' of nature and the ideal way of life for human beings. (I say 'ideal' because we have freedom to choose our way.) This ideal human way of life is called 'wu-wei', which literally means 'no action' or 'inactivity' but is more aptly understood as 'taking no action contrary to Nature', not interfering with the order of nature, but going along with it – which is seen as the way to fulfil one's own human nature. As is implied by my reference to human free will, our relationship to nature is a little more complex: we ourselves have creativity! But more on that later!

Reverence for nature is shown in Feng-Shui ('wind and water') which is another means of achieving harmony with nature's energy by conforming to nature rather than dominating it – letting nature's energy flow where it will, instead of blocking that flow.

Yoga, too, is a means of unblocking the flow of cosmic energy within the human being; and there are secular therapies based on freeing the flow of (cosmic) energy: acupuncture, acupressure (shiatsu), and indeed, massage.

Meditation

The primal reverence for nature was frequently accompanied by meditation. In the Celtic tradition, which was centred on the Earth Mother (remember the Paps of Anu and Sheila-na-gig), there were the druids, who frequently practised meditation – often in pairs, facing each other – at the vaginal entrance to the womb-like burial chamber where the dead were placed for rebirth. Like other shamans, these druids were believed to possess mystical knowledge and wisdom. Among the North American Indians, whose sun-worship and totemism are indicative of a felt mutual dependence of the human community and its surrounding fauna and flora habitat (its eco-system), young men were initiated, after being purified by the sweat-tent, by a period of solitude – perhaps on a hill or mountain – to develop awareness of their inner and spiritual resources in communion with the Great Spirit.

Taoism had its 'nature mystics', so called because they experienced oneness with the universe intuitively, sometimes in a trance-like state, achieving union with the cosmic energy, Tao. Such Taoist shamans were said to tap into the natural and spiritual energy of Tao, enabling them to explain the meaning of people's dreams and reveal their destiny, as well as to heal the sick and guide the souls of the dead to their appropriate places – the places where they would feel most comfortable – in the spirit-world.

No Eastern Split

Just as Taoism and Yoga enhance the quality (and perhaps the length) of human life by 'keeping body and soul together', so in the whole of indigenous Indian religion there has been no split comparable to the Western split between body and mind, world and God, and no sundering of the human being from the rest of nature. On the contrary, there is what might be seen as a glaring contrast between the meditative "life-negating"[25] ascetic or 'withdrawn one' (muni or sunnyāsi), who seeks brahman, the One behind or within the many natural phenomena and, on the other hand, the full and unashamed enjoyment of life's riches and participation in its creative energy (depicted, for instance, in the Kāma Sūtra). Nowhere is the contradiction seen more clearly, says Wendy O'Flaherty,[26] than in the "erotic ascetic" Shiva, who is the lord of nature's dance and also the great ascetic who stands at the still centre of the turning wheel and whose ascetic third eye (a spiritual eye situated between the eyebrows) destroyed the god Kāma ('desire'), but who spent a thousand years making love to his consort Parvati!

Hinduism is called by its devotees 'sanātana dharma' ('eternal truth') because, unlike most other religions, which can be traced to identifiable founders, it had no known beginning. Of course there have been contributory influxes into the Hindu tradition, including the Aryan and the indigenous Dravidian contributions; and in villages some of the local goddesses are thought to precede the Vedas, which include the earliest Hindu scriptures and are probably the oldest surviving scriptures in the world. But the ultimate origins of Hinduism are shrouded in mystery. (One could say the same about the origins of Hebrew religion, except that the nature-based religions were disowned by Moses: the sky-god Yahweh was divorced from the goddess and the Jews became motherless, separated from nature.)

Hinduism, like Taoism and other aboriginal religions across the globe, has a meditative component – and a very fundamental, intrinsic one. The co-existence of nature-worship and meditation 5,000 years ago in the Indus civilisation is reflected in the fertility and yogic figurines recently found in the mounds of Harappa and Mohenjo-daro. Possibly this blend of reverence for Mother Earth and mystic-meditative practice goes back much further in time, but any tangible evidence would have been made, not of metal, but of wood and would therefore have had little chance of surviving the ravages of time.

Perhaps it needs to be made clear that Sikhism should not be seen as a part of Hinduism. Founded by guru Nānāk during the Muslim Moghul rule in India, it is a Hindu–Muslim amalgam. But in adopting a rigorous monotheism, the Sikhs removed themselves definitively from Hindu tradition. The jealous god who says, 'Thou shalt have no other gods but me' belongs to the Jewish–Christian–Muslim tradition, but not to the Hindu tradition, which tolerates all gods but not a monotheism: monism, yes, but not monotheism.

One might say that what is worshipped in Hinduism is not gods but the divine, which is manifested in (or, for more philosophically minded Hindus, symbolised by) the gods; but the divine is present also in nature and in human beings – in any holy man or teacher, rishi or guru, but (in Upanishads and Vedānta Hinduism) also in every human soul.

Reflecting on how Indian religion links the remote past with the dawning future, Yehudi Menuhin points to how it combines "intuitive man's immediate responses with cultivated man's most abstract concept of a disembodied, unnameable power unifying creation . . . India had not pulled up the ladder on its journey through the ages, but only lengthened it".[27]

Rādhākrishnan said, "It does not matter what conception of God we adopt so long as we keep up a perpetual search after truth."[28] Exactly so! And one should not neglect the corollary: any way of envisaging or relating to God that prevents us from remaining open to all truth must be abandoned as false, unworthy of God and of the human being who has God within herself. (After all, even if one were wrong in supposing that God/divinity is in the universe, and there really is a deity 'out there' beyond the universe, one can still feel sure that such an anthropomorphic creator-god would be pleased to have his creation worshipped!)

Matter is truly wonderful. *There is no such thing as 'mere' matter.* Our spirituality – our thinking and our loving, for instance, and all that makes life meaningful for us has a physical base. *Spirit is within matter,* not separate from it. That is why we may properly declare that the universe is good, that nature is something to be wondered at and cherished and trusted.

Thomas Aquinas (1225–74) taught that much could be known with certainty about God, his existence and his attributes, by arguing from what our senses tell us about the natural world; and that what could not be known in this way – for example, the Christian Trinity and Incarnation doctrines – was a matter of faith, which requires, not an act of understanding or reason, but simply an act of will. Few theologians today would claim that Aquinas' five arguments for the existence of God amount to absolute and irrefutable proof; but some would agree that any viable attempt to provide a rational framework for belief in God must be grounded in human experience of the natural world – and, one must add – of oneself as part of that world.

Incidentally, just as Aquinas' shortcomings should not lead to an overall dismissal of that great philosopher's thought, so any unacceptable rituals associated with nature-based religion should not prevent us from accepting its fundamental reverence for and feeling of oneness with nature. Animal (sometimes human) sacrifice was practised in nature-cults; and recently, on the occasion of Kali's autumn festival in Calcutta, 800 goats were slaughtered. Earlier, in Canaanite religion, for instance, prostitutes were a temple accessory. I trust that my advocacy of a return to nature will not be interpreted as a recommendation of any such dubious appendages. Moreover, the return I wish for would mean an advance: from the backward-looking Western religiosity to a dynamic spirituality advancing alongside science (though not necessarily accepting all of science's technological offspring) towards ever fuller and surer truth.

The notion of God within things is mystical rather than dogmatic. *Mystic emotion is more fundamental than the varieties of religious creeds*: it has co-existed with monotheisim, polytheism, and pantheism and transcends all these. If I use the word 'mystical' to characterise the notion of immanent divinity, it is not in any elitist sense; rather, my intention is to suggest that this is a natural and instinctive response to the world. If it does not 'come naturally' to us, it may be because we are too much caught up – entangled and asphyxiated – in a terribly busy 'go-get-it' and 'can't-stop-to-gaze-and-wonder' culture (or should I say 'cultural void'?) that robs us of time or incentive to cultivate the basic human responses to the natural world – joy and gratitude, love and reverence – that characterised those ancient ancestors of ours who did not separate themselves from nature but strove to live in harmony with it, in kinship with it.

"If I chop down a tree that blocks my view", says Huston Smith, "each stroke of the axe unsettles the tree; but it leaves its mark on me as well, driving deeper into my being my determination to have my way in the world. Everything I do for my private well-being adds another layer to my ego, and in thickening it insulates me more from God. Conversely, every act done without thought for myself diminishes my self-centredness until finally no barrier remains to separate me from the Divine."[29]

It has been my good fortune to have made the acquaintance of a retired professional gardener who did not make a fortune for himself in monetary terms but more than compensated for that by the deep wisdom and behavioural rightness and dignity that his closeness to nature gave him – even more than sufficient to outweigh the effects of his unspeakable experiences as a Royal Marine Commando in the Second World War. He did not go to church, except for weddings, baptisms and funerals; his religion, like the unknown soldier, had no name – but it went deep into nature's mysteries. *Such is the substance of the religious attitude I wish to commend at a stage in human history when Western forms of religion are fast losing credibility.*

Where does one look to find divinity? Centuries of traditional Western theism have conditioned us to look upwards, where the spires of their great Gothic cathedral churches are pointing. One imagines how myriads of people may have gazed upwards at the twinkling stars in the night sky, wonderingly, even expectantly, only to be disappointed – because what they were looking for was not some property or quality of things that could be seen, but something other than and additional to – but also within – those things. Perhaps, like me, they had been told in Sunday School that God was something – or, more likely, someone – totally outside of things, totally Other.

What we should be looking for is not a thing, and not a person, but a *feeling*, in response to a *perceived property or quality* in things – beauty, goodness, rightness, awesomeness, mystery. The feeling will differ according to the perceived property, or quality: it may be bliss, peace, wonder, awe, reverence, joy, or gratitude. But the feeling will invariably express some underlying and perhaps vague awareness of something vast and not altogether known, namely, nature in its entirety.

Does this encounter cause a shiver of fear, as on seeing something alien? That may be the natural result of an unnatural cultural predisposition to associate ourselves with a world of man-made or machine-made objects – houses, motor cars, refrigerators, dishwashers, underground drains and high-rise blocks of flats ("machines for living in"), space telescopes and electron microscopes, and computers that are outdated almost as soon as they appear on the market.

But our estrangement from nature is not so deeply rooted that we cannot welcome a holiday in the country or at the seaside, or a walk in the park where we can watch swans and ducks and the ubiquitous Canada geese (and see them over-fed with super-refined white bread instead of nutritious grass!), breathe in more or less pure oxygen, gaze into the sky and listen to the sounds of nature, and also its silence (which is, however, always a vibration); and we may begin to wonder at the immensity and majesty and glorious variety of nature and to see it as it truly is – the one and only, stupendous miracle, which scientists have spent centuries exploring, and of which they are revealing newly discovered wonders almost weekly. For anyone with eyes to see and ears to hear, and a receptive mind free from distracting addictions, the worshipfulness of nature is unavoidable; and so is joy in its presence.

And if we look into ourselves . . . ? Perhaps "without a mystical element – namely, an experience of the immediate presence of the divine – there is no religion at all".[30]

From Divinity to Divinity

Our end is our beginning, rediscovered. One may object: "I have no wish to return to my childish beginnings. Whether ontogenous or phylogenous, such a reversion is contrary to evolution." Another may object: "If the human being is the apex and summation of evolution, is it not a perversity to place a thing (divinity = energy etc.) higher than a person (God)?"

But, first, consider: do not the philosopher and the scientist leave self behind in their search for (impersonal) truth? Are not painter and poet, sculptor of stone and composer of music bound to go beyond self if their works are to be anything more than mediocre or mundane?

To those who would object that, if people ceased to think of God as a person, it would mean the end of all belief in God, my reply is the whole of this book – or, more tersely: "Good riddance! Just look at the fruits of theism: bigotry and bloodshed, the triumph of dogma over reason, authority over truth."

An observation made in 1872, in Samuel Butler's *Erewhon*, is relevant here: the fact that people no longer think of justice as a goddess does not mean that justice is no longer respected.[31] We might even say that what that goddess represented continues to hold a special place of honour in the hearts and minds of people (and on the lips of politicians), not despite but because of its depersonification. It is the reverence in which justice was held that led to its deification in the first place!

Justice was only one member of a pantheon, and represented an aspect of human life that belongs to the relatively late city-state stage of civilisation. But what has just been said about this goddess applies equally to the gods of an earlier epoch, when gods represented the energy or forces of nature: the power or powers of nature were not held in awe because they were personified as gods and goddesses; rather, their deification was the *result* of their being held in awe. In other words, religion does not originate from a belief in a god or gods, but from the universal human experience of the world of nature, an experience that included an element of what has been called awe, a mixture of fear and fascination.

With the development of their intellectual faculties human beings have been able to make a less starkly emotional appraisal of their environment, seeing in it orderliness and consistency which answer to the same qualities in the human intellect, and therefore adding to their demeanour towards nature a new confidence in their ability to predict nature's behaviour and consequently exercise some measure – ever increasing – of control over it. But this does not necessarily mean a loss of wonder and awe; rather, for many people the reverse is true: the *modern scientist sees, and shows the rest of us, far more to wonder at in the universe than our Neolithic ancestors could have imagined.*

On the one hand, the religion of reverence must keep abreast of science so as to remain open to new insights and save itself from stagnating. On the other hand, this true religion must also keep abreast of science and its derivative technologies with a view to monitoring their impact on human values, particularly where the purposes served by science and technology are destructive of human life or any other part of the natural world. One thinks particularly of those new explosives that are a thousand times more powerful than the Hiroshima bomb, and of horrifying biological and chemical weapons. One aspect of the international race to amass the biggest and 'best' arsenal is the trillions spent in this enterprise that could have saved or improved the lives of millions of human beings in the Third World – and even in the so-called 'developed' but still unequal Western societies. Ironically, one hopes that this vast expenditure on weapons of mass destruction will be wasted; and in any case it is likely that the new weaponry will very soon become obsolete – if it has not already done so.

What can save us and the world from the inane childish masculine vanity that resorts to violence or the bullying threat of violence ('my bombs are bigger than yours')? Either intelligence and reverence, or nothing.

"There is money in armaments", say the bankers and company directors and shareholders. Is *that* the last word? Is *that* the true measure of humanity? Not if we perceive the divinity in things.

CHAPTER SEVEN

The Christian Doctrine of Incarnation

Restricted Immanence

"Church history is rich in evidence that Christians forget the manhood of their Lord with amazing ease: but they have done so only because they read the Gospels with veiled face."

–   H. R. MACKINTOSH[1]

"It is to be lamented that the history of [Jesus] was written and revised by Men interested in the pious frauds of Religion."

                                       JOHN KEATS, 1821[2]

"Oh, if only your heart could become a manger, God would once again become a child on Earth."

   JOHANN SCHEFFLER (1624–77) better known as Angelus Silesius, 'the Silesian angel'

Generally speaking, Christians have been outraged by or have just firmly refused to listen to the statements of people who value truth more than tradition. In particular, they cling jealously to what they call the historical element in Christianity: namely, the Incarnation of God in Jesus of Nazareth. Take away the Incarnation, they say, and what is left of Christianity?

In this they have received weighty support from theologians. Karl Barth, for instance, said:[3] "The reason for the Christian conviction, according to the Apostles' Creed, cannot be some general truth of an intellectual, sentimental or even metaphysical order. Rather it is founded upon an event which is the history of Jesus Christ . . . "

But what *is* this incarnation: what are its mechanics and its meaning? Church creeds, liturgy and popular hymns speak of God coming down, or sending his Son, to earth from heaven.

The view we take of Incarnation is all of a piece with the view we take of the relations between natural and supernatural, between man and God. Clearly, the Christian Incarnation doctrine is inextricably bound up with a theistic idea of divinity: God as a person, dwelling outside the physical universe, was made flesh in human form.

This is truly remarkable, given the stress laid in Judaism and in Christianity on the transcendence – the otherness – of God. It is as if the proverbial chalk and cheese became one substance. God and a man become Godman, completely divine and completely human.

Kenōsis

How was this possible? Some Christians have said it was the result of divine self-emptying ('kenōsis'), either of God or, as in Paul's epistle to the Philippians (2: 6–11), of the Christ understood as existing before all worlds as (part of) the eternal God. This emptying consisted in a relinquishing of all exclusively divine attributes (omnipotence, omniscience, omnipresence, and immortality), and thus becoming truly human. This doctrine is reminiscent of the divine status bestowed upon the Roman emperor as an embodiment of God, and also of the Jewish Kabbalistic pre-existent Adam Kadmon – the heavenly and primordial, archetypal man. Some Christian theologians of modern times have clung to this doctrine as symbolising an anthropomorphic deity's love for human beings, such that he was ready to live and die as a human being in order to save them from their sinfulness.

Albrecht Ritschl (1822–89) delivered a devastating blow to kenotic theories: to accept kenosis means that we cannot with any assurance believe that *God* was in Jesus at all. If stripped of all the attributes that depict Godhead, what *was* that thing that became Jesus? Don Cupitt remarked that it is *logically* impossible for God (the God of Christian theism) to cast off any of his attributes. To that one may add the question: if they *were* discarded, what happened to those cast-off attributes? and who performed the function (ascribed to God in Christian tradition) of sustaining the cosmos during that period of 35 years or so when God had relinquished his divine attributes? If it is to be allowed to survive, the notion of kenosis demands a universalist interpretation, that is, as a universal immanence of divinity, which has as its corollary the possibility that divinity may not always be given that name by people who experience it. All in all, reason and commonsense lead one to dismiss kenosis as an incredible piece of mythology, the sort of crass mythology that Homer depicts, of deities – both male and female – descending to Earth to mate with human beings.

Virgin Birth

Mark's Gospel

Indeed, the second enabling factor for the birth of God as Jesus of Nazareth bears a striking resemblance to those Greek myths. It is known as the Virgin birth. The earliest of the four canonical gospels, that of Mark, makes no mention of anything remarkable about the manner of Jesus' birth. Must we suppose that Mark got it wrong? Is it not more credible to suppose that Mark stuck to the observable facts and that later writers superimposed on those facts a theological myth?

Mark was not himself one of Jesus' disciples, but he acted as Peter's interpreter: his gospel preserves the content of Peter's public teaching. Moreover, Mark's Gospel has generally been understood as a simple expansion of the primitive 'kerygma' ('preaching'),[4] as distinct from the 'teaching' (didache') which was later added to the kerygma.

When Jesus was born, Mary, his mother was betrothed to Joseph. One might naturally assume, therefore, that Jesus was born out of wedlock, and either that Mark was ignorant of this, or that discretion led him to remain silent on the matter. But since the Jewish custom was to identify a person by naming the *father*, not the mother, the question, "Is not this the carpenter, the son of Mary ... ?"[5] would naturally be taken to mean that the father was unknown and the birth illegitimate. Had Mark been acquainted with any reference to a virgin birth, he would surely have made use of it – if only to spare Mary's blushes.

The purpose of the Virgin Birth was to remove Jesus from the inheritance of the original sin of Adam. Bishop Spong[6] tells us that in the time of Jesus the woman was not thought to contribute anything to the genetic make-up of a child; she merely provided nutrition for the male sperm. (Interestingly, Aquinas, in his attempt to save the Virgin Birth dogma, used Aristotle's false idea that the *male* contributed nothing physical to the offspring.)[7] When, in the 19th century, both these views had to be abandoned in the light of modern genetics, the protection of Jesus from humankind's hereditary sinfulness was supplied by the dogma of the Immaculate Conception of the Blessed Virgin Mary. (I wonder who got promotion for that ingenious piece of sophistry?) The Virgin Birth dogma and the creed's description of Jesus as "the only begotten son of God" are unfortunate: they both remove Jesus from humanity, with the result that Christianity's claim to be the religion of God-expressed-in-human-terms falls to the ground.

For a human being to reveal God it is not necessary to be born of a virgin: what is necessary is that the person respond freely and positively to the indwelling divinity. The person does not have to be a Jew or a Christian, just any man or woman.

Matthew's Gospel

The author of Matthew's Gospel was writing initially for Jewish readers,[8] and is at pains to present Jesus as a second Moses. Not only does he divide Jesus' Sermon on the Mount into five sections to draw a parallel with the five Old Testament books attributed to Moses and the fact that it was a *mount* where Jesus is said to have addressed the crowd – not on a plain as in Luke's Gospel – would immediately put his readers in mind of Mount Sinai from which Moses addressed the Israelites and delivered to them Yahweh's Ten Commandments.

Matthew also makes use of 'midrashim' – the name given to the stories told by rabbinic commentators on the scriptures, to illuminate the meaning of the text. One such midrash is Matthew's story of the Flight into Egypt: Joseph takes Mary and baby Jesus all the way from Bethlehem to Egypt to save Jesus from Herod's wrath and, on hearing that Herod had died, the holy family returns to Bethlehem. Here Matthew again presents Jesus as a second Moses: the first Moses had been placed in a basket on a river, whence he was transported by Pharoah's wife to the royal court; and as a man, Moses led his people out of their slavery in Egypt.

Another example of this story-telling is the rising of the saints' bodies when the veil of the Holy of Holies was rent in two[9] – not to be taken as factual. Yet another example is the visit of the three wise men ('magi').

The fact that Matthew traces the genealogy of Jesus back to Abraham certainly suggests that Matthew saw Jesus' birth as like any other human birth – especially if, for the present text's "Jacob begat Joseph, *husband of Mary from whom was born Jesus*"[10] we substitute the Syriac manuscript's "Jacob begat Joseph, *Joseph begat Jesus*". Luke also provides a genealogy for Jesus, but this one goes all the way back to Adam: Luke's gospel was intended for Gentiles.

Although the Gospel of Matthew shows signs of being written for Jewish Christians, it closes on a more universal note. In Matthew 10:5 we have Jesus forbidding his disciples to preach to the Gentiles, but in 28:18–20 he tells them to "make all the nations my disciples", the Jews having shown themselves unworthy to enter the kingdom of heaven (22:1–14). This volte face tells us that "Matthew does not work in a vacuum, but within the life of a church for whose needs he is catering . . . ".[11]

Luke's Gospel

Luke's gospel differs significantly from Matthew's. The latter makes much of the Last Judgment,[12] where "there shall be the weeping and gnashing of teeth", the Son of Man will "come in his glory" to judge humankind, sentencing some to "eternal punishment" and rewarding the righteous with eternal life. Luke, on the other hand, is more interested in the *humanity* of Jesus, and particularly Jesus' compassion The Good Samaritan parable appears only in Luke's gospel; whereas Matthew's version of the Beatitudes has "the poor in spirit" (meek and docile), Luke's version has simply "the poor". The parables of the Rich Man and Lazarus, the Unjust Judge, and the Pharisee and the Tax-collector[13] (the last two found only in Luke's gospel) all depict Jesus' concern for society's outcasts; and in the godly Simeon's song on the occasion of Jesus' circumcision (preserved as the Nune Dimittis in church liturgy) we see Luke's firm belief in universal salvation.

John's Gospel

With the Fourth gospel (written sometime between 90 and 140 CE) we come upon a totally divine Jesus. John gives us no birth story. Instead, he gives us a profound mystical theology of Incarnation in which the Christ is the eternal divine 'word' or 'reason' ('logos'). He gives us no account of Jesus' temptation or Jesus' last supper with the disciples, but he does have John the Baptist refer to Jesus as the Lamb of God[14] which may refer to the lamb sacrificed at the annual Passover festival: after describing Jesus' crucifixion, John says it fulfils the prophecy that not a bone of him will be broken – which was one of the regulations concerning the sacrifice of the Passover lamb.[15] On the other hand, he has Jesus declaring: "I am the resurrection and the life,"[16] and "Before Abraham was, I am."[17] Thus not only in the prologue but throughout the gospel, Jesus is acknowledged as the eternal (supernatural or spiritual?) Christ.

Jesus as Son of God

When Paul (who had not seen Jesus in the flesh but only in a vision after Jesus' death) began to preach in the synagogues of Damascus, he proclaimed Jesus as "the Son of God".[18] This was perhaps the first hint of what would become a long-lasting division in the Church. In the primitive Church Jewish Christians would certainly not have quarrelled with Jesus' appropriation of the title 'Son of Man', which was how Jews referred to their hoped-for Messiah. But not only Jewish but also many other Christians drew the line at accepting Jesus as the Son of God. They accepted him as '*a* Son of God' which in Hebrew and Aramaic meant 'a godly man' – which is how the Roman centurion described Jesus at his crucifixion. We may compare the Hebrew 'son of wisdom' (meaning 'a wise man'). Old Testament 'sons of God' (= 'godly men') included Moses, David and Israel. (Indeed, the Book of Genesis speaks of "the sons of God" taking beautiful human women as wives.[19] But this is a reference to ancient demi-gods or heroes, such as we find in early Greek mythology.)

One should also bear in mind what Jesus told the crowd and his disciples: "Call no man on earth your father: for one is your Father, which is in heaven."[20] Jesus here surely meant that we are all God's children. Similarly, where Matthew,[21] in his account of Jesus' baptism by John, tells of Jesus having a vision and hearing God say, "This is my beloved son, in whom I am well pleased", we do not have to see any Christological significance. (The creedal Trinitarian dogma was not formulated for another 300 years, and even then it was hotly disputed.)

The only New Testament appearance of the Trinitarian formula ("In the name of the Father and of the Son and of the Holy Ghost") comes at the very end of Matthew's Gospel[22] and is almost certainly a later addition by the Church. The *Shepherd of Hermas*, written *c*. 90 CE (before Matthew's Gospel), makes no mention of the Trinity, but says, "First of all, believe that God is One . . . ". Another book probably belonging to the age of the Apostolic Fathers but rejected by the Church is the Gospel of Thomas, which presents Jesus simply as 'a man' (which is what the phrase 'son of man' means). Jesus is not presented as 'Christ' or 'Messiah', or as a *unique* son of God; nor is anything said about any saving significance of Jesus' crucifixion; and no mention is made of an empty tomb.[23]

I have mentioned that Jewish Christians baulked at the idea of Jesus as Son of God. Six hundred years later the Qur'an was to insist, as the Jewish Old Testament had done, that God was one and therefore could not have a son. "They [Christians] say: 'Allah has begotten a son'? Allah forbid! Self-sufficient is He. He is all that the heavens and the earth contain. Surely for this you have no sanction. Would you say of Allah what you do not know?"[24] Al-Tabari (d. 855 CE), a Christian converted to Islam, said Christianity could *not be* true, since its Incarnation doctrine implied that Jesus was both creator and created, thus raising the question of whether Jesus is God, or a second God; and how could Jesus *be* God and be *sent by* God?[25] 'Sent by God' is a phrase used in the Hebrew Bible of prophets.

The Alāwi, an extremist Shi'a sect, believe that 'Ali, Muhammad's son-in-law, was an incarnation of Allah. But for mainstream Islam the idea of incarnation is blasphemous: the fundamental doctrine of Islam is 'tawhid' the 'oneness' of Allah. Veneration of the Prophet in Pakistan, and Sufi veneration of Sufi saints are tolerated but are, strictly speaking, contrary to Qur'an and Hadith ('tradition').

Meanwhile, Christianity revels in the 'scandal of particularity': only one incarnation, and that was Jesus the Christ.

The Messianic Secret[26]

Rudolf Bultmann (1884 – 1976) and other New Testament scholars have told us that Jesus was a simple but somewhat heretical rabbi. It is clear, however, that the early Church held Jesus to be the Messiah and the Son of God; and so, not finding sufficient grounds in Jesus' own teaching for this belief, the Church invented the 'Messianic Secret'. That is to say, throughout the synoptic gospels (Mark, Matthew and Luke) words were put into Jesus' mouth warning his disciples, and some of the people he cured, not to tell others that he was the Messiah.

Other scholars take a different view: that Jesus did see himself as the Messiah, but a purely moral and spiritual leader of his people; and, if he bade his disciples and others not to reveal his Messiahship, it was in order to prevent people (particularly those in authority) from getting the idea that he claimed to be the political and regal messiah of popular expectation. The Hebrew and Aramaic 'messiah' = Greek 'christos' = 'annointed'. The Kings of Israel were anointed at their accession and were referred to from then on as God's 'annointed one'.[27] They were also given the title 'begotten son of God'.[28]

Was Jesus Sinless?

If Jesus was God, surely he must have been incapable of sin; if he was human, he was surely capable (at least) of sinning. This conundrum is not solved in the gospels. Mark and Luke have Jesus protesting, "Why callest thou me good? There is none good but God." This does seem to suggest that Jesus did not think of himself as God. Was he *mistaken* in this? If so, that itself is surely evidence that he was human, not God.

Matthew (whose gospel continued to be the Church's favourite gospel for 700 years) has "Why askest thou me concerning the good?" This alteration was probably due to the fact that Matthew was writing at the end of the first century CE and was presenting the early Church's belief in Christ's sinlessness.

One argument that has raged in the Church was between those who maintained that Jesus could not sin and those who held that he could not-sin. This distinction is more clearly expressed in the Latin 'non posse peccare' and 'posse non peccari'. Here we see the important implication of the second statement: if Jesus was free *not* to sin, he must also have been free to sin. The possibility of the one cannot exist without the possibility of the other.

This piece of straightforward logic did not suit those who wanted to insist that Jesus was the only Son of God, of one substance with the Father, and believed – mistakenly – that the only way to do this was to claim for Jesus a different constitution from that of mere human beings; and therefore fitted him up with a unique divine supercharger. But what relevance can the life and teachings of such a unique, one-off being have for those of us who lack that supercharger? In order to command our attention Jesus needs to be seen as both human and divine; but what this means – and rationally can only mean – is that Jesus is divine in a way that is accessible to all human beings. *Any authority of his teaching (by word or example) lies in the correspondence between what he teaches from that transpersonal level of consciousness at which he is receptive to the indwelling divinity and what we ourselves may intuitively experience and accept at that same transpersonal level.*

By 'transpersonal' I do not mean 'supernatural' or 'superhuman'. We do not need to be supernatural or superhuman to have divinity within ourselves. Divinity is present in all natural things and therefore in all human beings. What counts, however, is *whether*, and *how* we respond personally to the indwelling divinity.

Was Jesus Perfect?

Christians habitually claim that Jesus was the perfect man. Do we – can we – really know? We cannot even define human perfection; we can only point out the ways that seem to lead towards it. We can aver that it consists in being open to God so that God can work in and through us. Perhaps this is all we need to say about the attributed perfection of Jesus.

Much depends on what you mean by 'perfect'. Sometimes we feel we have witnessed perfection when hearing an enthralling piece of music so well played as to express just what the music itself contains, with no addition or subtraction. In the same way, many people who witnessed Jesus must have felt they were in the presence of a perfect human being. But, just as we cannot assume that either the composer or the performer of the piece of music was perfect in all respects, so one might see Jesus as spiritually perfect without necessarily assuming that he was in every way perfect: for example, did he *know* everything?

The traditional Christian notion of God's own perfection is static. God cannot change, since any change could only be a move away from perfection. But, as we have seen (pages 10–11), A. N. Whitehead points out that such an understanding of perfection is not in keeping with our present understanding of the universe. Today we know that our own bodies are constantly, continuously changing: old cells die, to be replaced by new ones. One could almost say that we never touch the same body twice. On the grand scale, we know that the whole cosmos is constantly changing. At present it is still expanding as a result of the initial big bang. Perhaps it will at some time in the future implode, in preparation for another explosion. Within our solar system we see movement everywhere. On planet Earth we have evidence of evolution at the physical and chemical and biological levels; and we ourselves are capable of creating ourselves, transcending what we presently are.

According to Whitehead's definition, something is perfect if at any given time it is as good as it could reasonably be expected to be, but is always capable of going beyond what it now is. I am reminded of what Sartre said: that you cannot properly say what a person *is*; only – after the person's death – what that person *was*.

To be perfect in the traditional Christian sense, as applied to God, must now be seen as something less than complimentary – as if God were like the man who boasted that he had never changed his mind about anything! To grow is to change from what one now is – unless one is the old God-in-the-sky, which is dead.

Returning, then, to Jesus, one acknowledges the divinity in Jesus. He was assuredly a godly person, full of compassion for the suffering and the poor and needy; he was rightfully indignant at the Pharisees' loveless righteousness; and his way of life – ascetic and prayerful – as well as his preaching, suggests that he was a truly spiritual person. The same may be said of Mahatma Gandhi. An old Indian lady had spent a whole day standing, without eating or drinking, to hear Gandhi speak. When asked why, she said, "Because I believe he is an incarnation of God". Jesus was not meant to be unique.

Incidentally, if Jesus prayed to God, it should be seen, not as a denial but as a confirmation of his godliness, his union – but not identity – with the indwelling divinity. He rejects the heavy burden of the Pharisaic petty and punitive legalism and substitutes for it an "easy yoke", that of compassion and love in response to the promptings of the God within. Of course, praying is something human beings do, not gods. Indeed, it may be said to be the quintessentially human activity since it means being open to – aware and receptive of – divinity; but also because in prayer the human spirit is most fully engaged. In prayer there is no alternation of divine and human activity, of listening and speaking. 'Speaking' to God must be with attention, else it were not prayer but a mere form of words; 'listening' is not purely passive, since it implies the previous posing of a question – a positive, creative act on our part.

But Jesus is represented as having declared that the end of the world was nigh and could even occur within the lifetime of some of those who were listening to him, and, as Albert Schweitzer pointed out, this belief in an imminent day of judgment might account for the extraordinary demands he made of those who would be his disciples: forsaking home and family and work, in exchange for a life of celibacy, poverty and homelessness – extreme measures in response to extreme circumstances, what Schweitzer called a 'Notethik', an 'emergency ethic'.

Well, it is human to err, is it not? It is also human, all too human to cry, "My God, why hast thou forsaken me?" – one of Jesus' last utterances on the cross.

At the same time, words that the Fourth Gospel ascribes to Jesus, "I am the way, the truth and (the) life", may truly reflect Jesus' own conviction that the sole reason for his life was to allow the indwelling divinity to express itself in everything that he (Jesus, or the divinity within him? both, in unison) did or said. *Yet even in a man who was at one with divinity to such a high degree we must expect limitations determined by the when and where of the man's birth and life.*

This applies to other great spiritual teachers, to whom we must not turn a blind eye just because they almost inevitably display either the influence of, or their own opposition to, their environment. Does this not apply to Shakyamuni "the Buddha" ('the enlightened one') in 6th century BCE India, who bequeathed to the world a non-theistic religion but was himself eventually deified by many of his followers? And does it not apply also to those other known spiritual creative geniuses, the great composers and artists from medieval to modern times, and philosophers and scientists?

Jesus' Miracles

Like other great spiritual teachers, Jesus was credited with many "mighty works". He is said to have walked on water and to have performed other 'nature miracles' such as the stilling of the storm, the multiplying of locusts and fishes, and the turning of water into wine. Such feats were ascribed to godly people in other traditions. The story is told of a disciple of the Buddha who came running to his master to tell him, "I've done it! I've walked on the water". The Buddha is said to have replied, "So what? It is only a penny on the ferry." The Buddha did not encourage trivial pursuits.

In Tibetan Buddhism there has been a long tradition of what looks like magic, probably originating in the aboriginal Bon-po religion. It is based on the identification of energy and consciousness, the power of mind over matter, power that was used to control breath and heart-beat and even gravity, as well as taking the place of medicine. The Tibetan Buddhist Milarepa is reported to have flown through the air with the speed of an arrow and to have produced food as if by magic – just by joining his consciousness to the Eternal Mind. ('Yoga' = 'joining').[29] But one should add that for Milarepa himself the yogic goal was not to work wonders, but to enjoy the quiescent state of eternal bliss that is attained in meditation (Samādhi).

It is said of the Christian mystic Suso (14th century CE) that it seemed to him, in an ecstatic state, that he walked on air; and both Teresa and Catherine of Siena spoke of being lifted up bodily from the earth in a state of rapture.[30]

Did not Moses and Elijah perform such magic – the one causing the waters of the so-called Red Sea (but probably 'reed sea' i.e. marshland) to part, allowing the Israelites to escape from the pursuing Egyptian chariots, the other bringing rain from the skies to extinguish the pagan priests' sacrificial fire? According to his Shi'ah Muslim followers, Ali stopped the flood-waters of the Euphrates when they were about to engulf Kufah. Such wonders must be seen as legendary supports to the prestige and godliness of a religious figure.

Vincent Taylor (a dear man who gave me, as an impecunious student, his old copy of a Lexicon of New Testament Greek) suggested that Jesus' stilling of the waves was "probably a miracle of divine providence. Jesus trusted in God and his trust was not deceived."[31] That could well be the case. But I am inclined to see it as part of the trappings of celebrity. (One must acknowledge the effect of repeated positive affirmations, which can change one's attitude and expectations, making possible what had previously seemed impossible of achievement. But this should not be classed as miraculous: one can make sense of it, as of other mind-over-matter phenomena, without recourse to 'the supernatural'.)

As for the miracles of virgin birth, bodily resurrection, post-mortem appearances, and ascent into heaven, these must be classified as 'tales that are told', like the imaginative rabbinic midrashim. If resurrection and ascension are physical phenomena, could we not say that they occur if, after resuscitation, a person is put into a space rocket and sent off into outer space? In other words, what sense, if any, can be assigned to them if taken literally? India is rich in stories of holy men who rose after three days' burial, reduced their own body to dust or passed through solid walls.

Matthew's Gospel closes fittingly (as the Church's faithful servant) with the story of the chief priests giving large sums of money to the guards to say that Jesus' disciples stole the body at night while the guards slept. This prop for the resurrection dogma was followed immediately by Jesus' post-mortem appearance to his disciples in Galilee, telling them to preach the gospel to all nations and promising to be with them till the end of the world.[32] (Matthew was in Antioch, a centre for missionary activity, contrasted with the conservatively Jewish Jerusalem.)

Perhaps Jesus' *healing miracles* should be given a rather different kind of explanation. They might aptly be called faith healings, since Jesus insisted that the person in question, or someone accompanying the person, should have faith; and such faith healing persists in our own age, and is sometimes claimed to be effective even over long distances. Traditionally, too, shamans and yogis have been said to have healing powers; and the shaman who did not show prowess in this field would soon lose his patronage and his living.

Moreover, healing miracles seem to be all of a piece with Jesus' great compassion for the poor and needy, whereas those who tauntingly requested something spectacular were given a cold shoulder. Certainly, those who regularly practise yoga in a class will testify to the healing energy that fills the atmosphere and one's own body and mind; the teacher does not need to have supernatural powers, but only an egoless submission to the indwelling divinity, the source of energy and strength and control.

In this connection, it is interesting to note that there was an early Hebrew belief in the "extension of personality" whereby energy is transferred from healer to healed. This information comes from J. Mauchline who, in the course of his comments on the story of Elisha's resuscitation of the lady of Shunem's dead child, refers to A. R. Johnson, *The Vitality of the Individual in the Thought of Ancient Israel* (1949).[33]

At all events, we must not discount Jesus' attractive power over the masses – by word and deed – which eventually led to his crucifixion.

On the other hand, the power to work miracles should not be seen as a necessary qualification for godliness or – as in the Roman Catholic Church – for sainthood. The New Testament miracle stories are not to be taken as proofs that Jesus was God. It is certainly specious to ascribe the miracles to the agency of God whilst attempting to save the humanity of Jesus by some theory of kenosis!

We must entirely dispense with supernatural connotations of the word 'miracle'. The word itself simply means something to be wondered at. We may appropriately link this notion of the miraculous (something that arouses a sense of wonder) with the notion of divinity that is presented in this book. But this divinity is within nature, not a supernatural visitor.

Was Jesus God, or Godly?

Gibbon, in *The Decline and Fall of the Roman Empire*, was caustically critical of the bishops and theologians who, as he put it, quarrelled over a mere diphthong. He was referring to a long-lasting debate on whether Jesus was of the *same* substance (Greek 'homoousios') as God or of a *similar* substance ('homoiousios'). But this difference of substance was for the Church leaders substantial also in the sense that it was the difference between saying that Jesus was God and saying that he was a godly man.

Bp. John Chrysostom (= 'golden tongued') (*c.* 347–407) said we are entirely ignorant of God's nature but, since Jesus was of the same nature as God we could rely on Jesus to tell us what God's nature is! Full marks for ingenuity, but blatantly begging the question! Jesus' purpose, said Chrysostom, was to reveal his divine origin; so we must take note of occasions when Jesus healed people without uttering a prayer to God, rather than the occasion when he prayed over the tomb of Lazarus. The latter, said Chrysostom, does not mean Jesus needed help from God: the prayer was simply a model for his listeners to use!

There is no problem here for anyone who believes in the divinity that is in all things. But for a Church fixated on the notion of a transcendent and totally 'other' deity there could be no rational account of divine incarnation. The result *was mythology presented as historical fact, an unsustainable hybrid* – what might be called a 'condescending'[34] dogma, but not an intelligible concept.

H. R. Mackintosh,[35] referring to the Fourth evangelist's view of the relationship between God and Jesus, uses the phrase "mutual immanence". This felicitous phrase is easily transferable to a non-theistic scenario, in which it would represent a spiritual relationship between spirit and Spirit, requiring of the man Jesus a continual practice of the presence of God within him.

Origen, one of the Church's Fathers (*c.* 185–254 CE) and his contemporary Paul of Samosata, Bp. of Antioch, taught that the union of divine and human in the Christ was not a union of substances, but a dynamic relationship that permitted separation. In other words, its maintenance – and, indeed, its origin – depended upon acts of will (though one may say that these became, with time, an unwavering attitude or mind-set). Origen and Paul spoke of a gradual merging or commingling of divinity and humanity, so that the humanity of Jesus became deified. I certainly have no quarrel with this.

The man who really set the cat among the pigeons was Arius (*c.* 250–*c.* 336), who taught that it was nonsense to say that the Son was equally pre-existent with the Father: any son must, by definition, come into existence after the father. Arius quoted the gospels to confirm his teaching that Jesus was a spiritual and ascetic man, 'a son of God' (a godly man), but not '*the* Son of God' – for example, John ch. I verse 14, where the correct translation of the Greek is "as of *an* only begotten from *a* father" and ch. XIV, verse 28: "the Father is greater than I".

One cannot help seeing the influence of his namesake on the modern German-born theologian Paul Tillich (1886–1965) who, like the other Paul, spoke of God's *adoption* of Jesus. This is to be seen as an attempt to signify the godliness of Jesus as a consequence of an inner union with the indwelling divinity: and should not be dismissed simply because it is redolent of an early 'heresy' or because it would mean a break with tradition – after all, truth must take precedence over tradition, and it is never too late to mend an error. The earliest Christian conception of the relation between the divine and the human in Jesus may well be closer to adoptionism than to incarnationism: contrast Acts 10:38 (which tells how, at Jesus' baptism, " . . . God anointed him with the Holy Ghost and with power . . . for God was with him") with John 10:32ff (where Jesus speaks of being "sent into the world . . . by the Father"). As to the moment of adoption, it is significant that the earliest New

Testament gospel begins with Jesus' baptism and temptation (= testing), not with his birth.

What Tillich saw in the Christian Incarnation is the mingling of divinity and humanity, not as a 'miraculous', i.e. impossible, mixing of two substances that were generally believed to be incompatible, but rather as a personal *spiritual* union of a man with God. For Tillich, God was not a thing or person existing in addition to the things and persons that constitute the physical universe. Rather, God was "Being", understood as the ultimate reality from which all things and persons derive their existence; and the "depth", in the sense of anything that a human being holds to with absolute or "ultimate" seriousness.

Scottish theologian Donald Baillie (1887–1954) approached the mystery of Incarnation through that of *grace*. The experience of what Christians call grace is of a power within one's spirit which gives rise to action that is truly one's own, free and personal, but which one attributes to the 'grace' or power of God. Grace and freedom are correlative, not contradictory concepts.

Of course, Baillie thought and wrote as a theist; but if we discount his theism and interpret 'grace' as an equivalent of the indwelling cosmic 'creative energy' or 'divinity', we may see his affinity with the thesis presented in this book.

I believe that, just as there was a division between those who stressed the divinity of Jesus (represented by the Alexandrian school of theology) and those who stressed his humanity (the Antiochene school), so today we have the same division, plus the many who, consciously or unconsciously, shift the emphasis to suit their purpose on any given occasion whilst hoping to remain within the bounds of orthodoxy – whatever these are, or are seen to be.

What must be understood is that, if we remove either divinity or humanity from Jesus, we take from him any value as a revelation of the only God we can know – the divinity in nature and in the depths of our own humanity.

But did God *definitively* reveal himself in Jesus? Was God's *fullness* present in Jesus, and *only* in him? So the Church has claimed, although I believe few Christians would say they know God totally.

Here one can learn from the 10th century CE Sūfi mystic Jili who, when remonstrating with the Christian restriction of divine revelation to the person of Jesus, declared: "God said, 'I breathed my Spirit into Adam'; and here the name 'Adam' signifies every human individual. The contemplation of those who behold God in man is the most perfect in the world. Something of this vision the Christians possess and their doctrine about Jesus will lead them at last . . . . to the knowledge that mankind are like mirrors set face to face, each of which contains what is in all; and so they will behold God in themselves and declare Him to be absolutely One."[36] (The last sentence reminds one of the Celtic druids' practice of meditating in pairs, each looking into the face of the other.)

CHAPTER EIGHT

Incarnation and Atonement Mythology

"The sick and perishing – it was they who despised the body and the earth, and invented the heavenly world, and the redeeming blood-drops . . ."

NIETZSCHE, *Thus Spake Zarathustra*

"There is no Christian doctrine which arouses fiercer resentment and opposition [than the Atonement], just as there is none more passionately welcomed and confessed."

J. Z. MOZLEY, *The Doctrine of the Atonement*[1]

"The mythology of the New Testament is in essence that of Jewish Apocalyptic and the Gnostic redemption myths."
RUDOLF BULTMANN (1884–1976), N.T. scholar and theologian

Just as Jesus' (as distinct from the Church's) teaching on God would seem to deny incarnation even as a possibility, so it has nothing to say about making a sacrificial atonement for man's sins. Just as Martha's declaration, "I believe you are the Christ, the Son of God, he who comes into the world"[2] is a fragment of an early Christian creed; so the redemptive significance of Jesus' death and resurrection reflects the myth, popular in the Hellenistic period, of a dying-and-rising-again saviour-deity.

Close to the end of his life Jesus sees the thunderclouds gathering, the wrath of the Jewish priestly hierarchy, and realises that his end is near. At this point he climbs the Mount of Olives, a traditional place of prayer, and prays, "Father, all things are possible to you; remove this cup from me; however, not what I will, but what you will."[3]

Here we are still within the realm of history. The passage in Mark 14:32–42 is just one more repetition of a constantly recurring Old Testament theme of what German scholars have called "Heilsgeschichte" ('salvation history'). The Old Testament is not a book – or, more correctly, a series of books – chiefly concerned with history as mere facts; its writers and editors are at pains to teach the significance of the Chosen People's history in terms of that people's relationship with God. Broadly speaking, the events of their history express God's wrath or pleasure: e.g. defeat in battle, being carried off as slaves betoken his wrath at their disobedience or lack of piety; delivery from exile and slavery, or giving them a fertile land to live comfortably in, was a reward for their repentance.

The particular episode that is repeated in Jesus' prayer on the Mount of Olives is in 2 Samuel 15. David, convinced that his son Absalom has taken his place as King, walks barefoot up the Mount and confides to his companion: "If I find grace in Yahweh's eye, he will let me see once again his ark and his dwelling [the Temple in Jerusalem]. But if he says that he no longer cares for me, so may he do to me as he sees is good." The result of this self-effacing submission to Yahweh? In the battle between David's supporters and those of Absalom, Absalom is found dead, hanging from a tree. After bewailing his son's death, David rides down to Jerusalem on a donkey, as Yahweh's anointed one (King) re-entering his royal city.

As with David, so with Jesus. Having submitted himself totally to his Father's will, he too rides into Jerusalem on a donkey – to return, by way of an ignominious and painful death, to his Father's throne in heaven.[4]

The remainder of the story of Jesus is not midrash, but myth. Just as Jesus' (as distinct from the Church's) teaching on God would seem to deny incarnation even as a possibility, so it has nothing to say about making a sacrificial atonement for the sins of humankind. Just as Martha's declaration, "I believe you are the Christ, the Son of God, he who comes into the world"[5] is a fragment of an early Christian creed; so the redemptive significance of Jesus' death and resurrection reflects the myth, popular in the Hellenistic world, of a dying-and-rising-again saviour deity.

Without the myth, the Church's mission would have been a failure. What could Jesus' followers have offered the world? Of course there was a fine example of godly living, Jesus' life of loving, caring service of people in need; but that did not offer salvation, whereas the Hellenistic mystery cults did. His promised reign of God on earth had not materialised. A warning that people must prepare themselves for an imminent day of judgment? But on that score Jesus had lost credibility; and in any case the messianic theme might have made little sense outside Judaism. Christianity would probably have remained a minor Jewish sect had it not adopted the popular mythology of the mystery cults.

Mystery Cults

One of these was Mithraism, which came from Persia and was akin to the Amidha Buddhism that flourished in Japan and was centred on mystical union with the solar Buddha of the Land of Bliss. Mithraic novitiates were laid beneath a grill through which the blood of a slaughtered bull (representing the god Mithra) baptised them. Underlying the ritual was the belief that the spirit had to be freed from its imprisonment in the body, which was the source of evil. Thus, the initiate must himself die to the senses as a prelude to true – spiritual – life. Not surprisingly, women were not accepted as initiates in the Mithraic cult. Several mystery religions established themselves in Rome, and under Emperor Commodus (180–192) Mithraism was elevated to the status of official imperial religion. When Constantine in the 4th century made Christianity the official imperial religion, was it because he saw Christianity as a mystery cult, too? It would certainly appear so.

The Greek Dionysus, son of Zeus and Semele, and the Egyptian Osiris, son of sky-goddess Nut and earth-god Geb, were both human insofar as they both suffered and died; but both were resurrected and thereby redeemed their initiates, who would be resurrected after death and join Osiris in his eternal realm.

Evelyn Underhill explained that "The idea of Divine Union as man's true end" seems to have arisen in Europe with the Orphic mysteries in Greece and Southern Italy in the 6th century BCE.[6] The Orphic myth tells us that the human soul was the indwelling Dionysian–Orphic factor, imprisoned by the corporeal factor. Thus, 'soma–sema' (= 'the body [is] the tomb'). But by asceticism the body could be purified, thus releasing the soul from its fetters; and by meditation the initiate could become united with the indwelling divinity,[7] receiving full divine status after death. Significantly, some Christian catacombs contained drawings of Orpheus.

Hermeticism, a Gnostic cult of Hermes Trismegistus (a Greek equivalent of the Egyptian god Thoth), also sought emancipation from the flesh through rigorous asceticism.

The body–spirit dualism that characterised the mystery cults was present in the early Church, where it found dramatic expression in the desert anchorites known as 'the pillar saints'; and the question of whether and to what extent women should be allowed in churches has featured in the Church, in East and West, from the time of Paul to the present day.

Unfortunately, in its borrowings from the mystery cults, the Church has sometimes overlooked the mystical understanding of a spiritual merging of humanity and divinity. The word 'Atonement' says it all: Dionysus, Orpheus, Mithras; all these gods themselves died. But the Christian God had a Son to suffer and die as a vicarious sacrifice to save us human beings: from *God's judgment!*[8]

Nicholas Berdyaev rightly distinguishes[9] Eastern Christianity from Western, as being less attracted by ideas of atonement and of salvation (by faith or works) than by transfiguration and deification. We shall return to this Eastern perspective when we look at Origen's teaching on 'apokatastasis'. Meanwhile, let us stay with what may be called classical Christian understanding of Atonement.

The classical theories of Atonement tend to be grossly theistic. The Church rejected the polytheistic myths of Greece and Rome – the battles of gods in the heavens, and the thunder-producing marital quarrels of Zeus and Hera. But the dying-and-rising-again saviour cults were something different: they appealed to many intelligent people; the church quickly succumbed to these external forces, forces that had little to do with the historical Jesus who was the ostensible founder of Christianity – these were *foreign* forces that represented what might be called the religious band-waggon of the Hellenistic age (311 BCE–324 CE).

There is, however, a significant difference between the sacrifice of the Mithraic cosmic bull and Jesus' sacrifice. The Mithraic example shows death in a positive light, as a revitalising force that may be experienced within ourselves in the spiritual growth brought about by the willed 'death' (relinquishment) of the old materialistic self, the unenlightened ego. The Christian example, on the other hand, shows death in a negative light: Jesus Christ died on the cross to make amends vicariously for human sin, thus *saving us from the otherwise dire consequences of God's judgment.*

Many Christians would say that it was God's love for us that caused him to send his Son into the world to die on our behalf. "God so loved the world that he gave his only begotten Son . . . "[10] If so, why the need for a human sacrifice? Or was it a sacrifice of God by God to God? But how could that be necessary except perhaps for a pathological deity? a vampire deity? One is reminded of Abraham's readiness to offer his son Isaac as a propitiatory sacrifice to Yahweh. On that occasion Yahweh told Abraham to sacrifice a ram instead; and some scholars have understood this story as marking the time when the Hebrews abandoned the practice of human sacrifice. Whether or not those scholars are right, we must ask ourselves why God – the same God – insisted on sacrificing his own Son ("begotten before all worlds") as an appeasement. Could anything be more revolting than Paul's words about God "making peace through the blood of his [Jesus'] cross"? Why did God need his Son to die an ignominious and painful death before he could forgive human beings? What *sort* of God would require it? Had Jesus misunderstood God when he told the parable of the Prodigal Son?[11]

Original Sin

One answer to this is that, although it was humankind that had sinned and therefore *ought* to make amends, their sinfulness disabled them from offering anything acceptable to God. Only a perfect man – a God-Man, in fact – could make a sufficient offering. Moreover, that perfect being would have to be free, not only from all particular sins of commission or omission, but also from the *original sin*, or tendency to sin, that has been passed on by heredity to all human beings in all parts of the world. At a meeting of the Council of Trent in 1546 it was declared that "If any one asserts that the sin of Adam . . . which has been transmitted to all mankind by propagation, not through imitation . . . can be removed either by man's natural powers or by any other remedy than the merit of the one mediator our Lord Jesus Christ . . . let him be anathema."[12]

Hence the birth of Jesus from a virgin who, according to Pope Pius IX, had herself been immaculately conceived, i.e. without any taint of original sin. That was in 1854. Up till then there had been differing opinions: Anselm, Archbishop of Canterbury from 1093 to 1109, in his *Cur deus homo (Why God became man)* taught that Mary had been conceived and born in sin. Aquinas said she was conceived in sin but purified before birth. However, Pius IX settled the matter definitively, especially since, in 1870, he decreed that "the Roman Pontiff" (the pope) is "endowed with that infallibility with which the Divine Redeemer has willed that His Church – in defining doctrine concerning faith or morals – should be equipped: And therefore, that such definitions of the Roman Pontiff of themselves – and not by virtue of the consent of the Church – are irreformable."[13]

Adam's apple, the fruit of the tree of knowledge of good and evil, depicted in the Book of Genesis as Satan's gift, for which Adam put the blame on Woman, was in fact the gift of God. That is to say (if I may be excused for using the idiom of myth to explain the myth), eating the fruit of the tree of knowledge put the human being, male and female, on a level higher than the rest of the natural world: to be human meant having a degree of consciousness that included conscience. In other words, 'original sin' was concomitant with the acquisition of freedom, freedom of will. Where before there had been only instinct in creatures, now – in the human being – there came into existence the possibility – and necessity – of choosing good or evil, right or wrong, truth or falsehood.

But it is not as if humanity *chose* freedom. The freedom to choose was assigned by God or, as we would say today, by natural selection from random mutations. How unacceptable, then – both logically and ethically – is a myth in which God denounces the human being for the consequences of the freedom that God himself had, without consultation, bestowed upon him! Here, by 'human being' I mean not only Adam and Eve but all the billions of human beings descended from them. The Church, until recently, and still in some parts of it, has taught that newborn babies must undergo baptism to wash away the inherited original sin – in case they died early, with the taint of original sin still within them.

It is no longer acceptable to talk about sin as if it were a physical substance that can contaminate human offspring. What could be the use of such a notion, apart from buttressing the Church's authority? If so, what was once a support has now become an ethical and logical embarrassment, which can be removed only by showing more respect for truth. So absurd and horrific is the notion of original sin that no rational being could accept it unless there were no alternative. But there are alternatives. Why can the Christian God not just forgive, tout court? "Tout comprendre, c'est tout pardonner." This Christian Creator seems not to know as much about evolution as we do. Is this because those who invented this God were ignorant of evolution? Or had this Creator just forgotten that he had created human beings with in-built freedom? If we were charitable, we might put all this down to the Old Man in the Sky suffering from senile dementia. But if we are realistic and stand with our feet firmly grounded on earth, we must surely say: better no god than this one!

Atonement is not necessary in Islam. Original sin is not a part of Islamic belief: when Adam repented, Allah forgave him. No need, therefore, for a redeemer, let alone a redeeming sacrifice in which God is incredibly both the initiator and the sacrificial victim. It would appear that Allah was more reasonable on this score than the Judaeo-Christian God.

One question that occupied some of the Church Fathers (renowned theologians of the early Church) was whether Jesus' sacrificial death was addressed to God or the Devil. One who took the latter view was Gregory of Nyssa (4th century). He said the sacrifice was necessary to purchase our release from the Devil who, because of our sinfulness, claims us as his own. Gregory is thought to be the first to use the now famous (or infamous?) imagery of bait. Jesus Christ was the bait offered to Satan in the form of a huge fish who, having grown especially fond of a menu of human flesh and seeing in Jesus a particularly tasty morsel, swallowed the bait with alacrity – but got caught on the hook! The hook was God, hidden within the human flesh of Jesus, and deadly poisonous to the Devil. So it was that God, with a cunningly counterfeited ransom, saved us from the Devil.[14]

The Christian Church did not forsake mythology. It simply selected a mythology to suit its determination to become, and to be seen as, God's new chosen people (Greek 'ekklesia' = 'the selected') to replace the old, Jewish chosen people and become the religion for all people. Hence its readiness to adopt and adapt the mystery cults.

Mention of the Jews reminds me of what Campbell says about "an essentially Semitic attitude of dissociation from, and guilt vis-à-vis, divinity". Interestingly, he adds that whereas the ancient Sumerian belief in a cosmic dissolution was based on entirely mathematical grounds, the Jews saw this dissolution – the Flood – as the vengeful act of a God made angry by human disobedience and disrespect.[15] Freud's depiction of the guilt-complex (in *Totem and Taboo*) applies specifically to the Semitic forms of religion – Judaism, Christianity and Islam.

Christianity is somewhat sin-centred. The world it is interested in (apart from heaven) is the 'fallen' world, not the world of nature. (We can never sufficiently praise and thank all those ladies who have brought nature into churches with their beautiful flower-arrangements!) The conceptual and moral crudities of the Church's doctrine of atonement can no longer take refuge in mythology. How can one person's death make amends for someone else's sin? What human judge would accept the death of an innocent person as a substitute for the guilty? And no amount of casuistry can justify a god who creates humanity with freedom of will and takes umbrage when people's choices do not suit him. If the possibility of moral good requires freedom, this necessarily entails the possibility of choosing evil. Could the creator-god not foresee such a possibility? We may speak of a 'good' machine if it does what it was made to do, but that is not a moral goodness, since the machine has no freedom of choice: which is why we laugh when someone kicks his car because it does not start. But is it not illogical for this god to expect that human beings should always even *know* what is the right thing to do in any given situation? And if the sin that required expiation by a god-man was *original* sin, have we not already seen that this would constitute the illogicality to cap all illogicalities?[16]

Can anything be said in defence of the Church's use of the mystery-cult motif of a dying-and-rising-again saviour god? Has it got any redeeming features? Well, what cannot be redeemed is the sacrificial element, since there is no plausible mechanism by which the cause could bring about the effect. In other words, the notion of vicarious atonement requires a recourse to magic. The same applies to the Catholic doctrine of transubstantiation, according to which the bread and wine consumed in the Mass, or Eucharist, become – by virtue of the words and actions of the celebrant in the Prayer of Consecration – the body and blood of the Christ. (One should note that what had been the commemorative Lord's Supper was already by the 2nd century replaced by the Eucharist, signifying thanksgiving for Christ's sacrificial death.)

On the other hand, one may assert that the purpose of the Mass as a whole and of the consumption of the bread and wine in particular is to facilitate the spiritual union of every communicant with divinity, which means a conscious union or mingling of humanity and divinity within the communicant. In this, no magic is required, and no sacrificial death. The only sacrifice needed is that of the individual ego, to allow the union to take place; and this is a *creative* sacrifice, the relinquishing of something in order to achieve something of greater value.

Deification

This means that for the notion of atonement we need to substitute that of deification. This is a term employed by mystics who have achieved, or seek to achieve, oneness – which should not be taken to mean strict identity! – with God. This is the union that Jesus himself attained: a consciously cultivated mingling with the indwelling divinity. The 'unselfing' process that is involved in deification may be seen in Jesus' temptations (testings or trials) in the wilderness.

This is the only way to salvation. We should not rely on 'Other-power' – some supernatural power 'out there' – for salvation: as every Theravada Buddhist knows, salvation requires inner-power: a creative co-operation with the indwelling divinity. 'Salvation' means 'healing', 'making whole', and consists in progressive self-integration and self-realisation. Salvation is a process in which God/divinity is absolutely *necessary*, but not *sufficient*: if human response is lacking, God can do nothing to save us, nothing to lead us towards our complete fulfilment.

"If Christ is born a thousand times in Bethlehem but not in you, you remain eternally lost."[17]

It is worth stressing the connection of salvation with health. Not only should we acknowledge and utilise the positive power of mind over body; we should also recognise the connection of negative mind-sets or beliefs with psychic pathology and, in particular, the strong association of a mawkishly sentimental attachment to the crucified Jesus with an obsessive fixation on guilt, which may actually show itself in blaming *others* (for example, the Jews) or – more systematically – in blaming *oneself* and consequently disabling oneself from enjoying life and realising one's creative potential – the divinity in oneself. Such a person will characteristically set his hopes on a hereafter in which God will make all things right. But depending on a god out there, or up there, to forgive you only keeps the door wide open for doubts and anxieties: will God forgive me? can I expect him to? and is there really an hereafter?

Paul reminded Christians that reconciliation with God requires their participation: they must fill themselves with "spiritual wisdom and understanding."[18] Later, Origen said, "To know Christ crucified is the knowledge of babes."[19] He meant that the notion of a God-Man offering himself as an atonement for our sins is only for those who cannot rise to seeing Christ as the divine teacher within oneself. There is a striking resemblance here between Origen and Nietzsche, who said: Heal yourself, there is no need for any good tidings other than this; you do not have to believe any longer in the incredible mythology of atonement.

Martin Luther believed that looking for forgiveness and favour by going on pilgrimages or going to confession regularly and invoking the prayers of saints was evidence of a feeling of insecurity and a lack of oneness with God.[20] Is it not time for someone to preach a sermon in the manner of Dylan Thomas' delightfully redemptive *Under Milk Wood*, or alternatively in the manner of Nietzsche's Zarathustra; or else William Blake, whose identification of the Christian God with Satan was prompted by the traditional Christian notion of God sending his Son to die for us (which is why Thomas Altizer honoured Blake with the title, "the first Christian atheist")?

It was interesting to find in Clark's *Civilisation* the following passage: "We have grown so used to the idea that the Crucifixion is the supreme symbol of Christianity, that it is a shock to realise how late in the history of Christian art its power was recognised. In the first art of Christianity it hardly appears . . . The simple fact is that the early Church needed converts, and from this point of view the Crucifixion was not an encouraging subject."[21]

Peter de Rosa reminds us that the 'cross' carried by Constantine's soldiers in the 4th century was in fact the ☧, the first two letters of the Greek 'Xpistos' (= 'Christ'). No one dared to depict Jesus in his humiliation on the cross, presumably because the Church taught that he was the Son of God. The *empty* cross was allowed. Not till the end of the 6th century was it felt possible to depict Jesus on the cross, and the first representation – in the 10th century – of Jesus *suffering* on the cross was condemned by Rome as blasphemous. Soon, however, the Church gave way to the popular demand for a human Christ, one who suffered as ordinary men and women suffered in their lives.[22]

Such compromise with popular mawkish sentimentalism may be welcomed by some as a laudable piece of hierarchical condescension to the rank-and-file believer. If seen in that light, the fact that such condescension has become a fait accompli in Protestant churches as well as the Roman Catholic church should be heralded only as a triumph of emotion over reason.

What is the cost of such a triumph? The forfeiting of the positive for the negative, of the divine creative potential within humanity, for a squalid submission to a supernatural (and therefore merely invented?) Other-power; of the true self-fulfilment that consists in accepting our human role in the maintenance and promotion of spiritual values in human society and respectful interchange with our natural environment, for the self-negating sloth which leaves everything to a convenient god 'up there': all that is the price.

Note that it is *selfish* emotion that I am berating: ruthless greed for self-promotion, possessions and power – blinkered egocentrism that does not (want to) see the plight of others or the consequences of our actions – or inaction – in the world. There are nobler, more positive forms of emotion which might better be called passions: desire for truth and justice, adoration of beauty, a thirst for knowledge and understanding, and – towering over all – reverence for the divinity in all people and all things.

If we cease from cultivating negative emotions and open ourselves more fully to the positive ones, we shall have outgrown any need for Atonement. In its stead we shall increasingly enjoy and promote the positive products of our own and other people's divine–human creativity, readily distinguishable from the negative products of *mere* (godless – because egotistical) human 'creativity'.

Such are the dynamics and criteria of true salvation, for the individual human being and humankind as a whole, for planet Earth and perhaps the entire cosmos.

The Divinity within the Self Evolution and Creativity

"To conceive of Christianity exclusively as the religion of personal salvation is to restrict the area of the Church's consciousness, and to obscure the true life of God-humanity and the divine–human creative process of the world."

NICOLAS BERDYAEV [23]

A careful critical reading of the New Testament leaves one convinced that Jesus would not have acknowledged the Church's mythologising of him. His cry of dereliction, "My God, why hast thou forsaken me?" suggests that, if there was salvific sacrificial significance in his death, Jesus himself knew nothing about it. One sometimes wonders if the Church believes in its own mythology. "Extra *ecclesiam* nulla salus." In the 13th century the Roman Church introduced into the ordination service the phrase, spoken by the bishop to the ordinand: " . . . whose sins thou dost retain, they are retained." Both Eastern and Roman Catholic churches are alike in insisting that confession to a priest is necessary. Incidentally, Jesus' words to the thief crucified alongside him, "Today you shall be with me in Paradise", do not have to suggest superhuman authority. They retain their full meaning if translated into non-theistic terms, with God understood as the cosmic energy by which all things have their being and to which all things return in their death.

Certainly, the typical 21st century human being is unlikely to be either enthused or even amused by the Church's chameleonic Jesus Christ, divine in his heavenly pre-existence (where he was exactly coeval with his Father!), somewhat ambiguous in his conception in a virgin's womb, human in his birth and helpless infancy and in his temptation in the wilderness; divine at his transfiguration (represented by the Jewish conventional signs of God's presence, the shekinah and the bath kôl, blinding light and the voice coming out of the light) and, possibly, divine in his miracles, but human again in his suffering and death and burial; somewhat ambiguous in his post-mortem appearances, but divine again in his resurrection and ascension to his Father's right hand in heaven.

Our 21st century *Homo sapiens* recognises a fellow human being when he sees one, even when encountered in ancient religious texts, whether Buddhist or Christian. As for the idea of a father setting up his own son's death as a substitute for the death of sinners, our 21st century human being will not permit his reason and moral sensibility to be paralysed by such a distasteful scenario.

The Fourth Gospel gives us a less revolting description of divine redemption: "God so loved the world, that he gave his only begotten Son, that whosoever believeth on him should not perish, but have eternal life. For God sent not the Son into the world to judge the world; but that the world should be saved through him."[24] But the theistic Father–Son mythology persists even here; and the musical setting of these words in Stainer's *Crucifixion* oratorio (1887) does full justice to the popular sentimentalism of Victorian and Edwardian audiences.

Our typical 21st century *Homo sapiens*, however, will not feel at home with such outpourings, whether from Stainer or from evangelical pulpits and pews. Rather, he will take such renunciation of reason for what it is – the last despairing groans of a belief-system that is rapidly approaching fossilisation.

A 20th-century man, Mahātma Gandhi, in an address on Christmas Day 1931, said: "I may say that I have never been interested in an historical Jesus. I should not care if it was proved by someone that the man called Jesus never lived, and that what was narrated in the Gospels was a figment of the writer's imagination. For the Sermon on the Mount would still be true for me." This is surely a viewpoint that can be shared by many 21st century men and women: if something rings true, live by it – until some new circumstance arises which necessitates a revaluation. This does not imply that Jesus alone had divinity within him. Gandhi himself earned the title Mahātma ('great-spirit') by his deep spirituality and lifelong devotion to the cause of the outcast and exploited poor and powerless.

The Trinity a Final Word

"For as many as are led by the Spirit of God, these are sons of God. For you received not the spirit of bondage . . . ; but you received the spirit of adoption, whereby we cry, Abba, Father."

ROMANS ch. VIII, verses 14–15

"Christ is not outside us, but within us; He is the Absolute human being within us, He is our participation in the holy Trinity."

NICOLAS BERDYAEV[25]

Since the Christian Father–Son mythology must be consigned to oblivion if Christianity is to retrieve its lost credibility, there remains only one credible 'person' of the Christian Trinity – the Holy Spirit, which is identical with what I call 'divinity'.

When talking about the divinity in the human self, it is perfectly natural to speak of a meeting and confluence of 'spirit' and 'Spirit', the lower-case 'spirit' referring to the human spirit and the capitalised 'Spirit' to God, or divinity in toto. We all have God/divinity within us, but none of us can claim to have the *whole* of God/divinity: otherwise, there would be no God/divinity left for the rest of humankind. But in the case of 'divinity' there is an additional reason for lower-case lettering, namely, to indicate that what the word stands for is not any entity as such, but any perceived *quality* that rouses those human emotional responses to the natural world that may properly be described as *religious* – awe and wonder, reverence, love and ecstatic joy.

Spirit

So: let us use both words, 'divinity' and 'spirit' in lower case lettering; and let us welcome the opportunity to bridge the gap which presently separates Christianity from the world of human reason. The bridge is the concept of spirit. The gap is the Father Son soteriological mythology.

In relinquishing this mythology, which involves the Trinitarian dogma, Christianity would be free to assert unambiguously its commitment to the One that is acknowledged in all the world religions.

Moreover, a simple identification of God with spirit would enable Christianity to undergo a spiritual transformation, from dogmatic statism to the dynamics of divine–human synergy.

Dogmatic statism stems from two factors, the Book and Tradition. The clinging to scriptures as the ungainsayable word of God is a particularly strange phenomenon, since it would seem to be attributing to a large number of people – the authors of the 27 books of the New Testament and the 39 books of the Old Testament (and possibly the 14 books of the Apocrypha) – the same authority as that which the Church has officially restricted to Jesus Christ alone (who wrote nothing). But it has to be said that there are different opinions within the Church on the question of how much authority should be accorded to the various parts of the Old Testament.

Within the other factor, ecclesiastical tradition, one may include creeds and rituals as well as established stances in churchmanship ('high' or 'low', i.e., 'Catholic' or 'Evangelical'). Tradition is especially important in the Eastern Orthodox Churches.

Together, these two factors constitute a heavyweight dogmatic statism – or should one say, a dogmatic slumber? – that might seem to call for a mighty Samson or the mighty blast of Joshua's trumpets, but can be terminated only by the power of holy spirit. Christians should have no difficulty in accepting the indwelling spirit as a perpetuation of the living presence of Christ – as an inner guru, so to speak. That God is Spirit was a well established belief in Judaism. "In the life of the Church the Spirit occupies the place as counsellor that Jesus had taken in the days of his flesh."[26] Indeed, the most natural (as distinct from supernatural) way of understanding Jesus' contribution to human salvation is to see him as a guru, a spiritual teacher who showed us how to behave in such a way as to allow the divinity within ourselves full expression. This is to understand 'salvation' as a process of moral and spiritual growth inspired by Jesus' example. (Of course, such growth may also be inspired by other spiritual masters.) As a godly person who explicitly teaches love as the essential sine qua non of ethical conduct, he gives us the key to human happiness; and by his implicit teaching of proper self-love ("love your neighbour as yourself") and self-confidence (the parable of the talents) he gives us the key to self-fulfilment through the pursuit of spiritual truth and spiritual creativity. Such a process depends on our opening ourselves to the indwelling divinity, as Jesus did.

Spirit, however, is the inward presence of the *living* God and, as such, supersedes both Old Testament and New Testament, both Father and Son. God has not died or disappeared; God lives in the cosmos and in the microcosmic human spirit, or mind. As for the Church, where there is a will, there is a way. Did we not always regard God as Spirit? And they that worship him must worship him *in spirit and in truth.*

(Divinity, as the cosmic energy from which all things derive their existence, might conceivably be spoken of metaphorically as the universal Father; and consequently we might metaphorically call ourselves sons and daughters of that cosmic energy, provided that we extended the title not only to all living things (as Francis of Assisi did), but also to inorganic substances, which paved the way for life. But I am sure it is better to let the Father–Son imagery rest in peace.)

The imagery of spirit signifies the accessibility of God *within* us; it also allows the possibility of a credible link with science through the concept of *energy*. It reminds us that God is a dynamic reality, not an object, not static. Spirit means energy and therefore includes intelligence – *cosmic* energy and cosmic intelligence, and therefore *human* energy and intelligence. Let us hope that Christians will be led by spirit. They just have to let go of the clutter of dogmas and ritual and stand face to face with the naked truth, which is not an external authority (pope or bible or even tradition), but their own spiritual guru, the indwelling divinity. The true and universal divine incarnation is the spiritual presence of divinity within the whole cosmos and within ourselves. What would be the point of the incarnation of God in Jesus, if we did not have the potential for a divine birth – and growth – within ourselves? We have the whole mystery within ourselves – but of course we may choose not to acknowledge it. Christmas is an annual reminder to let God (divinity) be born or re-born in ourselves daily.

The 'mystery' of divinity is sometimes associated with darkness and terror: a dark wood, a lonely lake surrounded by grey hills; something wholly other, or terrifying. The mystery of divinity within oneself is often – initially, at least – experienced as the darkness of the unknown, unconscious depths of the psyche: one's 'other' or 'shadow', something that frightens us because we have not become properly acquainted with it. This is the unconscious, including Jung's 'collective unconscious', which is a store of wisdom inherited from our human (and perhaps pre-human) ancestors, the wisdom of the body, of nature and therefore of divinity. If we integrate the contents of the unconscious with our conscious mind (which requires a descent of consciousness into the unconscious), darkness gives way to enlightenment. Says Jung, "One does not become enlightened by imagining figures of light, but by making the darkness conscious." One should add: such descent of consciousness into the unconscious mind results in enlightenment of the whole mind.

Here we have the true death and resurrection, not a literal death and resurrection, but the blossoming of the human spirit that opens itself to *receive* the already indwelling divinity. Divinity should be offered our living-room, not our unlit cellar.

A Cosmic Christ?

With Paul a worthy theme made its appearance in the New Testament, that of the cosmic Christ: "for in him [Christ] were all things created in the heavens and upon the earth, things visible and invisible . . . ; and he is before all things, and in him all things consist ['hold together']."[27] In the prologue to John's Gospel the same theme is presented more fully: "In the beginning was the Word, and the Word was with God, and the Word was God . . . All things were made by him . . . in him was life, and the life was the light of men . . . and the Word became flesh and dwelt among us . . . "[28] Here the Christ is identified with 'the Word'. In the Greek this is 'logos', which also means that which word or speech expresses, namely, 'thought' or 'intelligence'. Thus, when the Christ is spoken of as 'the Word of God', it means that *Christ manifests the divine creative intelligence in the physical universe.*

This logos notion had figured already in Hellenistic Judaism (roughly, from the reign of Alexander the Great to the time of Jesus), where it was associated with the (frequently personified) notion of 'Wisdom' ('Sophia'). The books containing this idea are collectively referred to as the Jewish Wisdom literature: Job, Proverbs and Ecclesiastes in the Old Testament (and several of the Psalms) and the Wisdom of Solomon and Ecclesiastes in the Apocrypha. (But the Jewish notion of Wisdom was practical, ethical.[29] Jews could therefore accept Jesus as Messiah because he was a man who went about doing good, but not as God.)

The cosmic Christ may be equated with the universal presence of divinity, which constitutes the main theme of this present book and which we might speak of as the universal divine incarnation. It means, first, that divinity is *immanent throughout* the cosmos and therefore *within ourselves* and, secondly, that our supreme and all-embracing endeavour must be to *develop our conscious existential oneness* with that divinity, which is the ultimate source of all things. This endeavour is the path of self-realisation through self-transcendence, which is the positive and creative successor to the no longer acceptable notion of redemption as something attained not *by* us, but *for* us by the death of someone (God, the Christ, or a human being) some 2,000 years ago.

Salvation is cosmic as well as personal and individual. It is universal in the sense that its final product is the fulfilment – per-fection – of the universe. Salvation is the product of divine–human cooperation. All creativity comes from divinity, it is the *essence* of divinity. We may therefore say that salvation comes from divinity. But the indwelling divinity relies on us to accept and use rightly the creativity that divinity provides; if we do not, there can be no fulfilment, no salvation.

Incarnation *is* salvation. It may be called the mechanics of salvation, but there is nothing mechanical, in the sense of 'automatic', in the process of salvation. Salvation consists in a dynamic relationship of human and divine in which the human ego has to diminish in order to allow the indwelling divinity to expand and thereby enrich and fulfil the true nature of human selfhood. To use traditional theological language, salvation consists of both grace and works, i.e., the indwelling divine creativity and our proper employment of that creativity; and what activates the right use of divine creativity is the faith that all can be well in the best of all possible worlds.

In a universe that is still in process of becoming, what matters from a spiritual perspective is that we should strive towards our personal fulfilment and thus contribute to universal fulfilment. Salvation means fulfilment, personal and cosmic, and depends upon our human response to the universally immanent divinity.

The Hindu philosopher Shankara (8th century CE) was the father of the Advaita Vedānta ('non-dualist consummation of the Veda [= 'knowledge', i.e. the scriptures]), which taught that all that is needed for the soul's salvation is the removal of ignorance. Salvation is just a matter of realising that all phenomena are just that – appearances, not (ultimately) real. Ultimately there is only one, the One 'without a second', brahman. And we are one with that

One. We just need to *realise* that oneness. That is the Advaita Vedānta counterpart of the Western notion of salvation.

In the Upanishads (which cover several centuries, culminating in the 8th century CE) Brahman/brahman is described sometimes in theistic–personal terms, sometimes in impersonal terms. But whether with or without personal attributes, Brahman/brahman is understood as immanent; and certainly for most Hindus, even relatively uneducated people, the essence of Hinduism is knowing that 'ātman (our spirit) is brahman', the essential self of the human being *is* brahman, rather than the performance of sacrificial rituals.[30]

For a Theravāda Buddhist there is no salvation by some Other-Power. His aim is enlightenment, which means having a right view of things. If one is unhappy, it is because one does not have a right view, and one can free oneself of unhappiness by dealing with its causes, which are anger (aversion), desire (clinging) and ignorance. Since both anger and desire arise from ignorance (a wrong view of reality), the way to get rid of them is to realise the impermanence and ultimate non-reality of all things, including what we call 'self', i.e., ego. The wise person will not get attached to such things. This way of salvation (or more precisely liberation) is strictly do-it-yourself – even though a teacher may give support. A Tibetan (Mahayāna) Buddhist may differ in this respect, since he believes in the indwelling Buddha-nature or Buddha-mind as well as having the support of a master or masters, living or dead, whom he may invoke for guidance and strength in his endeavour to cleanse his consciousness of all illusion and achieve total enlightenment. In both cases, Theravāda and Tibetan (and other Mahayāna schools), *meditation* is the essential, indispensable practice, the royal road to freedom from illusion.

Incidentally, one may note that, whereas Jesus the Christ was crucified on a wooden cross to save us from his supernatural father's wrath or the jaws of an equally supernatural devil, Gotama the Buddha's life culminated beneath the shade of a tree, called the 'bodhi' tree because it was there that Gotama achieved enlightenment ('bodhi'), having found oneness with divinity.

"No religion has brought the mystery of the need for atonement or expiation to so complete, so profound, or so powerful expression as Christianity. And in this, too, it shows its superiority over others."[31] Such a boast based on such a mystifying and irrational dogma may prove terminal for Christianity as we have known it. Perhaps a transfigured Christianity based on the cosmic Christ will take its place; or, alternatively a Christianity based on an updating of L. S. Thornton's emphasis on the Spirit that led Jesus and leads all true sons of God.[32]

To be a Christian is to be led by the Spirit, as Jesus was. Any differences between us and Jesus lie, first, in the *extent* to which we allow the indwelling Spirit to lead us and, secondly, in the particular role each of us chooses, depending on his or her genes and environment.

God within Us

"The language of spirit and energy can open doors between different religious traditions, unburdened by religious dogmas."[33] It can certainly – and I hope it will – open doors between Christians and the divinity-hypothesis presented in this book. Here I say "Christians" rather than "Christianity" because I cannot presume to transform all the Churches – established Christianity – from a religion of creeds and ritual to a form of spirituality which is essentially a personal relationship between an individual human being and the divinity within the natural world and in oneself. To perceive the mystery of divinity *within* all things is to cut through the dogmas (or mythology) of Incarnation and Atonement to the spiritual reality itself and the interchange between self and Self, conscious ego and the indwelling divinity. The fullness of our union or at-one-ment with the indwelling divinity depends – just as it did with Jesus or Buddha – upon the extent to which we allow ourselves to imbibe and merge with it. Spirituality (as distinct from piety or religiosity) is essentially an individual experience and consists in developing an interior relationship with the divinity, in everything one does. This means living fully and intently – not necessarily tensely, but mindfully – in every present moment. This is not a relationship to God as Father, but an adult co-creative relationship in which one may say that divinity and humanity are interdependent.

It is an oddity of language that 'individual', literally meaning 'indivisible', has come to mean 'separate' or 'distinct'. Thus, to speak of ourselves as individuals is to emphasise the separateness of human beings and, in particular, our separateness from the divinity that is actually within all things.

As Caroline Myss points out, "divine energy is inherent in our biological system" and therefore "every thought that crosses our minds, every belief we nurture, every memory to which we cling translates into a positive or negative command to our bodies and spirits."[34] We can consciously participate in this divine energy within our own body, and consequently co-operate with divinity in promoting our own biological and psychological health.

In fact, we can, with the indwelling divinity (which is energy, intelligence and rightness) co-create our whole life.[35] This is not magic, or some dubious psychic process. It is the power of mind over matter, which is a problem only for one who supposes that mind is purely spiritual and matter purely physical. But we have seen[37] that an absolute spirit–matter dualism is becoming difficult to maintain. The power of mind over matter has been recognised and utilised not only by yogis and spiritual healers but also by today's psychologists and psychotherapists, and it is something many of us have experienced, or heard of from reliable informants. Think 'strength', and you will feel strong and be strong. Your yoga teacher will demonstrate this truth for you. The effects are *not* just in the imagination; the *cause* is in the mind. And – most important! – the energy within you is the cosmic energy, the same divine energy that gave rise to the universe.

CHAPTER NINE

Creativity, Divine and Human

"Creativity arises from the deep potentialities of spirit and freedom."
NICOLAS BERDYAEV[1]

"On Sundays we go to church. On six days of the week we go about our creative work. And our creative engagement with life remains unrecognised; it is not sanctified, it is not given a place in the religious view of life."

NICOLAS BERDYAEV[2]

In today's world we have to recognise that the universe is not static, but dynamic, forever in process. It is continually self-creative, and its creative energy is immanent. The religious attitude expressed in this book tallies perfectly with this scientific account of the universe. The religious way of looking at the world of nature is subjective: it expresses 'religious' feelings towards this self-creative universe by calling it 'divine' and responding to it with reverence, love and gratitude.

Following Whitehead's definition of 'perfect', we must say that our evolving universe is the best of all possible worlds, not because it is already all that it can possibly be, but because at any given moment it is as good as it can be expected to be, but always has potential for further development. In an evolving universe – and particularly in the human species, which has much fuller freedom than other species – it ought to be easy to forgive one another. As the spiritual teacher Barry Long used to say, it is irrational to have expectations of other people. If to sin is human, it ought to be human to forgive oneself and others, especially if we have a close relationship with the divinity in all things.

We are not first redeemed and only then brought into a positive relation with God; rather, 'salvation' (= spiritual fulfilment) is something we accomplish by conversing with the divinity within. Christianity has got it wrong; and many Christians are aware of this and are now attempting to put things right. Now the light is breaking through: we are beginning to realise that we have in ourselves all that we need for salvation, namely, the power of indwelling divinity – cosmic energy and intelligence and rightness. Our salvation demands, not the burying of our talents, but the employment of them to attain for ourselves – and to help others attain – the fullest possible realisation of our potential, our per-fection.

The cardinal sin is not pride, and the cardinal virtue is not grovelling humility. (Nietzsche was right in this respect.) Selfishness is bad only if it prevents a person from connecting with the indwelling divinity. Selflessness is good only if it is accompanied by a positive response to the creative divine energy within us. But a denial of one's own value is the greatest insult to divinity. (Self-negation posing as pious humility: how often have I been caught in that snare!) Meister Eckhart, a 14th century German Dominican, abandons all reserve on this point: "Our Lord says to every living soul, 'I became man for you. If you do not become God for me, you do me wrong.'"[3] An unknown 14th century Dominican wrote in the *Theologia Germanica* (mystical teachings that influenced Martin Luther): "Some may ask what it is to be a partaker of the Divine Nature, or a Godlike ['vergottet' = 'deified'] man. Answer: he who is imbued with or illuminated by the Eternal and Divine Light, and inflamed or consumed with Eternal and Divine Love, he is a deified man and a partaker of the Divine Nature."[4] Note the balance of intellect and emotion: light and love.

Transfiguration

What is known as the Transfiguration of Jesus[5] may be said to be the moment when his disciples recognised Jesus as a deified man. The symbolism used is from the Old Testament: the shekinah and the bath kôl, the blinding light and the voice coming out of the light, representing God. It means what the soldier said on seeing Jesus die on the cross: "Surely this man was a son of God", i.e. a godly man.

In a universalist understanding of divine incarnation, transfiguration should and can take place in us all as a consequence of allowing the inborn divinity to express itself in and through us. Not only that but, to the extent that human activity in the world is inspired, energised and directed by the indwelling divinity, the world itself will be transfigured and Blake's vision of the New Jerusalem will be accomplished.

Transfiguration has received greater recognition in the Eastern Orthodox than in the Western Churches. Why do not all the Churches renounce the horrors of hell and damnation and let themselves be led into all truth by the Spirit? Institutions and revolutions do not mingle? Well, then, so be it. Let Peter's Church continue to petrify, and let spiritually minded people turn elsewhere for guidance to the living and immanent Spirit.

Divinity within us means creative potential within us. As the universe is self-creative, so must human beings be. A. N. Whitehead declared that "Good people of narrow sympathies are apt to be unfeeling and unprogressive, enjoying their egotistical goodness, so far as their own interior life is concerned. This type of moral correctitude is, on a larger view, so like evil that the distinction is trivial."[6]

Jean-Paul Sartre

Jean-Paul Sartre (1905–1980) was strong on this point. What made Sartre an atheist was his perception that "existence precedes essence".[7] By 'essence' he meant that which makes a thing what it is. If everything were created by God (*theistically* conceived), the essence of all things would exist – in God's mind – *prior* to the things themselves coming into existence. But what we experience within ourselves is that we *first* exist, and *then* have to decide *what* we are going to be.

One might wish to quarrel with Sartre's premiss. Certainly, it is couched in anthropomorphic language; but it could easily pass muster in the divinity-energy–rightness language of this present book. We are aware that we have freedom to choose what we shall be. We can change our mind and our direction in life time and time again, if we so wish, so that, as Sartre said, one cannot properly say what a person is until the person is dead – and then one can say what the person *was*.

Sartre distinguished the human being, as "pour-soi", from objects, which are "en-soi". An object cannot change itself by an act of will, because it has no will. It is enclosed within itself, fixed and finished (unless some *outside* force changes its structure). Diagrammatically it may be represented thus: □

The human being, as subject, has freedom to create its own future self, and is represented thus: ⌐_ _ _ _ .

Of course, a person's death closes the possibilities. The person then becomes en-soi: an object. Thus we can say what that person *was*, but not what s/he *is*.)

Sartre spoke in the period of a post-war breakdown of traditional values and codes of conduct, a time when people had ceased to put their trust in those in authority, the well educated rich and powerful leaders of nations and prescribers of right and wrong. It was a time for abandoning 'their' truth and values and creating one's own.

Of course one's freedom is not unlimited. We are genetically and environmentally conditioned, so that we are more likely to behave in one way than in another way. But our choices are seldom, if ever, determined in any strong sense of the word. Nevertheless, we often choose to *live in fear* of freedom. We see a possible opening for further self-fulfilment, but allow fears and doubts – 'But what if . . . ?' – to cast a dark cloud over it. Freedom entails responsibility (as in a law-court where the decision between innocence and guilt may hinge on whether the accused was free to do otherwise than he did); hence, one's fear of freedom.[8]

Sartre spoke of the "inauthentic" person who attempts to escape from freedom – and responsibility – by simply playing a role – of parent, or policeman or waiter, priest or whatever – just doing what the role requires. Other examples of inauthenticity, or "bad faith", are conformism – doing what others do; fatalism – pretending one has no choice, that everything is predetermined; anything that may help one escape – or seem to escape – the anguish of having to make one's own decisions: a pope or priest or a holy book to tell us what to do, or a totalitarian government, or an imagined God-out-there who gave Moses ten commandments and sent Jesus to tell us what to do.

Some Christians even disregard conscience and fail to exercise it, choosing instead to conform their behaviour and their moral judgments to what 'the Book' or 'the Church' says. Such external authority provides refuge from the challenge of making their own decisions. Thus external authority, some of it 2,000 years old, takes precedence over the living, here-and-now inner authority of Spirit or, in other words, the indwelling divinity; or conscience.

People who take such escape routes from their freedom Sartre designated "salauds", or just "inauthentic". The authentic person, on the other hand, authorises himself to exercise his freedom and become self-creative, and accept responsibility.

Søren Kierkegaard (1813–55), a Danish philosopher regarded as one of the fathers of modern existentialist philosophies, said: "The man who can really stand alone in the world, only taking counsel from his conscience – that man is a hero."[9] Kierkegaard's "hero" and Sartre's "authentic" person exemplify all who are spiritually alive and self-creative through a conscious relationship with the indwelling divinity: conscience (literally = 'knowing with') *is* that conscious relationship with divinity. Both Kierkegaard's "hero" and Sartre's "authentic" one go deeply within themselves, beyond that superficial layer of self that Jung calls the "persona" (Sartre's role-playing "inauthentic" self) to the unconscious depths of the psyche where the conscious self begins to explore what will gradually reveal itself as both the true personal self and the indwelling divinity – though Sartre himself would not accept this, since he rejected depth psychology, and Kierkegaard had not even heard of Jung.

'No-Self'; and Brahman Ātman

The Hindu and Buddhist notion of 'no-self' (Sanskrit 'anātman', Pāli 'anatta') *denies the reality of the human self* and asserts that what we call 'the self' is illusory (māya). Only real self being brahman, the cosmic Self, which is the ultimate reality of and within everything (and therefore an equivalent of 'divinity'). Other Upanishadic formulations – 'tat tvam āsi ('that art thou') and 'brahman ātman' ('your self is brahman') would seem not to be denying the reality of the human self (or soul or spirti), but rather to be asserting its oneness – but not necessarily its *identity* – with the ultimate cosmic reality (brahman = divinity).

The present writer does not claim any special mystical knowledge, but is struck by the resemblance between these notions of the (potential) oneness of brahman and ātman, cosmic Self and individual self, and what seem to be the earliest holistic intuitions of *Homo sapiens*: his reverence for and conscious oneness with the surrounding world of nature and its tremendous energetic forces – intuitions which informed his behaviour. The mystic-meditative and the primitive intuitional wisdom may seem to be separated by vast stretches of time; but they are synchronous in the unconscious depths of the human mind. Whether we look within ourselves or outwards at the rest of nature, we are actually contemplating the ubiquitous presence of divinity.

Conscience

This divinity is not the God whose existence Sartre denied. Sartre's notion of God was incompatible with human freedom, and one must emphasise that the immanent divinity presented in this book does not, so to speak, do our thinking and decision-making for us. It may be useful to associate the indwelling divinity with what we call conscience. Conscience is an aspect of what we call imagination, which is the power to conceive what *might* be, as distinct from perceiving what *is*. Imagination functioning in conscience mode tells us what *ought* to be. But both imagination and conscience are our own human faculties, and therefore not infallible. To say that divinity is active in these faculties is to express one's *belief* that this is so. If I had, or could find, any reason for supposing that what I believe is true or right or valuable really is *not* so, I would have to abandon that belief, and with it any underlying conviction that it came from God/divinity. In short, one can create one's own tentative representation of divinity – if one lets ego onst the indwelling divinity,

This means, not that I have to abandon the notion of God altogether, but that I can never rationally assume that my understanding of God is total; it is – like a scientific hypothesis – provisional: some new experience or an old experience newly understood may necessitate revision of the hypothesis.

Even more disastrous is to cling to a divisive, separatist notion of 'my self', as if *that* were the ultimate reality. And yet, as Sartre reminded us, it is my self that chooses and makes decisions and therefore must accept responsibility for what I make of myself. The point is that we should as far as possible ensure that the self making our decisions is not the divisive, selfish, self-centred self, but the self that responds to and with the indwelling divinity. The more tightly we are bound to the self centred self, the less likely are we to experience joy, which requires that we be taken out of ourselves: 'ecstasy' means being taken out of (oneself).

Hegel said God achieves self-consciousness in the human being. Teilhard de Chardin said that evolution becomes self-conscious in the human being. So far as our concept of divinity is concerned, both Hegel and Teilhard are right: the high destiny of humankind is to allow the divine creativity to achieve fulfilment – or at any rate, some significant expression – in and through our engagement with one another and with the whole of our natural environment. This means behaving responsibly and reverently in our relations with our fellow human beings (pressing for a radical reduction of the gaps that separate the haves and the have-nots, or whites and blacks, or men and women, or the extremists of one religion or sect and those of another) and with the rest of the natural world (purifying the air and water that we have contaminated, and regulating our consumption of forests, and the flora and fauna we feed on, and the energy-sources we have come to rely on for heating and lighting our homes, cooking our food, clothing our bodies and transporting us from one place to another).

None of these things is easy of achievement as long as the two great monsters continue to hold sway over the human world – capitalism and power politics – the megalomaniac twin offspring of greed and callousness which persistently thwart the United Nations' efforts to bring peace to the human world.

A Buddhist who had been a monk for twelve years told me that, just as we need to use both legs equally in order to walk, so, in order to live fully and achieve personal harmony, we need to balance meditation and practical ethical activity in the world. This exemplifies the Buddhist 'Middle Way'.

Meditation and Creativity

Meditation requires withdrawal from our active engagement in the world into a passive, receptive state of mind and body. It is not an activity! It is a cessation not only of physical activity but also – and specially – of thinking. A mind full of thoughts or emotional clutter hinders clear perception or intuition of divinity. When not controlled by a need for concentration to fulfil some workaday task, most of our mental activity consists of worries and anxieties: self-recriminations concerning the past, or self-doubting and fears concerning the future. Meditation means being always *present* – here on this chair at this moment, not battling with the internal chatter of our worries or the sounds of the outside world. Buddhist monks say, "If you hear the cuckoo, do not reply." In other words, do not react to anything that enters the mind: do not get angry with it, and do not entertain it – just let it go.

Eventually the mind will become totally empty, void of all fears and all desires, and therefore void of self. If we persist with meditation on a fairly regular basis, even for a few minutes, without imposing any specific demands or expectations, we shall uncover our true Self (which merges with the indwelling divinity) and discover all that is needed for total fulfilment, or for the next step towards it.

This is the core – the heart – of meditation: the point where the false notion of 'I' as an individual reality separate from divinity (an 'ātman'-'soul' – separate from 'brahman' – 'world-soul') is transcended in an experience of one's oneness with divinity (brahman or whatever), one's oneness with the energy, intelligence and rightness of the universe!

What must be avoided or, failing that, remedied promptly is that rise-and-fall phenomenon in which, having been lifted in meditation to a numinous peace of mind and body, we shatter that peace by plunging precipitously into the hubbub of office or road traffic – just as, after listening to an enthralling piece of music, one may need a moment of silence before returning to 'real' life.

Needless to say, meditation of this kind will nourish and give direction to our practical engagement with the outside world. Meditation may provide a much needed respite from the world – the tension and bustle of the workplace and the roar of traffic. But that respite (Sogyal Rinpoche likens it to a child coming into its mother's arms[10]) should enable one to return to one's engagement with the world with a mind refreshed and strengthened by its renewed conscious oneness with the energy, intelligence and wisdom of divinity. Meditation and creative activity go together, like in-breath and out-breath. Meditation on the God within brings thinking and living together, and either brings meaning into the daily routine or changes the routine to one that can carry and serve the meaning of life. Meditation that does not lead to creativity has failed in its highest purpose, which is to allow the divine creativity to achieve fulfilment – or at least some significant expression – through our engagement with one another and with the rest of the natural world. That is humankind's high destiny: to give the indwelling divinity the assistance it needs in order to achieve liberation and fulfilment for all humankind in unison with all other living things. As the Viennese existentialist philosopher Martin Buber (1878–1965) put it, "We take part in creation, meet the Creator, reach out to Him, helpers and companions."[11] Buber clearly saw divinity as a power that assures us that life has a meaning that can be verified or confirmed within our own life.

Perhaps this creative enterprise is one in which it would be profitable for senior Christian clergy of all denominations and their counterparts in other religious traditions to confer with senior representatives of government, business and finance, science and technology, especially on pressing problems such as: inequality; the Third World and the constantly widening gap between rich and poor in the 'developed' countries; access to education; racial, religious and sexual issues. Such conference – and confrontation – if wisely directed and engaged in with frankness and tolerance, would surely provide a clarification of issues over a broad human spectrum, even though its discussions might have to be conducted on a purely unofficial and non-binding basis.

Nietzsche

We should even pay homage to Nietzsche for his positive stress on creativity as an expression of humankind's courageous 'Yes' to nature's irrepressible life-force. His Zarathustra may – understandably – shock us with his declaration that "Higher than love for your neighbour is love for the farthest, the future ones . . ." But if we substitute 'along with' for 'higher than', we have a proper emphasis on human self-transcendence and consequently on passing on to future generations the same commitment to the further development of the human species. Where one must part company with Nietzsche is in his cynical reduction of truth and goodness to whatever suits one's own purpose and his supercilious lack of respect for the common man or woman. (The fact that they are not likely to read his books does not exonerate him.) Both Nietzsche and Sartre are right in insisting that, to be truly human, one must cherish and exercise one's freedom, which means daring to become totally oneself, not a mindless pawn in someone else's game. Where both err is in their lack of recognition of an ultimate reality that not only gives existence to everything but is also within everything as the energy, intelligence and rightness which the human being may choose to acknowledge (with resulting benefits for the world) or deny (with resulting damage to the world).

There is bad as well as good creativity. Good creativity is that which comes from the divinity within with one's full consent. Bad creativity comes from selves that allow divinity no say. This applies to all forms of creativity: art, science, engineering and technology, love or the lack of it in society, family or one-to-one relationships, and self-creativity.

Again, what matters is not the label but what is in the bottle. One can allow or deny divinity without actually employing either the word or even the concept. The human creator – composer, writer, painter, physicist, or engineer or whatever – might speak of 'inspiration' or (in Schubert's words) "a state of excitement", or else say, 'It just came to me in a flash' or 'out of the blue' (sky, heaven?), or simply, 'I did it', rejoicing in the fact.

Artistic Creativity

Nevertheless, one may truly say, as William Blake did, that all genius consists in unreserved devotion to (what I call) divinity, which is present in and constitutes all that is properly deserving of worship. Wordsworth famously declared that poetry "takes its origin from emotion recollected in tranquility".[12] But when Wordsworth spoke of the awe he felt on looking

> "Into our Minds, into the Mind of Man,
> My haunt, and the main region of my Song",

Blake's retort was, "Does Mr. Wordsworth think his mind can surpass Jehovah?"[13] When we consider the difference of social background between the two men, we shall understand and therefore forgive Blake's unfair remark. Wordsworth's amour propre was that of a man who saw divinity in everything and everyone. Paul Tillich spoke of the human being as a "door to the deeper levels of reality". Surely that is a truth that Blake as well as Wordsworth would have accepted. We are fragments of the whole, but in each of us there is, so to speak, an aperture through which the whole may be perceived: prehended, if not fully comprehended.

When Mozart, in the depths of despair, wrote the brilliant Jupiter Symphony, handling its great complexity with what appears to be the greatest of ease, does not this suggest that he was able to rise above (or descend beneath) the ego to a level of the mind where humanity and divinity meet and mingle?

The music of J. S. Bach contains deep emotion ranging from despair to the heights of joy but invariably lifting the listener to a tranquil assurance of what I call the rightness of the universe. Many musicians begin the day with Bach's keyboard music, as breakfast for the soul.

Much of Beethoven's music is filled with heroic humanist defiance of everything that would seek to restrict human freedom and creativity, and an equally heroic resignation to what must be – including his deafness, his disappointment in love, his constant ill-health, and human mortality. His late piano sonatas and string quartets take the listener into the same spiritual realm as Bach, or Bruckner ("God's own musician") or Mahler or Pärt or Tavener or Jonathan Harvey – and without any make-believe piety.

Tavener said, " . . . I cannot separate composing, the act of working, from prayer." Of Bruckner it has been said that he "may be the lay apostle who with his work, which projects the divine idea into the world in its purest form, may touch the hearts of those whose ears are closed to the preaching of the churches. He can become the mediator leading from materialism to spirituality, from disbelief to true religion."[14] One might say the same of Mahler. The music of both these composers has been seen as a spiritualising of Wagner's profane sound-world – though there is surely some spirituality in the ecstatic Liebestod of his *Tristan und Isolde*. In any case, what is wrong with physical passion?

The morally dubious Wagner, who took what he could from others (notably the generous Liszt) and showed little gratitude, and was unequivocally anti-Jewish, may be said to have redeemed himself by what he achieved in the realm of opera. One does not have to be a saint to be a genius. One may dislike the frequent excessive loudness and occasional treacly vulgarity of his orchestral sound. But one must accept that, although divine creative energy is available to all, much depends on how one uses it. An English rabbi denounced Wagner's music and called for it to be banned, because the composer was strongly anti-Jew. The rabbi was a woman. Was she not aware of the archetypal feminine roots of Wagner's music? or did she find them objectionable? Was she afraid that his music would spread moral corruption? One may make a comparison with the way some people, particularly Christians, in the USA but also in Britain, assume that a person who has committed adultery is ipso facto unfit to be a political leader, regardless of qualifications and success in the job.

Daniel Barenboim, celebrated pianist and conductor, and himself a Jew, must be praised for his courageous defence of Wagner the artist and his refusal to appear in Israel unless he was allowed to perform Wagner's works there.

No one is perfect, i.e., totally good; and no one is totally evil, except perhaps for a very few psychopaths who cannot help themselves or be helped by others. It is said that Martin Luther was anti-Jew, but he is rightly admired for his heroic mission against the corruptions of the Roman Catholic Church of his day. His namesake, Martin Luther King, was also said to be anti-Jew, but again we have to acknowledge his courageous efforts to win freedom and equal rights for black people in the USA. Whereas Richard Wagner's anti-Jew trait was a more than trivial component of his character, one must see it in the context of the widespread European anti-Jewishness of his time; and, be that as it may, we must surely acknowledge divine creativity when we see – or hear – it.

The fact that an artist (Tchaikovsky, for instance) displays his own feelings in his work with little or no reservation does not necessarily mean that there is no room in it for divinity. There could be no human creativity at all without the divine creative energy that is in everything. The same applies to what has been called the 'Russianness' of Tchaikovsky's music: the presence of national or racial influence in a composer's or a painter's work does not mean that the work owes nothing to the universal creative energy, which is divinity. Divine creative energy is available to all; but much depends on how – or, indeed, if – one employs it; and this must often depend upon one's social, national and racial background, as well as on one's genes and education. The wonder of wonders is that divinity makes itself universally accessible and it is only human beings who can choose not to avail themselves of it, or – worse – to prevent others from doing so.

But let Tchaikovsky speak for himself: "If that state of the artist's soul which is called *inspiration* . . . were to continue unbroken, it would not be possible to survive a single day. The strings would snap and the instrument shatter to smithereens. Only one thing is necessary: that the main idea and the general contours of all the separate parts should appear not through *searching* but of their own accord as a result of that supernatural, incomprehensible force which no one has explained, and which is called inspiration."[15]

This comes from one who did not subscribe to any Christian creed and professed himself a pantheist, but could still be deeply moved by the Orthodox liturgy.[16] The beauty of the voices of unseen nuns – like all beauty – has its own kind of truth and should never be allowed to fall foul of dogmatic prejudice. The same applies of course to the aria of alto and chorus, 'Erbarme dich, . . . ' in Bach's *St Matthew's Passion*, or Britten's *Hymn to St. Cecilia*, and many more. Spiritual beauty surpasses all creeds, and is one of life's most glorious – and redemptive – mysteries. Such beauty and wonder in music can reveal the "unbroken wholeness in flowing movement"[17] that, according to physicist David Bohm, is at the heart of all reality.

Naturally, the inspiration : perspiration : ratio is bound to vary from artist to artist. Variables will include temperament, state of health (including state of mind), domestic and financial circumstances, the particular piece or type of work in hand, and the urgency of this and any other commissions. But what is crucial is that all human creativity – whether it be self-creation or artistic, creation of missiles or creation of good-will and peace – is essentially a divine–human process that would cease to be possible if either of the two components, divinity and humanity, were absent.

The minimalism that made its début in 1960s US is an interesting phenomenon. Speaking of minimalist 'sculpture' (read: 'any three-dimensional structure'), Eugene Goossens said, in 1966, "the spectator is not given symbols, but facts".[18] Just so. But if it is facts we are looking for, we should go elsewhere for them, not to art. A pile of excrement, a line of bricks placed on a floor at regular intervals, 184 bales of hay in a field, a 182.9 × 182.9 cm. square consisting of 36 thin zinc plates laid on a wooden floor, and a huge steel wall erected in a spot frequented at lunch-time by nearby New York office-workers (and later removed, on demand) are all just facts, nothing more. One supposes that Carl Andre's bales may have given spectators a breath of fresh air – but that is nature, not art. One might concede that Don Judd's ten painted steel rectangular frames set closely one behind another (*Untitled, 1966*)[19] have a pleasing symmetry comparable with that of iron railings.

Dan Flavin's *Diagonal 1963* is exceptional. It is certainly minimalist: a tubular fluorescent light mounted on a wall and rising from near floor level at an angle of 45 degrees. The tube is obviously a symbol of the erect male penis (Flavin called it "the diagonal of personal ecstasy").[20] The fact that a fluorescent light was chosen to carry the symbolism may suggest that Flavin wanted to share with us his fear that the enticements of modern technology might uproot us from our place in nature. If that were so, it is unfortunate that the immediate impact of the *Diagonal* is that of machismo. This is certainly Anna Chave's reaction to it. One wonders what Flavin feels about pistols and nuclear missiles.

Berdyaev said, "The meaning of art lies in the fact that it anticipates the transfiguration of the world."[21] We are meant to be creators, not destroyers. Divinity is energy; it is the universal drive towards further growth, further development. And the universe includes us, who as human beings constitute the potential vanguard of its Dionysian drive towards the beyond, the higher, the better. We must not forfeit our freedom to create or re-create ourselves and thereby play our leading part in the continuing creative process of the universe – as co-creators with God.

Peter Pan may be a fetching fellow in fairyland; but he is not to be emulated in real life in an evolving universe, where growth and self-transcendence are the order of the day, every day.

Any religion that would deny this high destiny of humankind is false religion. "When I survey the wondrous cross . . . ", the evangelical Christian sings with masochistic intent. We must instead survey the wondrous universe and our creative – and indeed, saving – mission within it.

> "Every act of love, of eros-love and of the love which is compassion is a creative act. In it something new arrives in the world, . . . and in it there is hope of the transformation of the world."
>
> NICOLAS BERDYAEV[22]

> "But the highest task of the human being is the creation of a new life."
>
> NICOLAS BERDYAEV[23]

We are not all gifted artists or engineers. Some of us are house-bound mothers, or office workers. But consider: the most creative – and saving – thing is love. (Here Christianity has got it right.) Love makes peace, not war. It is always creative, never destructive. Some may limit their love to family and friends and be hostile or indifferent to others. But this is an indictment not of love, but of lack of love. Love itself is never miserly; it overflows; it is essentially universal in its scope, all-accepting and all forgiving.

To realise just how creative love can be, think of what happens within a family where there is no love: children are – and feel – unwanted, of no value; the parents do not care or even notice if the children play truant from school; if the children live close to other unloved ones (in the same block of flats, perhaps), they may form gangs and, emboldened by numbers, give violent expression to their resentment, attacking anyone who can seem to personify the world that disowns them; stolen money buys firearms and drugs and alcohol; in prison they learn how to become more proficient in their criminal skills; and eventually they create new uncaring milieux for their own offspring.

On the other hand, children who know they are loved feel secure and grow in self-respect and confidence, have positive goals and expectations – and bring up their own children in similar style.

Love makes all the difference, between destruction and creativity. It is what our world needs most of all; and it lies within the capability of all human beings, except perhaps those who have been severely damaged by lack of it.

Love is the quintessence of the Sermon on the Mount. It is the one great enduring truth in Christianity. It is a pity that legalism and false piety and 'keeping up standards' should often combine to cast a dark shadow over that truth. This is the tragedy of Christianity.

Do I need to add: one cannot learn to love others if one has not first learned to love oneself?

Berdyaev said, "Beauty is the goal of all life, it is the deification of the world. Beauty, as Dostoievsky has said, will save the world."[24] Plato said beauty was the object and goal of 'eros' (erotic love), the love that desires to possess and contain its object. Physicists and mathematicians frequently speak of the beauty of a model or theory, quite as if beauty were a criterion of truth. Anyone who pursues (!) truth is motivated by eros. Goodness, too, is an object of desire as well as an object of duty. The classical Greeks would refer to a totally excellent thing as 'beautiful and good' (kalon k'agathon):[25] what was good was also beautiful and therefore desirable. May I suggest that Beauty, Truth, & Goodness, Plato's trinity, might be an acceptable and uplifting, truly saving trinity for our own millennium?

Jung said Christianity tore beauty and goodness apart. "It took more than a thousand years of Christian differentiation to make it clear that the good is not always the beautiful and the beautiful not necessarily good. The paradox of this marriage of ideas troubled the ancients as little as it does the primitives."[26] For Jung, by the way, the God-image was a symbol of the Self, or psychic wholeness.

CHAPTER TEN

Divinity and Ethics

The mention of love has brought us to a discussion of ethics. Love is the ultimate guarantor of ethical behaviour. Love may be described as a feeling that
can develop into a constant attitude embracing all that is. In his *Symposium*
Plato discusses the levels of love, beginning with the lowest. I choose to start
with the highest, the most universal level. This is what I call the religious attitude, which is a reverent, respectful awareness of and response to the divinity
in all things, including ourselves and all our fellow human beings.

Love is an essential feature of creative ethics. Mystics such as Julian of
Norwich use erotic imagery when they speak of their desire for union with God.
But when we become aware of the divinity within all things, love takes into itself
an empathetic and moral quality, and we become aware of our responsibility
within the cosmos, as partners in creation, the continuing creation of ourselves
and perhaps even the universe at large. Since our self-creating involves self-
transcendence – or, in moral terms, self-improvement – we may infer that our
duty in the universe is to play a part in cosmic self-fulfilment by virtue of the
divine energy and intelligence and rightness within us.

> "Rational religion is the wider conscious reaction of men to the universe in
> which they find themselves."
>
> ALFRED NORTH WHITEHEAD

> "A religion, on its doctrinal side, can . . . be defined as a system of general
> truths which have the effect of transforming character when they are
> seriously held and vividly apprehended."
>
> ALFRED NORTH WHITEHEAD [1]

This definition, it should be noted, may include bad as well as good religion. Muslim suicide bombers are so indoctrinated that they seriously hold
and vividly apprehend what they accept as general truths, and the result is a
devastating transformation of character in those vulnerable young people.
This is a warning that we must never abandon either reason or compassion,
no matter how glittering the inducements to do so in favour of illusory benefits in the here and now or in the hereafter. Emotions that are not bad in
themselves may have calamitous consequences if they are allowed to take the
place of reason.

"By their fruits ye shall know them." The fruits of the religious perspective
outlined in this book are manifestly good. Seeing divinity in all things and being

at one with the divinity in ourselves must inevitably result in feeling at one with all things and showing respect for all things.

Religion and Ethics

Before proceeding further, I wish to make it clear that I have no intention of reducing religion to ethics. William Hamilton, one of the American 'death of God' theologians, takes the kenotic doctrine (God's 'self-emptying') and extends it so that it becomes a way of saying that God is revealed only in what is not God. In other words, there is nothing metaphysical about God, and Christianity should focus, not on (a supernatural) God, but on Jesus: on ethics, not metaphysics. I am sure this formulation will be welcomed by many lay Christians; and it is very much what the present author is trying to say, but with one reservation: whilst agreeing with Hamilton that the notion of a personal supernatural deity is nonsensical today, I nevertheless regard the notion of *divinity* as an essential representation of a primal human awareness of a One within the many, an immanent dynamic and intelligent source and sustainer of all things.

Hamilton says, "We turn from the problems of faith to the reality of love."[2] In view of Jesus' focus on love, compassion, tolerance and forgiveness, and his lack of theologising, one has to say that Hamilton is in good company; and unquestionably he must be seen as one who is concerned to keep the heart of Jesus' message alive in an age that has said adieu to God, or more correctly, to the theistic concept of God. And surely anyone who does always what love requires is doing what God/divinity requires.

Yet I cannot subscribe to a simple reduction of religion to ethics. Religion is a certain kind of attitude towards the universe – including oneself – that has both an emotional and an intellectual component, the emotional component consisting in reverence and respect and wonder (love) and a feeling of oneness with the universe, and the intellectual component presenting the empirical grounding for the emotional component.

When a person realises that the same God/divinity that is in himself is also in others, he will not knowingly hurt others, because in doing so he would be injuring himself (by denying or disregarding the essence of himself).

People of my generation were conditioned not to see people as such, but only kinds of people. Sometimes there were only two kinds of people, 'our kind' and 'not our kind'. This was evidenced in the case of a lady of Banbury who, when she was asked in the course of a survey if there were many people in the town, replied to the effect that there were just a few – Lord so and so – and the major – and just a couple or so more. She left out at least twenty thousand other people who lived in the town. One supposes this was the attitude of army generals in the First World War who sent thousands of young troopers over the top in the face of heavy machine-gun fire. Those thousands were of no account: they were just 'men', not people, not 'gentlemen'.

Benjamin Whichcote (1609–83), one of the Cambridge Platonists, said: "No man's inferiority makes him contemptible."[3] It is not only royalty we should bow to. We ought to bow to the divinity in everyone and everything – as Buddhists do, and as Christian nuns and monks learn to do. Such acknowledgement of the divinity within all things would inaugurate a new era, not only for religion but also, as a consequence, a new era for ethics.

Marshalled against such a renewal are the massed forces of a greedy materialism that overrides the better feelings of humanity, and the de-humanised (but man-made and man-controlled) kind of capitalism that brooks no hindrance to profit (which here means, of course, monetary profit).

In the end, does it matter? Nature – divine nature – though abused and violated, will survive. If well fed power-crazed, unscrupulous bully-boys (but oh! so genteel, so civilised, don't you know?) precipitate a war to end all wars by annihilating billions of innocent human beings (including all those passers-by I see from my window – the young man who every Sunday buys a bunch of flowers, and the little toddler who trots along behind her parents), nature itself will survive, with new mutations to match new environments. The indwelling divinity of nature is infinitely resilient and infinitely tolerant!

If only we could emulate it! Why should we not? The same divinity is within us all. We just need to recognise and respond positively to it everywhere and always. Therein lie the true destiny and fulfilment and happiness of humankind. Right behaviour requires right motivation, and right motivation depends upon what we have made of ourselves, what we have done with our divine–human self creativity, which in turn depends upon the strength of our bonding to divinity. This is the connection between morality and religion. The nature and strength of our actions depend upon the nature and strength of our *attitude.*

No system of ethics will work without an appropriate attitude. For example, utilitarianism will not work without an egalitarian attitude. Jesus saw that the Jewish Mosaic code needed an attitude of universal, unconditional love or respect; otherwise it could only lead to 'Pharisaism',[4] the hypocrisy that assumes we are better than other people if we keep rules (even – or especially – practically useless ones) fastidiously.

In an evolving universe imperfection should not be a problem. As a young Christian I adopted a double standard, one for myself, the other for other people. But the more we expect of ourselves, the more likely we are to become smug and self-righteous – or else masochistic. Masochism is a neurosis that lies in wait for anyone who ventures to tread the path of self-denial. Jesus was right: one should love one's neighbour and, equally, one should love oneself. No one is absolutely perfect; and it is presumptuous to suppose that we ourselves are going to achieve absolute perfection. Can we even know what absolute perfection is?

Ethics and Rules

"If you are led by the Spirit, you are not under the Law."

PAUL, Galatians, 5:18

"Official morality has always been oppressive and negative: it has said 'thou shalt not', and has not troubled to investigate the effect of activities not forbidden by the code."

BERTRAND RUSSELL, *Sceptical Essays*[5]

Characteristic of geniuses is their readiness to break laws or long-standing tradition. Beethoven, Wagner, Chopin, Debussy, Mahler, Stravinsky; Copernicus, Newton, Einstein, Hawking; Gautama, Jesus, Gandhi, and Schweitzer are examples of this. Jesus is reported to have declared, "I came not to destroy but to fulfil . . . " This was possibly a diplomatic way of introducing his revolutionary anti-legalistic ethics of love, which was in effect an interiorisation and a universalisation of the Law (the Jewish Torah). Matthew's Gospel presents Jesus as "a second Moses", but the title fits Muhammad rather than Jesus. The Qur'an lays down – as did the Old Testament – laws governing the behaviour of individuals and their accountability to Allah, as well as rules telling them how and when to pray, where and when to perform pilgrimage, and the like.

There was a time in the West when religion, Christianity in particular, was regarded as the bastion of morality in society. This view seems to have been responsible for the mandatory statements concerning "religious instruction" in the 1944 Education Act. It was exquisitely expressed by the headmistress who, when graffiti appeared on the lavatory walls, demanded to know what the Religious Education specialist was going to do about it.[6] I wonder: did the R.E. teacher ask her to see divinity in everyone? or ask her what she thought the *reason* for the graffiti was?

Morality is sometimes understood as obedience to a set of rules, a legal code and or custom (the 'done thing', which even today may vary considerably from one social layer to another). I would not wish to impose any code of conduct on human beings (each person should construct his own and take responsibility for it); but I do wish that all human beings were truly equal, that is, equally valued, so that there would no longer be such an immodest gap between privileged and deprived classes as to incite the latter to adopt survival tactics that contravene the laws of the land. In such a case can one truthfully say that such 'criminals' are behaving unethically? Is it unethical to repudiate an unethical social order? The fact that immorality is institutionalised should not beguile us into accepting it.

What is needed is not world-renunciation, in the sense of turning one's back on it; nor a morality of mere obedience to laws imposed by governments –

though there is no denying that observance of some basic rules is essential for safeguarding us from physical or mental abuse. What is needed is a morality deeply seated in the human being by virtue of a conscious acknowledgement of the divinity in all people and things, and a pre-eminent awareness of divinity in oneself. This awareness of divinity in oneself must not be confused with megalomania, which is an exaltation of ego, the individual self separated from other beings and from the total cosmic organism of which we are integral members. Awareness of divinity is awareness of the possibility and the duty of self-transcendence, which can be achieved only through a divine–human amalgam.

If eros is the motivation for acquiring truth in other spheres, in the ethical sphere of 'right' and 'wrong' a fuller love is required alongside intelligence, a deep respect for people – all people, and all things – that are likely to be affected by this or that policy of behaviour or this or that particular action. 'Empathy' is the name we might give to this kind of love.

Furthermore, goodness is a concept capable of transformation. Yesterday's good may be today's or tomorrow's evil; and vice versa. 'Good' and 'evil' are categories whose perceived contents ought to change as we learn more about the effects of this or that action, or as our sensibilities become more refined and discriminating as a result of experience. Such insights are well and truly explored – along with others – in what has become known as 'situation ethics'.

Situation Ethics

Situation Ethics[7] is the title of Joseph Fletcher's presentation of love as the ultimate determinant of what is good and right in any given situation. Whatever love requires is good. This must be clearly distinguished from antinomianism, according to which whatever one *wants* to do is right.

As Fletcher himself points out, doing what love requires is not always plain sailing. He gives the example of a woman who, when a ship is sinking, is only able to save one out of two people; one is her father, the other a renowned medical genius. Not an easy choice for her to make! unless we assume that she will naturally choose to save her father. But the kind of love Fletcher has in mind is one that takes no account of self and relies upon an intelligent and objective understanding of the situation. The woman accordingly saves the genius, who has so much to give to the world.

This is the sort of love that one would find in anyone who is constantly aware of the divinity in all people: love, not specific rules. Such a person, like Fletcher's woman in the example given above, will take a utilitarian view and opt for the decision that will result in the greatest amount of good for all who are likely to be affected by the choice. In religious terms, this is a case of choosing the option that will allow the greatest amount of divine creativity to flow to the benefit of the greatest number of needy recipients. Love is dynamic, constantly growing, moving closer to per-fection. What love is seen to require may change from one stage of human development (individual or as a species) to another. Love entails *creative* activity.

To speak of ethics as creative is once again to distinguish ethics from law. Laws require only passive obedience. They leave us to decide – by making a moral decision – which of all the many things that law allows us to do we shall actually do or attempt to do; for instance, to transform the world of human intercourse from ruthless competition for the biggest slice of the cake to caring cooperation to procure adequate shares for all. Where ethics comes close to law is in situations where conscience forbids us to take a laissez-faire attitude – for instance, where we feel we must protest against practices which, if not actually illegal, are seen to be detrimental to health, say, or safety, or justice and equality.

Ethics and Freedom

My negative remarks on law should not be taken to mean that I consider law unnecessary. We do need laws, to protect us against assault and robbery and rape, against vilification of character and unequal treatment in the workplace or, indeed, in the law-courts, and to preserve our domestic peace and privacy and protect our human right to an adequate dwelling that will shelter us from rain and hail and snow and extremes of heat and cold, and to a sufficient income to cover the costs of buying or renting such a dwelling and clothing and feeding ourselves and family. In other words, basic human rights should be guaranteed by law.

Nevertheless, between law and morality there is a clear divide. No action may properly be called moral unless it is freely chosen. If we do something *only* because law requires it, we are not acting morally. If, on the other hand, I choose to disobey the law, this does not automatically mean my action is morally wrong. For instance, if I deliberately drive my car at speed into a car in which bank robbers are about to make their getaway, I have no idea what my car insurers would say; but my action, though strictly illegal, cannot be said to be morally wrong, even if the car did not actually belong to the robbers but had been stolen by them.

We might wish to argue that, since we did not vote for a particular law, we have every right to ignore it or flout it. But in a democratic society where we have a vote to cast in favour of this or that policy, we are duty bound to accept the measures enforced by the party that gained more votes than the others. We have a right to voice our disagreement or outrage concerning a particular measure, but must abide by it, perhaps until the next ballot takes place. In other words, we freely agree to having limits to our personal freedom where the exercise of unlimited freedom would run counter to the wishes of the majority. Otherwise we might – to take a rather extreme case – suffer the same appalling consequences of the breakdown of law and order as we have read about in such places as Cambodia and Bosnia, Rwanda and Sierra Leone. Such horrendous phenomena make it clear that order does not necessarily depend on obeying orders. It all depends on what the orders are and who gave them, and with what motive.

In short, we need a happy medium between law (and government) that takes little or no account of people's needs and wishes and, on the other hand, a misuse of freedom that may result in anarchy and bloodshed. The only trust-worthy arbiter and balancer is reason. But reason was no match against the smartness of an evil Saddam Hussein, who was able to manipulate United Nations peacemakers with his little finger (combined with rock-like stubborn-ness) and continued his savage massacres for a decade until American and British aerial and military bombardment and an international law-court finally put an end to his ignominious reign.

Having experienced the likes of Hussein and such ethnic 'cleansers' as Hitler and Milosevic, one seems to have only two options: resort to violence (the mere threat of it does not work), or else turn one's back on evil in an attempt to keep oneself "unspotted from the world." Is this second option really "true religion", as James believed?[8] even when thousands of lives are at stake? If so, religion has nothing positive to contribute to the world. I think I prefer Paul to James on this count: if Paul's intuition that a religious attitude based on the spirit of love supplies all that is necessary for a truly moral life is loosed from Paul's sexual inhibitions, we have a grounding for an ethic that is non-legalistic, undogmatic, ever open to new insights required by new circumstances – in short, a self-sustaining and dynamic ethic.

We may venture to say that detachment from the outside world is good if it means keeping oneself unspotted by aggressive money-making and exploita-tion of other people or indeed of other parts of the biosphere. But, like it or not, we are inevitably involved in 'this world': not doing anything about poverty and injustice or other forms of inequality that depend on human action or inaction is itself a way – albeit a negative way – of responding to such evils. To trick oneself into believing that one can opt out is to muffle or deny one's conscience, which is one's awareness of the indwelling divinity.

The ideal is to act *creatively*. But creativity may occasionally require some preliminary demolition. This is not an already perfected world. Our human business in it is to move it, or allow it to move, closer to its perfection. This is a moral imperative across the board, but perhaps especially in the realm of poli-tics, the realm of commerce, and at the interface of humankind and planet Earth:

> "Except the Lord build the house, they that build it labour in vain."
> PSALM 127, verse 1.

> "By their fruits ye shall know them."
> MATTHEW VII, 16.

It would be immensely presumptuous of me to say what 'the right answer' is to such complicated issues. But I am convinced that the fruits of the religious attitude outlined in this book can only be good. Seeing divinity in all things and being at one with that divinity (conscience, spirit) in ourselves must inevitably result in feeling at one with all things and therefore showing respect for all things. From then on is only (!) a matter of delving into the facts, the possibilities, and the likely consequences of each of those possibilities, with a view to arriving at a consensus.

The day on which I am writing this is International Day for Remembrance of the Slave Trade. Ken Livingstone (who, at the time of writing was Lord Mayor of London) has made a moving speech expressing on behalf of the City of London deep remorse for our ancestors' removal of black people from their homelands and the shameful flogging and torture and sexual abuse of them – men, women and children. One right-wing spokesman said he was not participating in the apology: he could not understand how one generation could apologise on behalf of another. But has he not shared in the material benefits of such ancestral bestiality? Perhaps, like Carlyle, he believed that black people were *meant* to be slaves.[9] What hope is there for the future – what justification is there for any future – of humankind if we have no respect for justice and for our fellow human beings?

Before considering the above-mentioned huge issues, it is essential not to lose sight of the need for balance. The balance in question used to be described as that between 'being *in* the world' and 'being *of* the world'. An understanding of an everywhere immanent divinity inevitably gives a new 'slant' to that balance: all is One, and One is all; spirit and matter are interdependent, not as good and evil may be said to be interdependent because relative, but in the sense that each needs the other for its expression. The relation between humanity and divinity is similarly reciprocal: true and total humanity is impossible without what the Christians call 'the grace of God', that is, the indwelling divine energy and inspiration.

Inspiration and expiration are a useful metaphor for the dynamic balance that is essential for all creative human activity in the world. Such activity needs the energising passivity, not merely that of sleep (which can be restive as well as restful), but the total passivity of meditation, which means total relinquishing of the egotistic self.

Religion is a way of looking at things – an attitude. To see the divinity in all things, and therefore the oneness of all things, is to be filled with wonder at and love for all things. From this, right action arises spontaneously – because oneness reduces and softens ego. In other words, this religious attitude is preeminently suited to serve as the foundation for a positive, creative ethic – an ethic of self-fulfilment and world-transformation. (Rather like Marx's last thesis on Feuerbach![10]) I believe Marx was a truly spiritual person vilified by people with vested interests.

The effect that awareness of the divinity in things has on one's actions must be clearly distinguished from the traditional theistic motivation for virtuous behaviour: that 'God sees everything you do, even if no one else does'. (The door of the classroom in an old village dame's school had an eye painted on it. When the teacher left the room for any reason, she pointed to the eye and said, "Children, behave yourselves. God's eye is watching you." The teacher was a sweet old lady; but my fifty-year-old son still remembers that ghastly eye.) By contrast, it is our own eye that sees the divinity in things; that vision is our own personal vision and valuation of the universe and all its parts. Divinity is not something or someone out there, keeping an eye on us; it is within us, our own essential self, our conscience.

But it is necessary to educate one's conscience. One should not totally identify conscience with divinity. 'Con-science' ('knowing-with') is our capacity for being at one with divinity. An uneducated conscience is likely to be bigoted, blistered, pompous or pretentious, pious or opinionated. Just as a creative artist may give all credit for his masterpieces to his ego (and become a pitiful victim of megalomania), so it is possible for us to believe that we have an infallible knowledge of what is good (and become insufferable prigs).

Duty and Beauty

"The mystical feeling precedes the moral."
NICOLAS BERDYAEV[11]

In the spiritual scheme of things virtue is not a result of conforming to a set of rules. Virtue arises, with an urgent intensity, at the moment we perceive the wonder and rightness of a cosmos in which all things arise from a single source. Oneness and wonder are the amalgam from which love and virtue arise spontaneously.

Creative ethics can only be prophetic and forward-looking, not enslaved to the past. Consequently it must have an erotic – yearning – component. Its good must transcend that of law, which is enforced by sanctions. The good in creative ethics commends itself by its own intrinsic quality; it has the same attraction as beauty: it is something we desire and worship voluntarily, effortlessly.

If what we perceive as good loses its attractiveness – perhaps because in the course of time its image has been debased or distorted, it will be abandoned. Its place may be taken by some other good-and-beautiful bearer of value. One such exchange may be good, another bad. This is because human beings may be pure or impure. If pure in their perception, they will easily and smoothly transfer their desire from a lesser to a greater good; if their perception is clouded by selfishness, their concept of the good and desirable may plummet accordingly.

This is the inherent *tragic* quality of human creativity, which can be good or bad according to the elevation or degradation of the human desire. The ultimate root of this tragic element in human life is freedom, the freedom to see or not to see the divinity in ourselves or, having seen it, not to accept it as our constant guide, as an inexhaustible well of wisdom accessible to us if we open our eyes to it, – or perhaps if we just *close* our eyes for a little while.

After that it is reason – an unegotistic and, where circumstances require, a scientific understanding of causes and effects – that must be allowed to point the way.

Sometimes it seems that truth is no longer respected: "If concealing the truth promises more profit, conceal it." "No one ever made an honest shilling by telling the truth." We may easily get the impression that not only that old salesman but present-day politicians all too seldom rely upon truth to sway popular opinion and have more faith in the power of enthusiastic rhetoric to win votes.

But that is only a part of the picture, and may well be a diminishing part, given more and better education, whether in schools or from serious discussion on television or in the more informative, less gossipy newspapers.

> "Who is the great dragon whom the spirit will no longer call lord or god? 'Thou shalt' is the name of the great dragon. But the spirit of the lion says, 'I will'."[12]

The dragon represents the authority of tradition, of age-old sacrosanct values. The lion represents the power to create new values, an ethic based on reason and freedom, not on external 'infallible' authority.

Can We do Without God?

Can we then do without God? If by 'God' one means the theistic notion of a person, emotional and usually masculine, who generally resides outside the universe, the answer is and, rationally and morally, *must* be, Yes. We can well do without that false god who is said to love us all and to punish those who disobey him; who gives us freedom of will and thought and expects us to use it as he wishes. This is – or would certainly appear to be – a psychopathological product of that portion of humanity that has been conditioned to think negatively about themselves – as sinful and worthless – or those who, having been nurtured in that way, use this poisoned view as a venomous weapon with which to threaten and attack those who entertain an altogether superior and happier view of life and hold superior positions in society.

If, however, one means by 'God' that everywhere immanent divinity that is the cosmic energy, the answer must be, 'No, we need it'. Not only do we need it, but we have actually got it and cannot do without it. We cannot even exist without it.

If to the notion of cosmic energy we add that of cosmic intelligence, or consciousness or mind, must we not acknowledge that our own mind or intelligence is a manifestation of that cosmic mind and intelligence? All that we have in us – minerals, chemicals, cells, organs and, to crown it all, mind – comes from the universe. Science has been able to trace our ancestry. We are not isolated from the cosmos either as a species or as individuals. We share with all other beings a single source that has been given various names: māna, God, Spirit, Nature, mind, energy, Big Bang. If I opt generally for 'divinity', it is chiefly with a view to preserving some link with Western religious traditions whilst at the same time pointing to a completely universal and, one hopes, a rational understanding of ultimate reality and meaning. But I would passionately beg my readers (I trust there is more than one) to read, if they have not already done so, *The Tibetan Book of Living and Dying*,[13] written by Sogyal Rinpoche. Those who are not acquainted with Tibetan Buddhism and associate it only with gongs and bells and a long didgeridoo-like instrument, prayer-wheels and flags, the chanting of mantras, or with the Chinese policy of ethnic cleansing (in which we see a stark juxtaposition of the bestial and the spiritual faces of humankind), should certainly read the book.

Sogyal expounds the notion of Buddha-nature that is common to all forms of Buddhism but receives special emphasis in Mahayāna Buddhism, which includes Tibetan Buddhism. Siddhartha Gotama is known as the Buddha because he is said to have achieved enlightenment ('buddha' = 'awake'); and this enlightenment is achievable by anyone. It is the knowledge of the one Mind that is in all sentient beings; and this knowledge brings awareness of our basic oneness with all such beings. This Mind is widely referred to as Buddha-nature and is equivalent to 'God' or 'Self' or 'brahman' or the Sufi 'Hidden Essence' of all things. The Tibetan word for it is 'Rigpa', which means primordial awareness of things as they are. Getting through to this primal awareness is the way to enlightenment, the realisation that 'my' mind is of the very same nature as divinity, or the cosmic intelligence. We may say that this is the Christian 'homoousios' (Jesus' being of the same nature as God) lifted from a particularist to a universalist level of understanding. From this perspective we can no longer separate or differentiate oneself from others. The same mind – the divine mind – is within all; all are therefore capable of enlightenment. All are therefore to be respected; to be heard and conversed with; to learn from.

Does Mind have to Make Up its Mind about Mind?

Gilbert Ryle's classic, *The Concept of Mind* (1949), argued against Descartes' view that thinking was not a function of anything physical, viz., the brain. Ryle said that, just as when we say, 'It is raining', we do not expect anyone to ask, 'What is [doing the] raining?', so we may properly say, 'There is thinking', without expecting to be asked what is doing the thinking. In other words, says Ryle, 'mind' is a useless concept, since it has no referent, no actual physical thing to which it refers. What we *can* see is brain, but not mind.

But is this not like saying one can hear sounds but not music, see a flower but not its beauty? Can one literally see intelligence or goodness? No; but are they – and beauty – unreal? Can one see vision or hear hearing?

If Ryle is right, we may say that thinking, like raining, is something that can have an impact on us, can influence what we do, what decisions we make. In other words, mind must be understood in dynamic, not substantive terms. If so, then what Ryle says is no more devastating than what I have said about divinity being the intelligence or mind of the universe. Mind – and likewise intelligence or consciousness – is a dynamic property of the universe.

CHAPTER ELEVEN

Religion and Science

If 'God' is said to refer to some supernatural being, one must dismiss as nonsensical any sentence that claims to say something about it. 'God exists' *looks* like a factual statement, such as 'The cat is on the mat'. But the similarity is only a grammatical one. Logically speaking, the two sentences are very different: 'The cat is on the mat' can be verified or falsified empirically: just take a look and see if the cat really is on the mat. But there is no empirical and objective way of showing whether a supernatural God exists or not; not even if it is said that 'God is in Jesus', and we have the man Jesus in front of us. Even if we were able to take a photograph of Jesus – even an X-ray photograph – there would be nothing to point to on the photograph that could be identified as a supernatural God.

If, on the other hand, we substitute 'divinity' for 'supernatural God' and stipulate that divinity is the energy of the cosmos, then the existence of energy is well attested by observation, but not divinity. As has already been said, I use the word 'divinity' to signify that whatever it is applied to is held in reverence, with wonder and awe and also with gratitude and love and joy, as the ultimate source and sustainer of all things, and as omnipresent so that human beings can consciously have access to the energy and intelligence (or mind) and rightness of this omnipresent divinity. In short, 'divinity' expresses a way of looking at – an attitude towards – the universe and our life within it, an attitude that fosters creative thinking and creative activity that are not only a means of self-fulfilment for the individual, but play a positive part in bringing the cosmos closer to its fulfilment.

Religion, then, is a way of seeing things. So is science. Science in Newton's day may be said to have rested on direct observation. Today's science goes beyond what can be verified by observation. In principle, observation could disprove any scientific theory: if, for example, some new empirical evidence came to light that contradicted the theory. "All swans are white" was regarded as a universal truth – until black swans were sighted in Australia. But no scientific theory rests solely on observation. Indeed, if science did not go beyond observation it would not be very useful. It is only by making universal claims – "If x, then always y" – that science becomes a useful tool for making reliable predictions which will enable us to negotiate the world safely and successfully by telling us what will happen if, for example, we heat a mixture of nitric and sulphuric acids with glycerine; or what is *likely* to happen if you jump off a high cliff onto rocks, depending on your weight, the suppleness of your joints, the distance from cliff top to rocks, and whether you have a parachute or not.

The philosophical understanding of scientific method has changed since Immanuel Kant came on the scene in the 18th century. Kant distinguished (somewhat as Plato had done) between noumena (things as they are) and phenomena (things as they appear to us), and he declared that science can tell us, not what things are, but only how they appear to our senses and mental interpretative faculties and the instruments we construct to aid and extend the range of our senses (e.g. telescopes and microscopes of various kinds) and our brains (e.g. computers).

A favoured conundrum is: Does a falling tree in a forest beyond human hearing make any sound? Obviously, phenomena will differ considerably for different creatures in accordance with their different sensory equipment: eagle and hawk have fantastic eyesight, but the birds they prey upon may only be able to detect the threat by distinguishing between light and darkness (the shadow or the actual dark body of the hovering predator). Some bats use laser beams for navigating in their dark caves; blackbirds can sense the vibrations produced by an earth-worm below the surface of the soil.

What does this mean for science? Hans Vaihinger, a follower of Kant, wrote a book called *The Philosophy of 'As if'*.[1] In it he insisted that, in order to be philosophically correct, all scientific statements that claim to tell us something about the universe or any part of it should have the prefix, "It is as if . . . " Thus, instead of saying there was a gravitational force, scientists should have said, "It is as if there were a gravitational force . . . " I give this example because Einstein tells us that gravity is in fact not a force, but a curvature of four-dimensional time–space around something. Sometimes science openly conforms to the 'as if' mode, as when it postulates – invents – entities ('gravitons', for example) to explain otherwise inexplicable observed phenomena; and scientific 'hypotheses' are exactly that: suppositions. It is important to add that hypotheses are put to the test by testing predictions based on them. But this does not mean that we then have to say that the hypotheses are necessarily telling us the truth about things as they are in themselves.

What seems *likely*, however, is that there is a consonance between the human brain and the universe that allows (or obliges?) the one to penetrate the secret parts of the other, and the implications of this human adaptation to the natural world would seem to be that we can trust our senses and our brains to give us trustworthy information about that world, especially if we assiduously check the rightness of our observations and arithmetic and honestly keep a look-out for phenomena that seem to 'disobey' our theories.

The Theory of Everything?

But the scientific enterprise is not yet complete. In physics various grand unified theories (GUTs) or theories of everything (TOEs) have been put forward. As far as I know, none of them has gained universal acceptance, perhaps partly because they include imaginative postulates (multi-dimensional models of the universe, for example) which are difficult to verify.

Energy

What is particularly significant is that the aforementioned avant-garde theories centre on the notion of energy as the ultimate source of everything, the all-pervasive essence of the universe. At present we recognise various forms of energy – electromagnetic, nuclear ('strong' and 'weak'), and gravitational (which Einstein describes as a curving of space–time). Now physicists seem to be approaching the one, ultimate factor or omnipresent component of physical reality, in terms of which everything else has its explanation: an ultimate cause, itself uncaused; the ultimate explanation, itself inexplicable. This, of course, is a definition of 'God' or 'divinity', but especially of 'divinity' as presented in this book.

Whereas it used to be only religion that claimed to give an explanation of everything, now science claims to be within reach of an authentic ultimate explanation of everything. In my understanding of energy as a manifestation – arguably the prime and fundamental manifestation – of divinity, all things, including the human mind, derive from it. Our freedom of choice means we can employ the divine energy that is within our mind (itself a fragment of the divine cosmic mind) rightly or wrongly, honestly or dishonestly. The scientific methodology contains inbuilt procedures for checking every postulate and every established theory. (Contrast the theological–ecclesiastical procedure, in which 'orthodox' teachings tend to be sacred and therefore taboo, untouchable. Quite rightly, new teachings are subjected to scrutiny; but often they are summarily dismissed.) Of course, science may be completely coherent, but nevertheless based on a fundamental error. That appears to be an unlikely possibility, given the proven successes of science; but the ultimate test will occur if and when science gives its definitive account of the ultimate ground or cause of all (other) things – namely, energy.

Energy, then, seems to be the area where religion (properly understood) and physics may be seen to meet. In battle, or in harmony? In a juvenile article printed in an undergraduate magazine, I pictured a physics student and a theological student engaged in mortal combat, the one armed with a retort stand, the other with a brass-clasped family bible. In those days theologians were in the habit of taking advantage of the fact that science had not got round to explaining *everything*, by conjuring up a 'God-in-the-gaps' who supplied an explanation wherever science had failed. Again, in those days logical positivism was in fashion, which dismissed God-talk as nonsense, since it was neither factual nor logical discourse. But now most scientists and most theologians are less extremist.

Karl Popper, renowned as a philosopher of science, said that the scientist's aim must be, not to verify a theory, but to falsify it: only thus could science progress to a fuller understanding of the way things are.[2] Stephen Hawking, revered as one of the greatest physicists of all time, comparable with Newton and Einstein, agrees with Popper: "Any physical theory is always provisional, in the sense that it is only a hypothesis: you can never prove it. No matter how many times the results of experiments agree with some theory, you can never be sure that the next time the result will not contradict the theory."[3]

In other words, 'We learn by our mistakes' applies to science – and not only *applies*, but is also fully *acknowledged* in science. Would that the same were equally true in religion!

But one must not exaggerate the difference. On the one hand, it is only recently that scientists have ceased to cling on to established theories just as relentlessly as religionists have clung to their dogmas and rituals; on the other hand, the last hundred years or so, alongside an ominous retreat into extremist fundamentalism which rejects outright anything that threatens it, have seen Christendom's growing openness to new insights.

Paul Tillich (1886–1965) was keen to bridge the gap between Christian theology and secular culture (depth psychology and existentialist philosophies in particular), boldly declaring that "The new is created not out of the old, not out of the best of the old, but out of the death of the old."[4] Teilhard de Chardin (1881–1955), as we have seen, was keen to bridge the gap between Christianity and science, centring on the human role in evolution; and Alfred North Whitehead's *Process and Reality*[5] (1929) gave inspiration to the Process theologians in the USA.

The Modernist movement in Roman Catholic and Protestant churches (perhaps notably in the Church of England) was sadly condemned in 1907 by Pope Pius X as "the compendium of all heresies" – a description that may be taken as a tribute to the sincere concern for truth and for the Church's continuing relevance that characterised that movement. *The Modern Churchman*, a journal that dared to accept avant garde articles that *Theology* refrained from printing, was published by the Modern Churchmen's Union.

Will Science and Religion Converge?

So, who knows? Perhaps we shall see a merger of science and religion, not a merger in which one or the other takes control of the other, but one in which each learns from the other, religion relinquishing its unacceptable dogmas and science jettisoning the remnants of its dogmatic neglect of spiritual reality. I can only speculate that there will be such a conjunction of science and the religious vision sketched in this book based on the equation: divinity = the energy, intelligence and rightness of the cosmos. But even the self-styled "devil's chaplain" believes that "Science can be spiritual, even religious in a non-supernatural sense of the word."[6] That is truly encouraging.

Science Ethics and Religion

Science, ethics and religion have different functions. Science's function is to increase our understanding of nature and therefore our control over it, so as to utilise its potential for meeting our needs, ranging from food, clothing and shelter, clean air and pure water, to ever more energy not only for cooking, heating and light and motor vehicles, but also energy on a rapidly increasing scale for continually updating weapons of war that could destroy all forms of life except some bacterial forms; not to mention biological and chemical warfare – deadly nerve agent VX, hydrogen cyanide, etc.

Science is objective, emotionless and a-moral. Ethics has the function of evaluating 'progress' in terms of its fruits – good or bad, creative or destructive, just or unjust. The consequences of scientific and matching technological developments may benefit both humankind and the rest of nature (which must be protected if only for the selfish reason that we are dependent on it for survival); but they may be disastrous for both – unless there is adequate provision for effective ethical control. Not that we must be 21st century Luddites or never allow anything to be done for the first time; but such newly realised possibilities as laboratory-born organisms that could produce innumerable cures and preventatives for diseases, for the dissolution of atmospheric carbons, and produce new sources of fuel, but could also be used for massacre and destruction on a global scale, obviously have to be looked at very carefully and, if accepted, be strictly controlled not with a view to how much money could be made out of them by commercial organisations, or how much power they could give this or that national government, but solely with a view to human welfare world-wide.

Religion that consists in a reverential feeling of oneness with nature functions as a foundation for creative endeavour and universal compassion, for science and ethics.

Transcendence and Immanence on the Personal Level

At this point I ought to try to clarify the relation between transcendence and immanence. On the personal level: if the human being is a self-reflective being, a "being-for-itself" (Hegel and, later, Sartre), then s/he is never completely identifiable with what s/he actually is at any given moment: there is always possibly something more to be achieved. "Werde was du bist" – "Become what you are". The human being becomes himself more fully, more truly, as he steps out of his 'facticity' into his 'transcendence' (Sartre's terms), for the human being is by nature a self-transcending being (Berdyaev's term).

What needs to be added is that the transcendence into or towards which a person steps is at once divinity/God and the person's own true Self. The stepping into transcendence is simultaneously a transformation of what was transcendent into something immanent. (As in Incarnation, properly understood.)

Progress in truth (or beauty or goodness – for the truth here is cosmic as well as human) means making immanent what was transcendent, in the encounter of spirit with Spirit. If that which is encountered in the mind is not transcendent, there can be no progress in truth; and if it *is* transcendent and *remains* transcendent, again there is no progress. *The transcendent is not made immanent by kenosis or any other supernatural magic, but by a relationship between the divine and the human in which both are active and in which it is not always possible to say where the one ends and the other begins, or vice versa.* This is the essence of divine incarnation and human deification: the two energetic processes coincide. If they do not synchronise, neither can occur – whether in Jesus of Nazareth or in you and me. Of course, we are talking about energy, and all energy – including 'our own' – is divine. But it is *we* who decide how – and indeed whether – to use it. As for *how* we use it, if we know that 'our energy' is divine, we shall surely be inclined to employ it for good ends, and reverently.

The conscious initiation of this relationship may be felt as an 'eruption' (Berdyaev's word) within oneself. If so, this may be taken to mean that God/divinity is within us from the beginning, from our conception (or – who knows? – even before). As Wordsworth says, we come into the world "trailing clouds of glory". When we open our eyes we are beguiled by the exciting busyness of the human-made world – until the moment when nature rekindles in us our pre-natal awareness of oneness with God/divinity. Then comes the eruption, which – please God! – will remain within our consciousness through life and death.

Here we have a coincidence of human self-transcendence and divine immanence, the first dependent on the other (via nature). The transcendent will always hover over us as long as we have not achieved per-fection. (And if perfection *were* attained, would there be anything left to live for? Yes, the bliss of contentment, say the enlightened; and the total love of all for all. For more, see the chapter to follow).

The same applies to our awareness of the divine in nature in toto, in the whole cosmos to the extent that we can experience or imagine it.

Divine Transcendence and Immanence

In religious use 'transcendence' and 'immanence' are not mutually exclusive. Even though the stress is more often on transcendence, both are predicated of one and the same thing, namely, God.

The problem I set myself is how to use the word 'transcendence' when one no longer believes in the creator-god of the Hebrew bible, adopted in all but detail by Christianity. I favour Santayana's (1863–1952) view of religious language as poetry. "Religion," he said "is the poetry men live by."[7] In other words, religious language is a language of the imagination. Languages of the imagination are commonly distinguished from languages of the senses, including those of commonsense and science: whereas the latter will talk about the *actual*, the former deal with the possible and – generally speaking, the desirable. But in fact the two kinds of language mingle; and where they do so, imaginative language – the language of what might be – is usually prior to the other. That is why Einstein, among others, stressed the value of imagination in science. Scientific hypotheses begin their life as statements of what *might* be the case.

One sphere of what *might* be is that of what *ought* (or *ought not*) to be: moral language belongs to the family of languages of the imagination. Religious language, I believe, is another. Much religious talk is moral talk: the Ten Commandments of the Hebrew bible, Hindu and Buddhist dharma, Islamic hadith, Jesus' Sermon on the Mount, and so on – and I have no desire to separate the inseparable. But there is a core of religious talk that may be distinguished from moral talk. That core is 'There is a God' (or gods), or some equivalent such as the 'buddha-mind' or 'buddha-nature'. To achieve – or realise – our oneness with divinity (or brahman or whatever) is the heart of religion, whether it be principally moral (doing what is believed to be consonant with our concept or inner experience of divinity) or mainly mystical (where one's mind consciously merges or mingles with the divine mind). The mystical embraces, at least in principle, the moral dimension.

I have already suggested that 'There is a God (or divinity)' cannot properly be classed together with the empirical statements of science and should rather be seen as a value-judgment *based* on our internal or external experience, but introducing and expressing a subjective, emotional response to that experience. In other words, a religious way of understanding things is an evaluation that involves the whole human being, body and mind, senses and spirit. Morally speaking, this means believing that the world – the universe – is good, in the sense that it contains the potential for per-fection, in all likelihood requiring human assistance for its realisation. In other words, the transcendent can be immanentised and – the same thing in effect – the immanent can participate in transcendence.

'Transfiguration' and 'Resurrection' may be seen as symbols of the possibility of the actual being transformed into the ideal; and this includes the 'deification' of humanity.

The Transcendent and the Ideal

Thus, 'the transcendent' may be seen as 'the ideal'. 'The ideal' is in itself a vague, indeed an empty concept. It needs filling. And the filling given it will vary from individual to individual, and with the same individual from one time to another. The filling is always provisional: when what was once supposed to be the ideal is *embodied* (in self or society or cosmos), the notion of the ideal may then assume a new filling. ('God speaks with a new voice'). That is why it is appropriate to call it 'the transcendent': the ideal always lies ahead of us;

when we *seem* to have embodied it, it is still soaring above our present reality, but in a new guise. 'The ideal' is always capable of receiving new connotations.

If the Buddhist 'enlightened one' or the Christian or Sufi mystic is credited with the whole truth and nothing but the truth, we must ask what this can mean. It can mean that the person has attained the heights of spiritual illumination as defined in the tradition s/he has espoused. If so, how can we who are outside that tradition make a valid judgment? We may not even *understand* the final stages of the discipline in question. In such cases we are forced to conclude that we cannot – and therefore should not – judge, since the posited truth we are talking about is subjective in the sense that it has to be experienced personally. This does not necessarily mean that the truth in question is invalid. Rather, it would seem that there are some things that can be truly known only by personal experience – like making love. The fact that we can know *about* them may encourage us and eventually enable us to achieve the same experience. *Then* we may judge it! As often as not, I believe, we shall find that another subjective religious experience is fundamentally the same as our own, only couched in different words.

Science, Religion and Ethics

Certainly, there is not always a sharp dividing line between aesthetic and moral concepts. 'Harmony', for example, is a moral notion so far as it represents what is believed to be an aspect of the ideal; but it is also an aesthetic notion, like 'symmetry' or even like 'love' and 'lovely', which may have moral as well as emotional or aesthetic connotations. Indeed, one's definition or account of 'the ideal' may be of something that kindles desire by virtue of what one would want to call its 'beauty', that is, by virtue of its appeal to the aesthetic sense. As Bertrand Russell pointed out, it is only the element of desire-fulfilment that can save the moral person from the hypocrisy of acting contrary to his inner disposition; and *desiring* what ought to be is certainly much better than doing what one thinks one ought to do even though one does not want to do it. Again, the word 'sublime' is frequently used in connection with or as a synonym for 'the transcendent'; and is not 'sublimity' also an *aesthetic* notion?

Although religion is not identical with morality, any true religion must bear moral fruits. Perhaps there is an analogy here with science. According to the pragmatist view expounded by Vaihinger and Popper (and discernible already in Kant), the function of science is not to describe the world as it 'really' is.[8] Rather, its function is to enable us to achieve control over the phenomenal world of nature so as to provide adequately for our human needs. Max Frisch (1911–91), Swiss playwright and novelist, sardonically defined technology as "the knack of so arranging the world that we don't have to experience it".[9] Whilst enjoying his wit, we can and should take seriously the fact that our technological revolution, like the industrial revolution, can estrange the human being from the natural world (which is his true home) to such an extent that he now feels at home only when surrounded by computers and other domesticated products of technology. Merging with – and perhaps inspiring – those creative human endeavours is the impetus of a cosmic vision in which divinity, the ultimate, transcendent and sublime reality, is *immanent* in all things. Such a vision is the religious counterpart of science. Religion is a reverent awareness of the divinity in things, an awareness that conditions our moral sense and transforms it from what it would otherwise be. If a scientist, or anyone else, were to insist that s/he had immense reverence for the natural world but that this did not mean s/he was religious, my response would have to be that s/he was probably mistaking particular dogmatic religions for the universal spirituality that I have attempted to depict in this book, an age-old spirituality that is still relevant and meaningful today.

Science enables us to use the divine creative energy and intelligence. But if science has no overriding moral direction (in both senses of the word) it may find itself being used – and even controlled – by those power-crazed elements of humankind that value science and technology only for their destructive potential. The religious vision of divinity in things requires a moral response in terms of reverence for all things and compassion for all suffering things; science provides the information and know-how that enable us to express our reverence and compassion in the most appropriate and efficacious ways.

Religion, morality and science: a truly venerable trinity! Add a sense of beauty, and we shall have an even more venerable and desirable quartet!

CHAPTER TWELVE

The 'Problem of Evil'; Providence

Is the Universe Good or Bad?

The problem of evil has employed the minds of human beings for several millennia – witness the explanations provided in mythology: some apprentice creator-god was allowed to try his hand, with dire consequences; or God sent famines or floods or epidemic diseases, or swarms of crop-devouring locusts to punish human beings for their wickedness.

In Western religion we have various answers to the question of the meaning of life, some positive and some negative: that all that happens in the world is due to the will of a benevolent deity and therefore serves a benevolent purpose (even though this may sometimes be difficult to discern); or that life is a dramatic contest between good and evil powers (God v. the Devil) which will end with a final vanquishing of the evil; or, on the other hand, that life in this world is totally corrupt and the only salvation for human beings lies in another, invisible world which may be attained either by a symbolic withdrawal from this world (= the monastic life) or by a joyless but determined fulfilling of our duties as a good Christian or Jew, or a good Muslim – duties which include miniature but regular retreats from the world, in church or synagogue or – in the case of Islam – in a mosque or, more frequently, simply on a prayer mat at the appropriate five times daily.

The most rational solution – or analysis, at least – of the problem of evil lies in the fact that we live in an evolving universe. I have already referred to Whitehead's analysis: that in an evolving universe one cannot properly apply the word 'perfect' in the sense of 'having all conceivable perfections within itself', meaning that it could not possibly change, since in a perfect thing any change must be for the worse. But the universe we live in is constantly changing, and has been changing for 15 billion years. Therefore 'perfection' in the absolute sense could not logically be applied to it. Instead, we must adopt a notion of perfection that *will* apply: namely, that something is perfect if at any given moment it is as good as it could reasonably be expected to be, but is still capable of becoming better. This may be called a dynamic definition, replacing the inappropriate static definition. I refer to the former as 'per-fection' to distinguish it from the old static 'perfection'.

If the world were perfect in the absolute sense, that would mean every one of us was perfect – which is obviously not the case. Indeed, many would say that the world is a very long way from perfection. We are constantly being told of some natural calamity – earthquake, volcanic eruption, tsunami, hurricane, famine, floods, epidemic diseases – to which we must add human greed and consequently poverty, injustice and inequality, wars and forever the threat of another war, or pseudo-religious terrorism.

Dostoevsky said he could not believe in a good God as long as there was even just one child somewhere in the world crying in pain. But Dostoevsky's God was a theistic personal, anthropomorphic deity. If, however, we believe in divinity, not as a person, but as the fundamental creative power of the universe, and also acknowledge that the universe is in process of evolution and therefore cannot be expected to be perfect in the absolute sense of the word, then catastrophes, great or small, do not cause us to relinquish our faith in the rightness of things – especially since we know that randomness is, in the process of cosmic evolution, a necessary prelude to human freedom.

On a different level, an Autumn 2007 poll in the USA revealed that a considerable portion of the population (30% or 40%, depending on the particular issue) believed it would be wrong to have children, in view of climate change, terrorism and immigration. A world in which God is believed to sanction 'holy war' to oust an indigenous population to make way for His Chosen People, or terrorism against people of another religious persuasion (or none), and in which many 'civilised' people show little concern for the natural environment on which they depend for life: such a world may well cause fundamentalist Christians or Muslims to believe the Day of Judgment is imminent, or Hindus to describe the present state of the world as a Kāli-yuga, the dark and evil age that marks the end of one huge epoch and the opening of a new cycle (Incidentally, this Indian karmic view of life assumes that justice is a built-in principle of the cosmic process.)

Tax-payers, particularly but not only in the USA, are being required to provide astronomical amounts of money for the provision and constant updating of nuclear and chemical weapons of war – money that could solve the global problems of poverty and starvation in undeveloped or developing countries but also in the world's developed countries, where the gap between rich and poor is growing wider and wider exponentially. We have already reached the stage where the head of a company is allowed an income 400 times that of his lowest paid employee. It reminds me of Jesus saying: "To them that have shall more be given; and from them that have not, shall be taken away that which they have." Jesus was referring, not to money, but to spiritual understanding; but ironically it has become an unacknowledged law of uncontrolled capitalism: as the rich become richer, the poor inevitably become relatively even poorer. Is not this the obscenity of obscenities?

Destiny and Creativity

As Adair Turner shows clearly, "The biggest threat to America's ability to create a more humane form of capitalism lies . . in a political system which gives too much influence to specific businesses opposing valid environmental and social objectives."[1] And "European welfare states are affordable if people want them. Price-based incentives to pursue environmental responsibility can and should be introduced without significantly reducing growth. Europeans can stop selling arms to brutal regimes and ignoring human-rights abuses at only minimal cost to their economies. Developed rich societies are largely free to choose their own destiny."[2] What is lacking is not the means, but the will.

If nations can choose their own destiny, so can the individual human being, within the constraints imposed by environment, government and gross domestic product. There may be providence; but one cannot help thinking that it is something handed down – in the West, anyway – from biblical times, when any tragedy or period of trial (Job is the classic example of innocent suffering) was put down to God either punishing or testing people. The historian Arnold Toynbee tells us how a nation faced with a challenge may be spurred by it to achieve greatness, whilst another nation may crumble under the challenge. Absence of challenge typically results in complacency and consequent decline; too great a challenge proves overwhelming. Yahweh, unfortunately, had not read Toynbee.

However that may be, the preservation of one's freedom is the paramount consideration. One must never relinquish one's freedom; one must never hide behind providence as a shield against any agonising decision-making. Martin Heidegger (1889–97), existentialist philosopher, said that the sense of destiny arises from a sense of the wholeness that one should achieve out of what the past (heredity and environmental factors) has given one. In other words, destiny is a matter of conscience, which requires us to use our freedom so as to transcend our "facticity" (what we are as a result of determinism) and achieve wholeness, our true and total self. (Compare Jung's "individuation".)

Some will agree with this but want to ask how they can decide what purpose to give oneself. The brief and portmanteau answer is: become what you truly are, fulfil yourself and enjoy life as much as you are able – and try to remove or reduce any inability. "Become what you are" means becoming a partner to the divinity within you. Know yourself and love yourself (including that indwelling divinity – or guru or wisdom), and the rest will follow: whatever your limitations, your awareness of oneness with the divinity in yourself and in all things will unleash your creative potential. We cannot all be concert pianists or Nobel prizewinners, but we all have something to give to the world; and the power of love and compassion is a match for any nuclear reactor, and less ambiguous in its effects. (What I have in mind is genuine love, not smothering or possessive love.) To the young: Get your parents to give you the education that you feel would best suit you (and their pockets!): be alive to the world around you, and to the needs of your body, and – again – stay constantly in touch with and responsive to the inner wisdom. If you yourself are disadvantaged, do what you can to ensure that others will not be. There are always so many channels for creativity in the world. Choose one that will also foster your own *self*-creativity. Discriminating between good and bad channels and between those that suit us and those that do not is sometimes easy, sometimes an arduous process of learning from one's mistakes. Once you are sure of your destiny, keep faith with it.

A great obstacle to creativity is depression, though it often accompanies creativity. Several great composers have had to battle with it. But not only creative artists have suffered from it: comparatively few people, it would appear, escape its visitations.

Strictly speaking, depression is not a physical disease, but it may have physical effects. Dorothy Rowe, a world-renowned clinical psychologist who specialises in depression, says: "It is something which we create for ourselves, and just as we create it, so we can dismantle it."[3] Depression can be a psychologically crippling condition, and the sufferer invariably looks for help from outside himself. (Initially, says Rowe, he does not want to be cured and just leans on the nearest person, whose nervous energy he proceeds to sap.) Ultimately, however, and the sooner the better, he must, as Rowe puts it, transfer from outer guru to inner guru for the necessary wisdom and strength. This inner guru is the person's own true self, the indwelling divinity. Know, trust and scrupulously obey your inner guru, and depression's crippling hold will slacken and release you.

Yes, who said God is useless? It depends what kind of God one has in mind (yes, *in* your mind).

There are, as far as I know, no precise means of measuring evil (even jurists may differ in their calculations). Science as such does not recognise good and evil; nor does mathematics (though music had its devil's interval, now accepted as respectable), Seismologists measure the force and predict the probable effects of an earthquake; and after the event we can count the dead and estimate the damage to crops and buildings; and in this way we arrive at some assessment of the evil in such cases of natural disaster and in cases of human slaughter and destruction in warfare, or mindless spoliation of Mother Earth. Science and technology are morally neutral, or neutered: weapons of destruction are provided on demand, and so are means of ameliorating the impact of climate changes and funding non-toxic substitutes for fuel sources that are close to exhaustion.

Where would we be without science? Some of us (wise after the event?) believe we would have been better off without it: no industrial revolution and the concomitant degradation of the working classes, smog in the air and noise in the streets; just idyllic back-to-nature peace and quiet and contentment. But we cannot fail to see in science and technology an amazing evolutionary epoch in the history of humankind. Such creativity, it must be acknowledged, belongs to the essence of humanity; and that essence is the cosmic divinity. It is not *less* *science* we need, but more intelligence in general and more wisdom and rightness: prudent and ethical control alongside of our creativity.

We are the vanguard of evolution, at least as far as our own planetary system is concerned. We may be replaced in future by natural selection, but until that happens we must honour and fulfil our magnificent and hugely responsible role. Only if we fail in our mission – our purpose and destiny – shall all-wise nature replace us.

Does the Universe have a Purpose?
Or does God play Dice?

"God does not play dice", said Einstein. Stephen Hsu maintains that "Not only does God play dice with the universe, but if he did not, the complex world we see around us would not exist at all. We owe everything to randomness."[4] Particularly significant are the random genetic mutations without which there might not have been any biological evolution. Many of us will have wondered about the seeming waste of material and time and energy involved in the evolution of the universe: surely a really intelligent creator could have done it, not perhaps in the six days allotted for it in the *Book of Genesis*, but certainly more speedily and with fewer false starts and dead-ends – those dinosaurs, for example, and those Ice Ages.

I have followed Berdyaev in seeing randomness as the physical base for the spiritual freedom we enjoy (or are burdened with, according to one's disposition) as human beings. To this must be added the notion of divinity as the creative energy, intelligence and rightness of the universe; and, of course, our present-day knowledge of quantum randomness.

Hsu's approach is cosmological and starts at the very beginning of the universe – "the first split second of its existence", as Chown puts it. Hsu calculated the size of the universe before the big bang and the amount of information it could contain: a mere 10^6 bits, compared with the present-day universe's requirement of at least 10^{86} bits. Says Hsu (*pronounced* 'shu'), the 'inflation' – the unidentified force that caused the inflation of the universe – filled the microscopic patches of space with different amounts of energy; and this resulted in "a fantastic amount of randomness across the length and breadth of the universe".

Chown tells us that physicists before Hsu believed that random fluctuations in the inflation field provided the seeds of today's galaxies. Hsu, however, goes further: "What I'm saying is that, when you go back . . . to the ultimate cause of anything, it's a random quantum event, something which happened for no reason."

Hsu's "for no reason" suggests that he is assuming that, since there is randomness in the initial stage of inflation, there can be no purpose in the cosmos (presumably excepting the purposeful behaviour of human beings). But consider Berdyaev's hypothesis that God deliberately created a universe in which there could be freedom, i.e. intelligent life-forms that are not mere robots doing only what their maker told them to do, but organisms that can make their own life-choices and therefore, within the limits set by their genetic make-up (which is itself randomly produced) choose what to make of themselves, what to allow in their behaviour and what to disallow. Such a form of life, able to determine its own destiny, is the human being.

Berdyaev thought in theistic terms. We need to discount that and add, first, that what at the macroscopic human level we call freedom corresponds to randomness at the subatomic level and, secondly, that the freedom of the human being includes the capacity to choose whether or not to acknowledge the divine presence within himself.

Seen from this perspective, the fact that it has taken an exceedingly long time to produce the human species ceases to be problematic. True, the cosmic energy (divinity) has taken much longer than the Hebrew creation stories tell us; but those stories did not take randomness into account. Why would it take a dozen chimpanzees who had never read Shakespeare's works much longer to produce those works by random tapping of typewriter keys than it took Shakespeare himself to write them? Because Shakespeare did not work randomly, but the chimpanzees do.

If this is a subjective way of making sense of the universe and our place within it, it is one that is in perfect harmony with a scientific understanding. As Lawrence M. Krauss, professor of physics and astronomy, says, "The big bang . . . can be interpreted in terms of a divine beginning, but it can equally be interpreted as removing God from the equation entirely."[5] From a purely scientific point of view God or divinity (along with beauty, goodness, love, justice and duty) is dispensable. But that does not mean that there are no other valid viewpoints from which such notions are seen as meaningful and necessary.

Owen Gingerich, Harvard professor emeritus of astronomy and of the history of science, says: "Frankly, I am psychologically incapable of believing that the universe is meaningless. I believe the universe has a purpose, and our greatest intellectual challenge as human beings is to glimpse what this purpose might be." He adds: "Understanding emerges . . . in the still small voice of the universe itself."[6]

I empathise with these sentiments. The universe is an *expression* of the divinity that is within it and produced it. In this sense we may say the universe is '*the word* of God'. There is a way of understanding the universe that is just as valid as the scientific understanding; and this other way, though subjective, is not incompatible with science but is fired by a desire for what might be called a philosophical and existential meaning, a meaning for the whole person – heart and mind – not *mere* factual knowledge and know-how. It is wisdom – an amalgam of feeling and instinct – that opens us up to a spiritual dimension of reality that transcends the limited, blinkered scientific perspective that does not allow the wisdom and rightness of the right-hand brain to speak.

Randomness and freedom, the first a scientific quantum-theory concept, the second a moral-spiritual concept, are the key that unlocks the riddles, 'Has the universe a meaning, a purpose?' and 'If it has, is it a *good* meaning or purpose?'

Was there anything *before* the universe? Perhaps there were other universes; or else there is only one universe, which explodes and implodes continually. But before all that? Perhaps just a void without any filling; just pure potential, as yet without any definition. Who knows?

Let us above all rejoice in the gift of life, the life around us on planet Earth and the life within us; our potential creativity and the exhilarating human enterprise in which we are all equipped to participate in some way: the cooperation with the divine energy and intelligence and rightness of purpose in the cosmos, to save the world from the egocentric human madness that could otherwise keep on desecrating and abusing it; and to restore our ancient predecessors' reverence for it and feeling of oneness with it. As Elie Wiesel, humanities professor, puts it, "Though God created the world, it is up to people to preserve, respect, enrich, embellish, and populate it, without bringing violence to it."[7] So be it.

All in all, one can properly say this is the best of all possible worlds. It may not be perfect (in the absolute static sense), but with a little bit of help from us, it could come closer to its per-fection.

The Workings of Providence?

"I am constrained every moment to acknowledge a
higher origin for events than the will I call my own."
                                        EMERSON [8]

"[Opportunities for enlightenment] occur continuously and
uninterruptedly throughout life and death."
                                        SOGYAL RINPOCHE [9]

A period of uncertainty by its very nature "creates gaps, spaces in which
profound chances and opportunities for transformation are continuously
flowering – if, that is, they can be seen and seized."
                                        SOGYAL RINPOCHE [10]

Sogyal gives an example to illustrate his meaning: You come home and find it empty: everything has been stolen. First of all you frantically try to make a list of all the items. But following this there comes a blissful, peaceful acceptance of the situation: after all, you have no choice. Thus from having lost precious possessions you find inner peace and strength: " . . . if you really rest in that gap, looking into the mind, you will catch a glimpse of the deathless nature of the enlightened mind."[11]

Later in his book Sogyal shows how suffering may provide an opportunity for a person to develop compassion.[12] Similarly, learning that you are soon to die can bring about a determination to cast off one's inhibitions and let people know how much you love them, how thankful you are for what they have done for you, how sorry you are for not having expressed your love and gratitude sufficiently in the past.

Please do not misunderstand me. I am saying, not that suffering is good, but that from it we may gain wisdom, or new and better values, as well as learning compassion for others. Perhaps more to the point, there are two ways of dealing with suffering: one is noble, unselfish, centred on divinity; the other is base, self-centred, short-sighted.

A Jewish contributor to the BBC Radio 4's *Thought for the Day* series said, "I don't believe we have a right to be happy – we have to earn the ability to be."[13] I beg to differ. When we become aware of the divinity within all things and relinquish an egocentric in favour of a divinity-centred perspective, we begin to see that we have no right to be *un*happy! If we are unhappy it is because we are self-centred and have no consciousness of the divinity within everything. If we are suffering, it is because we have not achieved oneness with the divinity within us, our authentic self, which does not suffer, is never hurt, is never frustrated – and does not die when the body and ego die. Jesus realised his oneness with God ("I and the Father are one"), and spent the last few years of his short life teaching people that they should and could do the same – that this was the meaning of life.

Always there is a way of turning a negative into a positive – if we look for it. For example, one of my yoga teachers tells us, when despondent or hurt, to hug ourselves and say, "I love you, Eric" (or whatever your own name is). The healing power of such a simple gesture is simply marvellous. The secret, of course, is to allow oneself (another yogic teaching) to relax into a constant state of acceptance and trust, what I would describe as a firm conviction that everything works for good for the person who trusts in the rightness of the universe. Let Sogyal Rinpoche ('Rinpoche', by the way, means 'Reverend') speak: "The danger we are all in together makes it essential now, that we no longer think of spiritual development as a luxury, but as a necessity for survival."[14] Wise and apt words.

Destiny and Freedom

We choose our destiny; or, rather, we *should* choose it, not just let it happen. If we have an inkling of what we think might be our destiny, perhaps we should consider it at length and carefully: is it possible? is it really me? If fully convinced, mention it to parents or friends, and take seriously whatever they say. Then give the notion some time to ripen . . . . And if events prove you were mistaken, change tack, but carefully, not precipitously. Above all, see it as an invitation to get to know yourself better – and to converse with the indwelling divinity, the wisdom of your true self. Even our errors cease to be negative if we learn from them.

Like it or not, we have freedom of choice. We cannot pretend that our life is pre-determined; to do so is to invite disaster and regret, perhaps enslavement to a masochistic or guilt-driven overdrive that paralyses our creativity and self-esteem. When considering Incarnation and Atonement we made the acquaintance of the devil, Adam's apple and original sin, a supposed inclination to evil inherent in us all (evil, in the context, meaning disobedience to God). This religious doctrine may have been well designed to keep simple people in thrall to Mother Church, but at what cost in terms of human dignity and proper self-esteem, true self-understanding. The truth is that we have freedom, and therefore wrong choices and wrong behaviour may be expected. But this fact should not give permission to any preacher to hide from people their true, creative, self- and world-transforming potentiality. All human beings should learn from birth, at first by looks and smiles, warm cuddles and sweet-sounding syllables, later, by loving words and tuition, that they are loved because lovable, valued because valuable – having the sublime gifts of freedom and creativity; and eventually they should learn that what people have called 'God' is in fact the cosmic energy, intelligence and rightness that are in varying degrees immanent in all things, but pre-eminently in human beings. And all should learn that 'noblesse oblige': it is incumbent on those of us who are better endowed than other human beings to enrich their lives as much as possible, and all humankind should show respect to other forms of life.

The Chāndogya Upanishad teaches us that we can trust the world of nature because its true nature is brahman. Even where something shattering befalls us – disease, or bereavement or unemployment, or whatever – faith in the overall rightness of the total scheme of things (the holistic instead of the egoistic view) can – if we let it – dissolve the pain.

There is no better antidote to discontentment and disbelief than nature itself: "Man may rise to the contemplation of the divine through the senses."[15] Beauty, energy and vitality, and rightness are all revealed in the world of nature.

Karma

The Indian notion of karma is commonly associated with fatalism. But karma (whether in Hinduism or in Buddhism) is the fate we create for ourselves. 'Karma' literally means 'action', and thus behaviour, and the (good or bad) energy of the action or behaviour. Eat the right foods and you will be healthy (other things being equal); eat wrong foods and your body – and therefore you – will suffer. Karma, then, is the opposite of what we call 'fatalism', which refers to something imposed upon us from some higher being or force.

In India karma is widely thought of as operating from a previous life or lives. For example, low-caste status has customarily been accounted for in terms of sinful actions in a past life. But always the suffering associated with karma is not an arbitrary product of gods, but a natural effect of a natural cause. In Jainism, a very strict offshoot of Hinduism contemporary with Buddhism, the law of karma is absolute: there is no escape from it except by eating the fruits of one's karma. There is no question here of any favour or punishment from gods. It is your virtuous acts that constitute good karma and purge you of bad karma.

My feelings about karma are not altogether positive. In the Hebrew bible God tells Moses he was a jealous God, "visiting the iniquity of the fathers upon the children, upon the third and fourth generation . . ."[16] Take away the anthropomorphism and we have karma. We see the same mechanism at work in the less salubrious streets of 18th century London and in the poorer quarters of today's cities and towns, except that where there was pickpocketing there is now armed robbery and gang warfare. In such milieus what chance is there that anyone will be uncontaminated? This is karma, and in the days of a strictly observed caste system, Hindus upheld that as an instantiation of the law of karma.

Here we must take a rational and moral stand. We must not stand by and watch generations of innocent newly born children getting entangled in this karmic trap. We are all in some measure responsible for others' sins by our neglect. We may shrug our shoulders and exclaim, "There will always be such people!" But there need not be, given appropriate undoctrinaire caring and research and sufficient government funding for what might be a long-term undertaking involving individual counselling and costly re-housing and employment projects. Such projects, however, would be more fruitful – and perhaps no more costly – than cramming into already overcrowded prisons (state-funded colleges of crime) young people who have been more sinned against (by society) than sinning.

With the possible exception of the hermit committed to the attainment of illumination, an unforgiving law of karma is intolerable. But the rest of us live our lives in touch with other people's lives and cannot properly be judged without taking into account the influence, good or bad, of others. I trust I am not being too squeamish, judging nature as if it, or the divinity within it, were a person. But I believe it is necessary to attribute not only energy but also intelligence and rightness to nature; and this belief is the root of true religion, which is reverence for nature.

Barry Long speaks of the karma accruing from the evergrowing "vicious injustice and imbalance" between rich and poor, haves and have-nots, in a world where might is right. "Since there is no one to take responsibility for the world, or because no one is able to take responsibility for such a dreadful mass of injustice, the karmic adjustments are made automatically from one generation to another as the endless alternating pains and gains of existence. Owing to the enormous time-lag caused by the massed unconsciousness of what is happening, the debts and reimbursements due to any generation fall on other generations yet to be born."[17]

Another obvious example of the sins-of-the-fathers syndrome is the greedy and thoughtless, but profit-making, pillaging of Earth's resources, for which succeeding generations have to pay the price.

We may plausibly take the view that the cosmos is such (so designed?) as to leave us to choose our own purpose in it. Not inconsistent with this is the conviction that, if one makes a genuine attempt to keep in touch with one's indwelling divinity, "all things work together for good" – big things as well as little things, e.g. finding solitude when needed or finding a lost hearing aid when looking for something else.

When such happy coincidences occur, the believer may involuntarily utter a silent 'Thank you, God'. It is a subjective thing, depending on one's attitude. Religion itself is an attitude.

Some theologians have argued that God, being outside time – eternal – is able to see all points in time past, present and future. My own experience strongly suggests that some startling ability of that sort is possessed by some human beings: at a time in my life when I was not sure what course to take, a clairvoyant told me not only that I would marry the woman who accompanied me (she herself was not sure which way to go), but also correctly predicted the number and gender of the children we would have, as well as how the marriage would end. One cannot explain such phenomena; nor can one easily discount them. That one person can look into another person's future would seem to suggest that predestination might be a reality. On the other hand, there is the firm conviction that I do – whether I like it or not – have freedom of choice and must take responsibility for my choices, or at least *share* responsibility with external factors that may have contributed to my choice.

What sort of God would endow his creatures with free will, only to override that freedom by predetermining all their choices? (For 'God' one may substitute 'intelligent universal energy'.)

In the end I must confess that I find it difficult to resist a sense of providence, but not predestination. The critical difference between these is that in providence the human free will is not overridden, whereas predestination is the very antithesis of freedom.

Material losses and even emotional impoverishment may be the means by which one learns that to be human is to be self-transcending, continually leaving an old self behind.

As Barry Long used to say, what upsets us is not the event itself but the interpretation we – or, more precisely, our emotional self – gives it by looking into the past or into the future. "Don't interpret. Don't analyse. You must see the event only as it is, without putting any imagination or conclusion onto it."[18] I take this as a warning not to read some special providence at work in events, i.e. seeing them as bad (and meant to punish us) or good (and meant to reward us).

And this means being ready to let go of the emotional self – the whole egoistic self – at the time of our death.

CHAPTER THIRTEEN

Death – and Beyond?

"The sick and perishing; it was they who despised the body and the earth, and invented the heavenly world and the redeeming drops of blood . . . Beyond the sphere of their body and this earth they now fancied themselves transported, these ungrateful ones. Yet to what did they owe the convulsion and rapture of their transport? To their body and this earth."

NIETZSCHE, *Thus Spake Zarathustra* I: 3

"To travel hopefully is a better thing than to arrive, and the true success is to labour."

ROBERT LOUIS STEVENSON (1850–1894)

"The doctrine of the enduring soul with its permanent characteristics is exactly the irrelevant answer to the problem which life presents. That problem is, How can there be originality?"

ALFRED NORTH WHITEHEAD[1]

"When it is time to die, even in the hardest death, just be still and be where you are. Stillness will get you through."

BARRY LONG[2]

"It is better to die forgetting oneself . . . "
MIKHAIL LERMONTOV (1814–41)

Recycling?

That we die is well known. We know that all living things die. What is not known is what happens to us after death. The body, if not quickly reduced to ashes by cremation, will disintegrate slowly. There is an old Yorkshire song that makes no bones about it. It is called *On Ilkley Moor baht'at* ('On Ilkley Moor without a hat'), which is the chorus line repeated after each verse. The verses are:

'Where hast thou been since I saw thee?'
'Thou's been a-courting Mary Jane.'
Thou's bound to catch thy death of cold.'

'Then we shall have to bury thee.'
'Then t'worms will come and eat thee up.'
'Then t'ducks will come and eat up t'worms.'
'Then we shall come and eat up t'ducks.'
'Then we shall all have eaten thee.'

Biologist W. D. Hamilton, who presented a modified version of Lovelock's Gaia hypothesis, also provides us with a more sophisticated version of 'Ilkley Moor'. He expressed the wish to be laid out, at death, on the bed of the Amazon jungle, to be interred by burying beetles as food for their larvae. "No worms for me, or sordid fly; rearranged and multiple, I will at last buzz from the soil like bees out of a nest – indeed, buzz louder than bees, almost like a swarm of motorbikes. I shall be borne, beetle by flying beetle, out into the Brazilian wilderness beneath the stars."[3]

Eternal Life or Immortality

"Earth to earth, ashes to ashes, dust to dust", says the clergyman officiating at a burial, but adds "in sure and certain hope of the resurrection to eternal life . . . " 'Eternal life' is ambiguous. Literally, it means 'life outside time'; but it is commonly taken to mean 'everlasting life' or 'immortality'. If we choose to take it in the first sense – 'life outside time' – we are faced with the questions: What *is* life outside time? How does timeless life differ from no life at all?

Perfection and Heaven

The only perfection available in a timeless realm would be the static perfection ascribed to God by those medieval scholastic theologians who said that God's perfection was such that he must be immutable, since any change in him could only be for the worse. Where there is no time there can be no development (can there even be continuance?), and therefore in an eternal hereafter there could be nothing to hope or aim for, nothing to engage our imagination and creative intelligence. Such a heaven might suit hedonistic lotus-eaters, but other human beings would not be likely to find it fulfilling.

Would we prefer 'everlasting life', 'immortality'? At least this is easier to imagine than timeless life. But the more one imagines it, the less attractive and less justifiable it may seem. Must we not say that only what is perfect deserves to be immortal? Is not this so, whether we take 'perfect' in the absolute sense, in which it would be changeless because any change would be for the worse, or else in Whitehead's evolution-friendly sense of 'perfect' (or 'per-fect', as I prefer to describe it), as always being open to further growth, further improvement? If any one generation of human beings were to be immortalised on earth, would that not prevent any further development of humankind? Do we not hope that future generations will learn from our mistakes and, by standing on our shoulders, they will enjoy a truer and grander vision of humankind's place and purpose on planet Earth and in the cosmos?

Granted, progress requires freedom and freedom entails the possibility of wrong choices, sometimes (especially with ever-increasingly powerful technology) with disastrous consequences. But "Error is the price which we pay for progress", says Whitehead;[4] and one trusts that later generations will ensure that ethics and international control accompany technological progress.

To return to Ilkley Moor: death is necessary for life. Not only do the decline and death of one generation of human beings in deference to the next generation make possible further progress towards whatever we regard as human perfection; but if the basic chemistry of the earth is not replenished by dead or dying organic matter, life of any kind cannot continue. The humble earthworms or beetles that disintegrate corpses thereby regenerate the earth; and now it is known that our body has its own self-degenerating mechanism, which is automatically switched on at death – a self-sacrificing ecological gesture if ever there was one! After all, if the death of the things we eat is the sacrifice we demand for sustaining our own life, should we not be prepared to return the favour at our death?

Heaven and Hell on Earth

As was said earlier in this book – and as Karl Marx said more than a hundred years ago – one must sympathise with those victims of enforced poverty and long hours of hard labour in 19th century Britain who looked forward to a reversal of fortunes in an hereafter when God would cause the ruthless rich to suffer the torments of hell. But as hell is created on earth by human beings for human beings, so can heaven be created on earth in the form of peace and happiness, love and justice and equality, by human beings who acknowledge and respond positively to the indwelling divinity in all things. Alas, this heaven can be prevented, degraded or destroyed by those human beings who, perhaps through not fault of their own, are ignorant of divinity and for whom therefore nothing and nobody has any inviolable, sacred value. This is one of the most serious and demanding challenges to social order and world peace, requiring not only such things as more, and more affordable, housing for indigenous people but also for poor and threatened immigrants, but also such things as more provision in school timetables for the development of awareness and empathy: through drama lessons in which scenarios are enacted where one learns what it is like to be 'different', 'not one of us' – black or foreign or homeless or homosexual or, indeed, of the opposite sex or a different generation or a different religion, if any. Economics, too, is a school subject that has – or should have – an immediate bearing on the inequalities that help to constitute the heaven-hell divide in the human here-and-now world.

If we identify nature with divinity, we shall confidently acquiesce in nature's requirement that, along with every other individual living thing, we ourselves should die. To win a pseudo perfection at the cost of becoming static is too high a price for an inferior commodity. Much more preferable is the per-fection which allows always further development, further enrichment. And this per-fection requires time, indeed is inconceivable without time. The spatio-temporal world is where this superior kind of per-fection is to be looked for. Looking for it there and working for it there: that is cosmic optimism and cosmic patriotism.

Cosmic Love and Selfish Love

Cosmic love or selfish love. That is the question: respecting and accepting the wisdom of nature, or berating nature for her apparent ruthlessness. Or is that really the question? What makes us the present apex of evolution is our degree of freedom, which is itself a consequence of randomness in the primal order of the cosmos. We may say that the whole cosmic process, from the big bang to the present day and beyond, has the appearance of an experiment. Let us not presume to anticipate the final result of the experiment. In any case, our response to the experiment is bound to be subjective.

Religion has taken many forms and continues to do so, depending upon one's total – emotional, moral, aesthetic and intellectual – attitude to the world of nature. Any religion should be judged by its fruits; and good religion is not a desire for personal perpetuation, but rather a desire for the well-being of a universe within which we live in a relationship of interdependence that demands our gratitude and reverence.

'Pie in the Sky'

The promise or hope of heaven after death – 'pie in the sky' – may have served as a consolation (along with gin) for the poor and powerless victims of an oppressive society; and in our own time we have witnessed the religious zeal that drives suitably indoctrinated young people to achieve martyrdom and its consequent rewards in paradise. Yet, although we may occasionally hear the now quaint chiding, "You'll never go to heaven if you don't mend your ways (stop drinking, or swearing)", it is usually spoken lightheartedly and received in the same spirit.

In any case, to do things for reward is to act prudentially, not morally. The only motivations consistent with any morality that is not mere conformity to what is presently 'the done thing' are love for the good and desire for the better: again, cosmic patriotism and cosmic optimism, reverence for the divinity in all things and compassion for all that suffer.

Bereavement may be shattering, but not irretrievably so for one who believes in the divinity in all things. Death may be frightening; but death puts an end to fear.

May we not also say that death puts an end to suffering? When asked if he did not feel sad at the thought of death, Buonarroti Michelangelo "replied that this was not so, because if life was found to be agreeable then so should death, for it came from the hands of the same master".[5] That is fine if you have had an enjoyable life. But what if you haven't? What if you live on the brink of starvation or under a reign of terror and persecution, or are a woman physically battered by her male partner? What if you have escaped such a fate but have some other deep sorrow, with no redeeming talent, or love, or joy?

Wishful Thinking

Is it possible that my feelings about the universe – reverence, love and trust – are just a product of wishful thinking? a theoretical construction that shields me from despair? Well, all things are possible. But all my thinking life, from childhood on, I have sought truth, even though it has not always been a painless process. Moreover, the truth-seeker – scientist or philosopher or whatever – can never allow herself to suppose that she has acquired the whole truth and nothing but the truth. However, I am convinced that, if my optimism is based on subjective responses to and evaluations of the universe as I perceive it, these responses and evaluations and perceptions are not inconsistent either with reason in general or, more particularly, the (not yet complete) scientific account of the universe. But yes, optimism is an option; pessimism is also an option.

Trust

Just as the lover trusts the loved one, so the scientist has faith in nature, believing that the account that nature gives of itself to human reason is not intended to deceive him. Faith is something we all need; and especially is this true with regard to death, our own or that of others.

As parts of nature, must not human beings die, as do other animals and plants – even centuries-old trees? Of course. The question is: what happens to us after death? And, again, must we not say that *all* living things share the same hereafter – whatever it might be? Or should we believe that the human spirit survives the body's disintegration, but other living organisms have no spirit and therefore no hereafter?

Survival of Energy – and Spirit?

We may say that what does survive is energy, and all things have energy; and is not this energy, in all cases, that of the indwelling divinity, which we must suppose does not die? Yes, indeed; but the energy that survives the death of Eric Ackroyd or the little piggy that goes to market or the tiny microbe or noble cedar cannot be said to be *owned* by any of these. Energy is generally believed to be indestructible, but capable of undergoing transformation. (And there is, I am told, one particular form of energy that may actually become defunct.) Energy is constantly entering and leaving one's body. It enters with food and water and sunlight and with every in-breath. It leaves in every out-breath and through all the orifices of the body. This is the universal phenomenon of energy-exchange, which I choose to see as the dynamic immanent divinity. Without this exchange nothing could exist for long. But this does not necessarily mean that any *particular part* of the universe is everlasting.

What may be said to be immortal is divinity itself. But the fact that divinity is in all things does not necessarily mean that all things are immortal. What one can say, with support from a physicist's view of energy, is that divinity is in a thing just as long as the thing exists! As the *Bhagavadgita* has it, "These bodies are known to have an end; the dweller in the body is eternal, imperishable, infinite."[6]

I have suggested that energy and spirit are one and the same thing; and this one thing is invisible, known only by its effects. At this juncture it may be appropriate to register Berdyaev's rejoinder to those positivists who spoke of spiritual things as mere shadows of reality, 'epiphenomena': "spirit is not an epiphenomenon of anything, everything is an epiphenomenon of spirit."[7] Truth is itself spiritual communion with spirit. Ideas are spiritual; mind, thought, imagination; beauty, truth and goodness (and evil) are spiritual realities. To say, with Berdyaev, that everything else is an epiphenomenon of spirit is to say that divinity is the essence of all things. As we commune with the divinity – the spirit – within us, we find truth. (Any truth you seem to find in this book is actually found within yourself, in your own communion of spirit with Spirit).

Will the Human Species Destroy Itself?

What if the energy contained in the so-called 'advanced' nations' stocks of nuclear and chemical weaponry were to destroy humankind altogether, and perhaps Planet Earth as well? What I can say is that I trust in nature's ability to survive, with or without humankind. Perhaps *Homo sapiens* will cease to be compatible with the best of all possible worlds and is therefore destined to bring about its own demise by what Hindus and Buddhists call the law of karma, according to which every action is an inevitable consequence of a previous action or actions. The theistic equivalent is a personal deity's wrath, which – as seen earlier in this book – is quite illogical and morally indefensible since it was that same deity who gave us freewill. (Even if it were the devil who caused us to have this freedom, it would still be seriously illogical if the deity punished *us* for its consequences.) The fact that human beings now play a significant part in conditioning the future of the cosmos, or some part of it, may be seen to add a new perspective – potentially hopeful or, as presently, horribly pessimistic – on the question of the future of the universe. We seem to have miscalculated – or not even bothered to calculate – the amount of spoliation, pollution and degradation that planet Earth and its environs can tolerate. It is worth being reminded of the October 2007 USA poll which revealed that 30 or even 40 per cent of women in that country do not feel it is right to bring children into such a world. On reading this I fell into a trough of despair; but I was comforted – strengthened – by a very dear lady who reminded me of Julian of Norwich's "All shall be well . . . ". Those two ladies together quickly restored my faith in the divinity in things. And it is the same faith that removes death's sting.

Our Death is a Moral Requirement

In this same way I know that all will be well after death: I trust the universe, the divinity within it, nature's energy, intelligence and rightness, the reliable trinity. We may and should do what we can in our life to make the human world better, for our own and future generations; it is not sinful to hope for the sort of immortality that might be gained by such efforts, namely remembrance by some of our successors. But perhaps the best contribution we can make to the historical time that continues after our death is just that – our death. Just as the good teacher aims to enable his students to exceed his own achievements, there comes a time when parents must stand back and allow their offspring to direct their own lives, find their own truth and fulfil their own destinies; we all have to die, and our death should be the sacrifice we are happy to make in order that humankind may continue to grow in wisdom and spiritual stature.

The younger generation is not necessarily wiser and better than the older generation; it does not necessarily learn from the mistakes of the older generation, or even recognise them as mistakes. Nevertheless, what the constant succession of generations does guarantee is the *possibility* of improvement, of greater motivation for creativity and less destruction, increased tolerance and a lessening of hatred and prejudice, more awareness of the divinity in things and an accompanying diminishing of ego. I cannot believe that I am the only father who sees better qualities in his children than in himself.

Body and Spirit

Does death mean a separation of body and spirit? In all three synoptic gospels we are told (by Jesus) that there will be no physical sexuality in the afterlife: in heaven we shall be as angels.[8] That, I think, is a very common understanding of what happens at death: only the body dies, and what is called the Spirit leaves the body, entering a spiritual realm where other disembodied spirits live. If one is contented with such an imaginative conjective, one might not want to change it. Others might, quite understandably, require some explanation of how this event could take place; and of what the spirit *is* that behaves like a Jack-in-the-box or a pilot catapulted from his stricken aircraft and borne safely away by his parachute.

Spirit is not a purely physical object, or a collection of such objects; nor is it a container of things, like the cranium. Spirit is something non-physical: one's character, or one's thoughts or beliefs and values; qualities such as truth and falsity, goodness and evil. Spirit is also energy, which is itself invisible and reveals itself only in its effects. Earlier, I spoke of 'spirit' as equivalent to 'māna'. Since truth and beauty and goodness activate human endeavour, one feels obliged to classify them – or, at any rate, *love* of them – along with spirit, as divine dynamic forces. (If we love evil and are motivated by evil, one might be tempted to say we are possessed by 'the devil'; but I prefer to avoid anthropomorphic personifications, and will describe this phenomenon as a human degradation of the divinity within us.)

Does the Universe Die? and Resurrect Itself?

If spirit is energy, may we say that energy can survive the death of the body? This spirit, which is the true Self (as distinct from the ego), is divinity; and it should be clear that divinity, as posited in this book, is immortal. In Hindu tradition there is what amounts to a belief that energy can even create a new universe upon the death of the old, producing another big bang and explosion to take the place of the preceding implosion; just as if divinity (brahman) were an intelligent and right-thinking creative energy capable of re-casting the mould (or shaking the dice again?) to see if evolutionary enterprise – and, particularly, a future replacement for humanity – would turn out better than its immediate predecessor.

Redemption or Liberation?

What we have here, however, is a continuance (after a catastrophic cessation) of life; not, as in the traditional Christian scheme of things, a deliverance from that continuum by God's sacrifice of himself (or his son) to himself (or to the devil). In the Hindu and Theravāda Buddhist traditions, not salvation but liberation is the goal, not a deliverance from sin by 'Other-power' but self-liberation from ignorance by a self-induced awakening to the truth, which is that the whole phenomenal world is illusory and that all reality is brahman (or Buddha-nature), the omnipresent but all too frequently unacknowledged divinity. And "That art thou" ("tat tvam āsi"): the essential you – but not ego! – is divinity.

Facing up to Death

Facing up to death is a true starting-point for understanding death and what may lie beyond it. The 16th century sceptic Michel de Montaigne suggested that the only way of coping with death was to think of it every day. Better known perhaps is the medieval hermit's practice of keeping a human skull on his desk. While I would not recommend the monastic practice, I do approve of Mikhail Lermontov's (1814–41) recommendation: to die forgetting oneself. One might also make a daily practice of consciously forgetting oneself as one falls asleep (the 'little death').

This is what the Western spiritual master Barry Long had to say: "Unless you die continuously to your notional self while you are living, you will always fear death as it approaches."[9] This notional self is what I have referred to as ego. The true self, said Barry, may be glimpsed, if you are alert, at the very moment of awaking from sleep, "before you come to realise that you have a body."[10] Barry identified life with pure awareness; and this, he says, is what you are before conception. Does this not make you think of Wordsworth:

> "But trailing clouds of glory do we come
> From God, who is our home:
> Heaven lies about us in our infancy!
> Shades of the prison-house begin to close
> Upon the growing boy."[11]

Two Worlds or Two Aspects?

If so, does it remind you of Plato, who influenced Wordsworth? Although I have chosen to understand both Wordsworth and Plato as referring to two aspects of reality, rather than of two separate realities or worlds, and have been supported in this view by Teilhard de Chardin, I am not ready to dismiss a two-worlds theory as impossible. In his dialogues Plato refers to what he calls 'Ideas' or 'Forms'. In *Parmonides* he speaks of the forms, 'the Beautiful' and 'the Good', as being *ideals* of which we have only more or less imperfect copies on earth. For a simple example we may take the ideal, true line. This has no thickness; all the lines we draw are therefore imperfect: when we think we are drawing a straight line, we are in fact drawing a (very narrow) rectangle. In *The Republic* Plato seems to present them in mythical form, as if they actually existed in some supersensible world where all is perfect and static, whereas in the terrestrial world everything is in flux (à la Heraclitus). Again, in *The Republic* we are given the myth of the cave, in which the human being is depicted as perceiving only the projected shadows of things (phenomena), not the things themselves (noumena). Only if he turns himself round through 180° (conversion!), to gain a mystical vantage point, will he see things as they really are.

Ideals are indispensable, but only as reminders that we must not rest content with whatever little truth or goodness we have achieved. But as a static other – perhaps hereafter – world, they might well appear to be a dead end (if you will forgive the unintended pun) where there is nothing to achieve and therefore no point in living.

Could it be, then, that 'this world', the physical world, is only illusory and the real world is spiritual? For thousands of years and in most parts of the world, shamans have been revered on account of their reputed X-ray knowledge of the human body and facility in curing the sick, but also on account of their knowledge of the spirit world and their consequent ability to convey the spirits of the dead to the parts of the spirit world where they would be well received and feel most comfortable.

In our own day there is no lack of people who lay claim to powers that enable them to liberate spirits that for one reason or another have not been able to detach themselves from some earthly location, and pass them over to spiritual guides (psychopomps) who will conduct them to their appointed place in the spirit world.[12]

Perhaps time and space are not ultimately real and, where the selfish ego has been left behind and spiritual union with divinity achieved, one is present in an eternity that is an eternal present, in which only what is true and good and beautiful has existence. Such a disembodied state, where only the *idea* of beauty – not beautiful things – can exist, could be entered and enjoyed only by one who has attained the total detachment that we may associate with the consummate Buddhist monk, or Jesus of Nazareth.

On the other hand, the fact that we experience divinity *within* nature, as a *quality* of nature, so that nature *expresses* divinity, suggests that there might be a *cosmic* dimension that has not yet been explored – except perhaps by mystics, who may *perceive* it (correctly or incorrectly?) as another, supernatural world.

We experience divinity within ourselves, too, and yet as transcending our ego. 'Self' is the name of our true self, which is where the human and the divine meet or merge. Divinity is always immanent, but when we become aware of it, we perceive it as transcending what we had previously taken to be our self, namely, the individual and separate ego. Here, I believe, lies the true mystery behind the mythical Christian Incarnation and Ascension; but we should not succumb to a false piety that bows down to a totally other deity in the belief that this deity will transport us to his totally other dwelling-place.

That mystery is what some mystics have called 'deification', the process that is both fulfilment of our true self and the nurturing and expressing of the indwelling divinity. And should we not say that what survives the death of the body is that portion of divinity, and its fruits? One essential fruit is the fulfilment of Blake's vision of Jerusalem in the streets of London, to build heaven here on earth. After all, we can easily get more than enough of hell on earth if we choose to: that is, if we allow our emotional ego-centred self to take possession of our thoughts and determine our attitude to life.[13] "The whole scheme of existence," says Barry Long, "depends on what is done on earth. Only on earth is freedom from ignorance attained." We have seen that freedom from ignorance lies in forgetfulness of ego. But Barry goes on to say that "the real work" begins after death, when you will have left your body and will be simply "a point of consciousness" from which, initially, you will observe life on earth, but then pass through hell, which Barry tells us is a positive kind of purgatory – like a laxative, one might say; but what is being purged is your attachment to what Buddhists call 'māya', 'illusion'. Then you will see what was "missing from your life on earth" and would "make you more true, more real, if there was to be another chance." In this process you are forming your new psychic body and life.

Caution: if your divine Self "has not been sufficiently realised through living on earth" you will die unconscious, with the result that your life after death will be nothing but a dream. So: stay close to the divinity within you; forget yourself, and stop craving for anything. As Barry says, " . . . hell is craving."

At death you go into hell; at birth you come out of hell as a lusty ego looking for an embryo you can impregnate "with your missing life, your missing self – your life to be." Thus you are "the eternal contradiction: Through sexual union and by sacrificing your immortal awareness to mortal existence, you crave the extinction of your own craving, so that you may crave and live again, to die and crave again." This is the endless karma spoken of in the Hindu–Buddhist tradition, from which Barry Long himself imbibed much. So far, then, you might be said to be immortal, since you are bound to the ever-turning wheel of samsāra (reincarnation), with temporary 'retreats' (we might call them) in which enlightenment may be gained. When enlightenment has been achieved, you are released from immortality – the ever-turning wheel – and move into eternity, from whence you will see *through* the ego and see *through* the notion of hell, which is really "the eternal flame" of "the eternal spirit", says Barry.

Note that in Barry Long's account of death and the hereafter there is no hint of pre-destination, no reduction of human freedom, and therefore no reduction of human responsibility. *The process begins in the here and now.*

I believe that in Barry Long we were given a god-send, a true spiritual teacher for the present-day Western world. I bow to his remembrance. He went further than I can go. Is that because he writes as a myth-maker, telling a story? But for me the story rings true: it tallies with my firmest beliefs: in human freedom and human responsibility; the indwelling divinity that gives us both confidence and humility and enables us to be creative and sensitive; and, above all, to put first things first, spiritual before material gains and growth; compassion and love before blame and self-righteousness (and indeed before self-denigration). To crown all, the vista that Barry Long opens up for us is one that satisfies Whitehead's concern that there should always be something worthwhile to live for, some originality therefore in life – and in death!

But is Barry's captivating account true? In the nature of the case, one can neither verify nor falsify it. What may properly be said is that his story *ought* to be true; and, that being so, that one ought to live *as if* it were true.

Consciousness without Brain?

Perhaps some readers will falter where Barry tells us that when we leave the body we are " a point of consciousness". Not only the practised meditator, but anyone who is aware of the indwelling divinity may have experienced this – but while still in the body. It is quite a leap – a leap of faith – from that to the belief that one can have the same consciousness when detached from the body, including the brain and the nervous system. Whether consciousness is possible without matter is something we cannot know. What we do know is that, if one's brain is destroyed or put out of action, one loses consciousness. One may, then, *believe* Barry Long but not *know* the truth of what he says unless one experiences that truth for oneself.

We have seen how Teilhard de Chardin argued that matter and spirit were inseparable. Perhaps he was acquainted with Jung, who said: "Psyche cannot be totally different from matter, for how otherwise could it move matter? And matter cannot be alien to psyche, for how else could matter produce psyche? Psyche and matter exist in the same world, and each partakes of the other, otherwise any reciprocal action would be impossible. If research could only advance far enough, therefore, we should arrive at an ultimate agreement between physical and psychological concepts."[14]

Forgetting Oneself

Perhaps someone will enlighten me if I am in error. Otherwise I shall be content if I can die forgetful of ego (Eric Ackroyd), but conscious of and trusting in the all-indwelling, omnipresent divinity, nature's own wisdom and power. Nature or the same by any other name, is all-knowing and knows best. Have not all our happiest moments been moments when we have forgotten ourselves, been taken out of ourselves, left ourselves behind? We can fulfil ourselves only by leaving our present self behind; may we not surmise that death is itself a further stage in our self-transfiguration, or a doorway that leads to such transfiguration?

It might seem that the Hindu notion of an infinite cycle of birth and death and re-birth is preferable to the traditional Christian and Islamic view of heaven. Certainly it is essential that the *human* world – the blot on Earth's landscape – should receive constant surveillance and ministration, constant reform and redemption. And does not this require a constant flow of 'new blood' (and therefore a constant recycling of 'old blood'?).

Reincarnation?

If it occurs, reincarnation is to be accepted gratefully and responsibly, in a glad and positively creative cosmos-serving liaison with divinity. But if it is a clinging to self that motivates one's desire for reincarnation, it might be better if there were no reincarnation. Buddhists speak of bodhisattvas, people who, having achieved Buddha-nature, qualify for nirvāna but choose to return to Earth to assist other human beings to achieve the same oneness with divinity, the same invincible bliss. But that is "something else", as the saying goes.

Barry Long says we choose our own rebirth. In a Hindu or Buddhist context, choice is conditioned by habit built up by previous choices and associated values. This is the law of karma ('karma' = action). Thus, "If my every effort in this life is the selfish acquisition of wealth or power or pleasure, chances are I will die wanting more."[15] Sogyal Rinpoche, however, tells us that death is potentially salvatory, providing opportunities for us to 'see the light' and choose it.[16]

We cannot be sure of rebirth, but the mere possibility of it adds to the reason for forgetting one's present and past self at death. Clinging to something imperfect would be contrary to evolution. "If you die to that personal self, if you face up to the falsehood of it, you are immediately reborn, instantly freed of that part of the old person or false self that you were."[17] This rebirth, this liberation, this achievement of enlightenment can take place in this present life on earth. *Possibly*, it may take place in an unknown hereafter. But why wait for something that may be merely imaginary when that something is available for the choosing (but there's the rub!) in the here and now? "The process of dying and rebirth is the same, whether you die psychologically, emotionally or physically. Something dies within you. It is you but it is not you."[18] In any case, we have to say that it is the individual person that dies. (Does that not remind us how inappropriate it is to speak of God as a person?). *What survives is the One, the divinity that is within us all; and who can say what new form or forms that divinity – that energy – will assume?*

As for death, Epicurus (*c.* 342–270 BCE) gives us the bottom line. "Get accustomed to the idea that death means nothing to us. For all good and evil consist in sensation, and death is only the deprivation of sensation . . . So death is nothing to us, for as long as we exist death is not present within us, and when death comes then we no longer exist."[19] Well, one can hardly get more basic – more minimalist – than that. But it is the dictum of a philosopher whose laudable aim was to relieve humankind from anxiety and fear.

At this point I feel obliged to redress any gross imbalance I may have been guilty of in my repeated preaching of self-forgetfulness. Hedonists, and particularly utilitarians have something to teach us. The rightness of happiness is part and parcel of belief in the divinity of things; indeed, from this perspective happiness has to be seen as the greatest good. Just as world religions speak of the bliss of nirvāna or the delights of paradise or the total happiness of heaven, so we may include the feelings of great joy and love and wonder that we derive from our experience of the world of nature among our strongest intimations of the divinity within things. The reward for any creative endeavour, any act of love, is the happiness it gives to both giver and receiver.

Darwin and the whole of science have made it clear that human beings are part of nature; and it has been said that death is a problem only where this fact is not accepted.

Our primitive (primeval, but not stupid!) ancestors, who lived close to and in harmony with nature, did accept this fact. But the belief in rebirth became widespread. The Celtic goddess Sheela-na-gig, depicted above (p. 18), represents the ambivalence of the fertility goddess, who gives birth to all forms of life and at their death receives them back into her womb for rebirth; so does the Celtic womb-like burial mound with a vaginal tunnel-entrance. Death is for rebirth. That ancient Egyptian religion also included a belief in a physical afterlife (for pharaohs and their entourages, at least) is clear from the fact that corpses were mummified and entombed (sometimes with a toilet!),[20] and letters were written to the dead begging their assistance in emergencies.[21]

The advaita Vedāntist philosopher Shankara taught that when the human soul (ātman) attains the knowledge that it is in fact brahman (which is the self, or soul, or essence of all things and is itself pure intelligence), it – the soul – is liberated from all that is material, and therefore becomes imperishable. As the priest and mystic Johannes Ruysbroeck (1293–1381) put it, "In eternity all creatures are God in God". To realise fully the oneness of self and Self is to attain eternal peace and bliss. If we *are* conscious after death, nothing is lost. In either case we shall never have the experience of being without God.

Tibetans celebrate, not a master's birthday, but his death, which is seen as "the moment of final illumination."[22] For Tibetan Buddhists death is a transition ('bardo') in which, if one is attentive, one will see 'opportunities for transformation."[23] One sees here a resemblance with Barry Long's account of death; and also in the caution Sogyal administers: "At the moment of death, abandon all thoughts of attachment and aversion."[24]

In 1950 the astronomer Fred Hoyle believed that the universe was everlasting, a steady-state universe. This view has been superseded by the Big Bang theory, the evidence for which, says a more recent astronomer royal, is "convincingly strong".[25] Scientists tell us that, at an extremely miniscule fraction of a second after the start of the explosion, the universe was about the size of a pea. Now its size is unimaginably vast and, so far as can be known, still expanding. But the universe (the one we know: there may be others) is not necessarily everlasting. It may implode and perhaps explode again, in a different form. With this we may compare the ancient Hindu myth that tells of Brāhma creating the universe by his out-breath and terminating it on his in-breath, and so on ad infinitum, each breath lasting millions upon millions of 'years', i.e., 'mahāyugas', 'great years'.

Perhaps we must accustom ourselves to viewing everything as transitory, in constant flux. That is how the ancient Greek philosopher Heraclitus saw the universe; it is also how the modern mathematical physicist and philosopher Alfred North Whitehead saw it, and how present-day scientists see it. Paul Davies tells us that grand unified theories predict that the proton – and therefore all matter – is unstable and likely to decay.[26] The existentialist philosopher Martin Heidegger described human existence as "being-towards-death", and said it is this sense of an ending that encourages human creativity, the fulfilment of one's destiny.[27]

And so we come back to our starting point: a universe in process requires us to justify our existence within it by transcending ourselves and thereby assisting in the spiritual self-transcendence of the universe, the great cosmic organism of which we are intelligent cells, cells which, like those within our own body, die and have to be replaced. What we can be reasonably sure of is that the life-force within those cells is everlasting. That life-force is the divinity I speak of, which is our own true self and the true essence of everything. So rejoice in this wonder of wonders; be happy and grateful, and dare to be creative and optimistic: not the fatalistic 'whatever will be will be', but the totally trustful 'all will be well'.

It may well be that what Origen said about Jesus' body – that at death it was absorbed in divinity – applies to all bodies. If so, it would have to take into account the known physical degeneration of a dead body, its absorption in the universe – in the air, in the soil (perhaps via absorption into the bodies of other life-forms). This would mean positing some equation between divinity and cosmos. And has not this book done that?

Shamans and today's mediums are reputed to have mental access to a spirit-world. The mind of the modern astrophysicist can traverse space–time without stirring from his seat. The mind of the mystical or spiritual person can be aware of and respond to the divinity in things.

Perhaps, then, it is not unreasonable to suppose that at the death of the body, mental energy (or spiritual energy) may become – or remain – at one with the divinity that is the mind and energy of the universe. If so, one might say that the Ilkley Moor scenario represents the physical dimension of this process, and that Jesus' ascension is a mythological representation of its spiritual dimension.

On the other hand, there is a strong case for believing that mind (or spirit) is inseparable from brain and nervous system. This remains an open question. Science has not yet said its last word on the ultimate form or essence of energy in general and mental energy in particular. Meanwhile, one can only speculate that spirit and energy are one and the same property of what I call divinity.

Thus, God will be all in all, and all in God. This I accept. But it is a mystery, in the contemplation of which the tongue must come to rest. More mundanely, things disintegrate, but energy – creative energy – continues. Those who do not believe in the divinity in things must be content with the mundane. Like Blake and Wordsworth and many many more (though I lack Blake's mystical intensity), I am wedded to the mystery that I call the divinity in things. Correction: I am married to the *notion* of divinity in things; I trust that I may become more hospitable to divinity itself. And I do believe that this is best achieved, not by concentrating on oneself, but by forgetting and forgiving oneself.

Blake saw death as like going from one room to another, and rejoiced in his own death, assuring his devoted wife that they would always be together. My own view – that death is a return to our divine source – coincides with Blake's up to a point. That point is where the visionary Blake sees beyond death a realm of freedom and glory. I too see freedom in the sense that the vacuum created by the death of a life-form may be seen as a potentiality for something new. As for glory, I can see it altogether appropriate for one who, like Blake, was constantly and consciously, mystically one with divinity and detached from worldly goods. I, too, may expect what is appropriate for me, but I cannot be sure what that will be – except that it will be what it ought to be, and I trust that I shall not quarrel with it. Should I quarrel with the creative source of the whole cosmos?

Now read the whole of Wordsworth's *Intimations of Immortality*, which his excellent biographer Juliet Barker regards as his greatest ode,[28] and see if you can resist the belief in *pre*-existence – which the Christian faith has reserved for the Christ alone. And, if pre-existence, why not post-existence?

And "carpe diem":[29] welcome and enjoy, and make good use of every day.

Epilogue

The present 'big thing' may be the current economic crisis. But this is only one of several slumps that have occurred within the author's lifetime, the first of these – probably the most devastating for working-class people – coinciding with his birth. There is nothing unusual about economic slumps. Karl Marx forecast such disasters as an inevitable corollary of a capitalist economy. Their ultimate cause is greed, the ruthless greed of multi-national corporations and the millions of super-rich individuals. And it would seem that governments do not dare – or are they just unable – to increase taxes on the rich to assist the increasing millions of unemployed and further millions of struggling pensioners and poor young people having their homes repossessed by irresponsible lenders.

Bad as this is, there may well be bigger, even more disastrous 'big things' in store for our descendants. We are being told that our efforts to check global warming and atmospheric pollution and to provide viable new sources of energy to maintain the survival of our civilisation are economically doomed; our positive practical responses have been too late to be effective. Of course that might be a good thing in disguise. Perhaps it would mean a return to an economy and a lifestyle that would bring us closer to nature and therefore closer to the indwelling divinity.

Meanwhile, however, money has been found in plenty for nuclear weaponry that could bring about a speedy demise of the human species and probably the rest of Earth's biosphere, except perhaps for some bacterial form of life from which biological evolution could start all over again.

Do not such considerations prompt a new look at religion, such as the one presented in this book? We sorely need to learn to trust divinity, nature's own intelligence and energy and rightness. Nature knows best; and we must learn to submit ourselves willingly to the wisdom of the best of all possible universes.

Since none of us is an island, please allow me to acknowledge here my indebtedness to my mother and particularly my stepfather, without whom my intellectual development might never have got under weigh; headmaster Mr. Beaton and Senior English master Mr. Burrell; chairmaster Mr. Scott; Dr. Matthew Black, lecturer in New Testament Studies; Arthur Widdess, my excellent tutor at St. John's College, Durham, and Vice-Principal Geoffrey Cumming, whose benign and unassuming presence I found deeply supportive; my first boss, Reginald Haw, the vicar of St. John's, Newland, who had the unenviable task of knocking into shape an arrogant curate who had already set his sights on a deanery. To these must be added, of course, those very special people to whom I have specially dedicated this book.

Notes

CHAPTER ONE   Is God Dead

1   Exodus 15: 3: "The Lord is a man of war"; Joshua 6: 13: he is a "Lord of hosts [= armies]". This title for Yahweh occurs frequently in the Old Testament.

CHAPTER TWO   The Western Split I: Transcendent Deity, Desacralised Nature

1   'Profane' comes from the Latin 'pro fanum', meaning 'in front of – or before – the temple', i.e. 'outside the sacred place or space'.
2   Genesis 12: 'The Yahwist' is the title given to the unknown author(s) of the presumed earliest strand of the Old Testament literature.

CHAPTER THREE   The Western Split II: God's Otherness, Humanity's Degradation

1   Feuerbach's thesis, in his book *The Essence of Christianity*, was translated into English in 1854 by George Eliot, no less!
2   German original, *Die Kirchliche Dogmatik*.

CHAPTER FOUR   The Western Split III: Gender Discrimination, its Origins and its Consequences

1   The quotation comes from the entry on 'Gaia hypothesis' in *Dictionary of Science*, ed. Peter Lafferty and Julian Rowe (Oxford: Helicon Publishing Ltd., 1997).
2   See Leon Lederman, *The God Particle* (London: Bantam Press, 1993), p. 83.
3   Richard Dawkins, *A Devil's Chaplain* (London: Orion Books, 2004), p. 203.
4   *Timaeus*, 30D.
5   Quoted in Berdyaev's *Der Sinn des Schaffens*, p. 61. (My translation from the German).
6   Genesis 1: 27.
7   See above, p. 33–5.
8   Wilding in *The Guardian*, May 25, 1983.
9   Gustave Glotz, *The Aegean Civilisation* (London, Book Club Associates/Routledge & Kegan Paul, 1976), p. 243.
10 Genesis 5: 1–2.
11 Genesis 3: 20.
12 See for example S. G. F. Brandon, *Religion in Ancient History*, 1973, pp. 13–17.
13 For this, and more, see K. S. Latourette, *A History of Christianity* (London: Eyre & Spottiswoode Ltd., 1955), pp. 166 ff.
14 *Paradiso* XXXIII, I.
15 Latourette (1955), p. 535.
16 Dante Alighieri, Paradiso XXXIII, quoted by Joseph Campbell, *Creative Mythology* (1968), Arkana edn, 1991, pp. 48–9

17 See John Renard, *The Handy Religion Answer Book* (Canton, China: Visible Ink Press, 2002), p. 346.

18 This painting may be seen in Edinburgh at the National Gallery of Scotland.

19 See Genesis 3.

20 For the often insufferable position of women in Islam see Nawal El Sa'adawi, *The Hidden Face of Eve* (London: Zed Press, 1980).

21 Quoted by Moyra Doorly, in her article in *The Guardian*, 25 May 1983.

22 See Kenneth Clark, *Civilisation* (London: BBC Books and John Murray, 1969), published 1987, pp. 61 ff and pp. 250 ff.

23 For a detailed and balanced treatment of this war see A. J. Coates, *The Ethics of War* (Manchester: Manchester University Press, 1997); look for 'Falklands War' in index.

24 See for example J. Moussaieff Masson's book, *The Oceanic Feeling*.

25 See for example his book, *The Destiny of Man* (London: Geoffrey Bles, 1937; 4th edition, 1954), pp. 63–4.

26 Ibid., p. 64.

27 See Joseph Campbell's *Primitive Mythology* (vol. 1 of his *The Masks of God*), (London and New York: Penguin/Arkana, first published 1959, 1976 edn), p. 416.

CHAPTER FIVE **Energy and Divinity**

1 *The Divine and the Human* (London: Geoffrey Bles, 1949), pp. 6–7. Berdyaev sometimes contradicts himself. On page 9 he says clearly God is "not force, not power". From my reading of almost everything he wrote, I would say that he saw God as dynamic, but not forceful in the manner of a tyrant, but Spirit. For me, 'spirit' = 'energy'; and God is within nature.

2 The English anthropologist R. R. Marrett was the first to argue (in 1900) that this belief in an impersonal power or force preceded animism, against E. B. Tyler and others who defended the view that animism was the earliest phase of religion. In 1967 Jan de Vries (*The Study of Religion*) denied that the māna concept was found in the most primitive tribes (Australian Aborigines and African Pygmies). He also expressed the fear that this concept might open the door to "a stage at which no god existed" (ibid., p. 110). That is precisely the most significant point about māna!

3 See Hopkins, *The Hindu Religious Tradition* (California: Dickenson Publishing Co. Inc., 1971), p. 19.

4 Ibid., p. 20.

5 Often Hindus gave 'brahman' a capital "B"; but, in keeping with 'divinity', I shall employ lower case.

6 For this particular instance see Mircea Eliade, *Patterns in Comparative Religion*, (London: Sheed & Ward, 1979, original publication 1958), p. 234.

7 Mirca Eliade, *Patterns in Comparative Religion* (London: Sheed & Ward, 1979), p. 11 (Eliade's italics), original publication 1958.

8 Gustave Glotz, *The Aegean Civilisation* (Book Club Associates edn, 1876), p. 231.

9 Ibid., p. 240.

10 Fritjof Capra, *The Turning Point* (London: Flamingo/HarperCollins, 1983), p. 82 (original publication Simon & Schuster 1982).

11 Paul Davies, *Superforce* (Penguin Books, 1995 edn), p. 38 (original publication 1984).

12 The italics are mine in both places.

13 Gospel of St John, 4: 24.

14 'Hinduism' in *The Legacy of India*, ed. G. T. Garratt (Oxford: Clarendon Press, 1937), p. 277.
15 Bishop J. A. T. Robinson's phrase.
16 Acts of the Apostles 5: 8.
17 See Ajit Mookerjee and Madhu Khanna, *The Tantric Way* (London: Thames & Hudson, 1977), p. 51.
18 Ibid., p. 54.
19 Fritjof Capra, *The Turning Point*, pp. 18–19.
20 See Ajit Mookerjee and Madha Khanna, *The Tantric Way* (London: Thames & Hudson, 1977), p. 51.
21 Represented by the centre of the Shri Yantra (a mandala used in meditation), figure 54 in ibid., p. 74.
22 *Oriental Mythology*, p. 29.
23 Chandogya Upanishad VI, 13, quoted by K. M. Sen, *Hinduism* (Penguin, 1973), (original publication 1961), p. 54.
24 Ibid., pp. 54–55.
25 *The Christian Experience of the Holy Spirit* (London: Nisbet, 1944), p. 243; original publication 1928.

CHAPTER SIX   **Divinity Within**

1 Paul Davies, *Superforce* (Harmondsworth: Penguin Books, 1995, supplemented edn), particularly pp. 142–149. (Original publication 1984, Simon & Schuster).
2 See Ajit Mookerjee and Madhu Khanna, *The Tantric Way* (London: Thames & Hudson, 1977), p. 51.
3 For having my attention drawn to this derivation I am indebted to Matthew Fox's *Sins of the Spirit, Blessings of the Flesh.*
4 Arne A. Wyller, *The Planetary Mind* (Aspen, Colorado: MacMurray & Beck, 1996), p. 219. Quoted by M. Fox (2000), p. 48.
5 See his book, *The Blind Watchmaker* (Penguin Books, 1991; originally published in 1986 by Longman).
6 In the encyclical *Humani Generis*, 1950.
7 Nicholas Berdyaev, *Der Sinn des Schaffens* (*The Meaning of Creativity*), J. C. B. Mohr, Tübingen, 1927, German trans. by Reinhold von Walter, p. 339. My translation into English.
8 Jeffrey Masson and Susan McCarthy, *When Elephants Weep* (London: Jonathan Cape, 1994). p. 208.
9 Ibid., p 193.
10 Ibid. p. 191.
11 Steven Fischer, *A History of Language* (London: Reaktion Books, paperback edition, 2001), pp. 11–13 (original publication 1999). The whole of this book is worth reading.
12 Ibid., p. 55.
13 Paul Davies, *Superforce*, revised Penguin edn, 1995, p. 39.
14 B. Long, *Only Fear Dies* (London: Barry Long Books, 1994), p. 1. (original publication 1984).
15 John Schwarz of Caltech, quoted by Timothy Ferris in *The Whole Shebang* (London: Weidenfeld & Nicolson, 1997), p. 222 (original publication 1992).
16 Cf. what was said above (p. 48) about the realisation of the universal self in one's own self as the highest achievement for the human being.

17 Alfred North Whitehead, *Religion in the Making* (Cambridge University Press, 1927), (The Lowell Lectures of 1926), p. 30.
18 Voltaire (1694–1778) in his novel *Candide*.
19 *Pippa Passes*, pt. I, l.228.
20 1343 – died after 1413. The quotation is from her *Revelations of Love*, 13th Revelation.
21 William Paley's *View of the Evidences of Christianity*, 1794. (This was a view that had already been declared untenable by the Scottish philosopher David Hume, e.g. in *Enquiry Concerning Human Understanding*, 1748).
22 See above, pp. 29–31 for remarks on freedom and determinism.
23 *In Memoriam*, ll. 56 and 54
24 Shakespeare's *Macbeth*, Act V, Scene V: Macbeth's speech in verses 17–18.
25 Schweitzer's phrase, in his *Indian Thought and its Development*, passim.
26 In her splendid book, *Shiva*, 1973.
27 Y. Menuhin, *Unfinished Journey*, p. 337.
28 Sir S. Radhakrishnan, 'Hinduism' in *The Legacy of India*, ed. G. T. Garratt (Oxford: Clarendon Press, 1937), p. 275.
29 Huston Smith, *The World's Religions* (San Francisco: HarperCollins, 1991), p. 38. Quoted by K. R. Nicholson, *The Prospect of Immortality* (Draper, Utah: Homeward Bound Publishing Inc., 1964/1999), p. 338.
30 Paul Tillich, *Christianity and the Encounter of the World Religions* (New York: Columbia University Press, 1964), pp. 88–9 (first published 1963). Tillich is expressing the view of Christian mystics.
31 See the Wordsworth edition, 1996, pp. 106–7.

CHAPTER SEVEN **The Christian Doctrine of Incarnation: Restricted Immanence**

1 *The Doctrine of the Person of Jesus Christ* (Edinburgh: T. & T. Clark, 1912; 2nd edition 1948), p. 10.
2 In a letter in which he expresses the great respect he had for Jesus. Quoted in Robert Gittings, *Selected Poems and Letters of Keats* (Heinemann, 1966), p. 112.
3 In *The Faith of the Church*, Fontana edition, 1960, p. 66. For Barth's doctrine of the Incarnation one must study his *Kirchliche Dogmatik*, vol. I, 2, pp. 1–221; for the present context see pp. 3 and 17. (English translation, *Church Dogmatics*).
4 C. H. Dodd, *The Apostolic Preaching*, 1944, pp. 46 ff., cited by R. McL. Wilson in *Peake's Commentary on the Bible*, p. 799, § 696b.
5 Mark 6: 3
6 John Spong, *Why Christianity Must Change or Die* (New York: HarperCollins, 1998).
7 A. E. Taylor, *Aristotle* (Thomas Nelson and Sons Ltd., London, Edinburgh, Paris, Melbourne, Toronto, New York, 1943), p. 108. First published 1919.
8 His gospel ends on a more universalist note. See *Peake's Commentary on the Bible*, p. 770, § 673f.
9 Matthew 27: 51.
10 Matthew 1: 16.
11 K. Stendahl, in *Peake's Commentary on the Bible* (original publication 1962), § 673 c and f, (London: Nelson, 1975 reprint).
12 Matthew 24 and 25.
13 Luke 16: 19–31; 18: 1–8; 18: 9–14.

14 John 1: 29.
15 John 19: 36.
16 John 11: 25.
17 John 8: 58.
18 Acts of the Apostles 9: 20.
19 Genesis 6: 1–4.
20 Matthew 23: 9.
21 See Matthew 3: 16–17.
22 Matthew 28: 19.
23 See Marvin Meyer, *The Secret Gospels of Jesus* (London: Darton, Longman & Todd, 2005), p. 5.
24 See *The Koran* in English translation and notes by N. J. Dawood (Harmondsworth: Penguin Books, 1977), p. 70 (original publication 1956).
25 See David Waines, *An Introduction to Islam* (Cambridge: Cambridge University Press, 1995; 1998 reprint), p. 57.
26 For the following account of the 'Messianic Secret' I am much indebted to J. W. Bowman's article, 'The Life and Teaching of Jesus', in *Peake's Commentary on the Bible* (London: Nelson, 1962; 1975 reprint, p. 736, § 641c–f.
27 There are numerous references to this in 1 and 2 Samuel, 1 and 2 Chronicles and Psalms.
28 See Psalm 2: 7 and Psalm 89: 27 (referring to David's accession).
29 For this and more see *Tibetan Yoga and Secret Doctrines*, ed. W. Y. Evans-Wantz (Oxford: Oxford University Press, 2nd edn, 1958), (original publication 1935).
30 See Evelyn Underhill, *Mysticism* (London: Bracken Books, edn 1955), pp. 188, 376 and 577.
31 Quoted in J. W. Bowman's article, 'The Life and Teaching of Jesus', in *Peake's Commentary on the Bible*, p. 737, §642e.
32 Matthew 27: 11–15, 16–20.
33 See *Peake's Commentary*, §301b, pp. 348–9.
34 I believe Don Cupitt used this word in *The Myth of God Incarnate*.
35 *The Person of Jesus Christ* (Edinburgh: T & T Clark, 1948, first published 1912), p. 112: for Origen, see pp. 164ff.
36 Quoted by R .A. Nicholson in his article on 'Mysticism' in *The Legacy of Islam*, 1968, ed. by Thomas Arnold and Alfred Guillaume (Oxford: Oxford University Press, original publication 1931), p. 232.

CHAPTER EIGHT **Incarnation and Atonement Mythology**

1 Duckworth, London, 1947, Preface, page v. (first published 1915).
2 John 11: 27.
3 Mark 14: 35–36; also in Luke 22: 42.
4 For this New Testament repetition of an Old Testament motif see Thomas L. Thompson's excellent book, *The Bible in History* (Pimlico, 2000,) pp. 21–3 (original publication 1999, Jonathan Cape).
5 John 11: 27.
6 See her *Mysticism* (London: Bracken Books, 1942), p. 24, footnote (original publication 1911).
7 For much of this glimpse into the Orpheus–Dionysus cult see Joseph Campbell, *The Masks of God*, vol. 3, *Occidential Mythology* (Arkana, 1991), p. 183 (original publication 1964).

8 Some 3rd century Christians believed that God himself died on the cross. If they were right, the modern cries of 'God is dead' are rather belated! Who has been standing in for God all these centuries?

9 In his *Freedom and the Spirit*, pp. 350 and 352–3.

10 A line from Stainer's *Crucifixion*.

11 Luke 15: 11–32 .

12 *Documents of the Christian Church*, ed. Henry Bettenson (Oxford: Oxford University Press, 1946), p. 366. (original publication 1943).

13 Ibid., p. 382.

14 An illustration in the 17th century CE manuscript of the Norse-Germanic Prose Edda shows Thor catching the cosmic serpent on a fish-hook. This attempt failed – luckily, since the cosmic serpent held the world together. See Sheila Savill, *Pears Encyclopaedia of Myths and Legends* (London: Book Club Associates, 1977), p. 65. It is interesting that the cosmic Christ was said to hold the world together (Colossians 1: 17).

15 Joseph Campbell, *The Masks of God*, vol. 2: *Oriental Mythology*, p. 392.

16 See above, pp. 100–2.

17 "Wird Christus tausendmal zu Bethlehem geboren Und nicht in dir, du bleibst noch ewiglich verloren." – Angelus Silesius, quoted in W. R. Inge, *Mysticism in Religion* (London: Hutchinson, n.d.), p. 164.

18 Colossians 1: 9–11.

19 See H. R. Mackintosh, *The Person of Jesus Christ* (Edinburgh: T. & T. Clark, 1948, p. 168 (original publication 1912).

20 See K. S. Latourette, *A History of Christianity*, p. 711.

21 Kenneth Clark, *Civilisation* (London: BBC Books and John Murray, 1969), published 1987, p. 29.

22 See Peter de Rosa, *Vicars of Christ* (London: Corgi Books, 1993, p. 4), (original publication 1988).

23 In his *Freedom and the Spirit*, pp. 342–3.

24 John 3: 16–17.

25 Christus ist nicht ausser uns, sondern in uns; Er ist der Absolute Mensch in uns, Er ist unser Teilhaben an der heiligen Dreifaltigkeit," *Der Sinn des Schaffens (The Meaning of Creativity)*, p. 277.

26 John Marsh, 'The Theology of the New Testament', in *Peake's Commentary on the Bible*, Nelson, 1975 reprint, § 667c.

27 Colossians 1: 16–17.

28 John 1: 1–14a.

29 See, e.g., Psalm 53.

30 For fuller exposition see E. Loth, *Vedanta Approaches to God* (London: Macmillan, 1980).

31 Rudolf Otto, *The Idea of the Holy* (Harmondsworth: Penguin Books, 1959), p. 71 (original publication 1917).

32 See L. S. Thornton, *The Common Life in the Body of Christ* (London: Dacre Press, A.&C. Black, 3rd edition, 1950, original publication 1942).

33 Caroline Myss, *Anatomy of the Spirit* (Bantam Books, 1997), p. 64.

34 Ibid., p. 67.

35 Ibid., p. 67.

36 See above, p. 33.

CHAPTER NINE   Creativity, Divine and Human

1 Geoffrey Bles, *Freedom and the* Spirit (London: Centenary Press, 1935), p. 307.
2 "Sonntags gehen wir Kirche. An sechs Tagen der Woche gehen wir unserer schöpferischen Arbeit nach. Und unser schöpferisches Verhalten zum Leben bleibt ungerechtfertigt; es ist nicht geheiligt, es ist mit dem religiösen Lebens-prinzip nicht mit untergeordnet." *Der Sinn des Schaffens* (*The Meaning of Creativity*) (1927) German translation by Reinhold von Walter (Tübingen: J.C.B. Mohr), p. 365.
3 Quoted by Evelyn Underhill, *Mysticism* (Bracken Books, 1995), p. 418 (original publication 1911).
4 Ibid., p. 419.
5 See e.g., Mark 9: 2–8.
6 *Religion in the Making* (Cambridge: Cambridge University Press, 1927), p. 85.
7 See his *Existentialism and Humanism* (London: Eyre Methuen Ltd., 1975), pp. 26ff. French edition published 1946 as *L'Existentialisme est un humanisme*.
8 *The Fear of Freedom* is the title of a best-selling book by Erich Fromm, psychologist.
9 See Kierkegaard's *Journals, 1850–54*.
10 *Tibetan Book of Living and Dying* (London: Rider, 1992), p. 63.
11 *I and Thou* (New York: Charles Scribner's Sons, 1958), p. 16. (original publication in French, *Je et Tu*, 1923).
12 In Preface to 2nd edn.of *Lyrical Ballads*, 1802.
13 See Walford Davies' Introduction to *William Wordsworth: selected poems* (London: Dent / Everyman's Library, 1984), p. xi (original publication 1975).
14 Max Auer, in 1946, quoted in Hans Hubert Schönzeler's *Bruckner* (London: Calder & Boyars Ltd., 1970), p. 169.
15 From a letter to his patroness Nadezhda von Meck, quoted in David Brown's *Tchaikovsky* (London: Gollancz, 1982), Vol. II, p. 230 (original publication 1978).
16 Ibid.
17 D. Bohm, *Unfolding Meaning* (London: Ark, 1987).
18 In *Art of the Real*, p. 11, quoted by Anna C. Chave in her article, 'Minimalism of the Rhetoric of Power' in *Art in Modern Culture*, ed. by Francis Frascina and Jonathan Harris (London: Phaidon, 1992), p. 266.
19 *Art in Modern Culture*, plate 47. The item itself was given to the Whitney Museum of American Art, New York.
20 Quoted by Anna Chave, op. cit., p. 267, where plate 46 shows the tube.
21 *The Divine and the Human*, p. 144.
22 From "*The Beginning and the End*".
23 "Die höchste Aufgabe des Menschen ist aber das Erschaffen eines neuen Lebens." *Der Sinn des Schaffens*, German translation by Reinhold von Walter (Tübingen: J.C.B. Mohr, 1927), p. 281 (original publication 1926).
24 Nicolas Berdyaev, *Freedom and the Spirit*, p. 332.
25 I have given the phrase in its neuter form as Jung did; but it was also used in feminine and masculine forms.
26 Jung, *The Archetypes of the Collective Unconscious, Collected Works of C. G. Jung*, vol. IX, Part 1, p. 28, para. 60.

CHAPTER TEN   **Divinity and Ethics**

1   A. N. Whitehead, *Religion in the Making* (Cambridge: Cambridge University Press, 1927), p. 31.

2   See Altizer & Hamilton's, *Radical Theology and the Death of God*, 1966 (Penguin edn, 1968), p. 58.

3   Quoted by W. R. Inge, in *The Platonic Tradition in English Religious Thought* (London: Longmans, Green & Co. Ltd., 1926), p. 53.

4   Pharisees were not always 'pharisaical' in the sense assigned by Jesus (or the early Christian Church) in the Gospels. (And not all Christians deserve the criticisms I make of 'Christianity' or 'the Church').

5   Page 83 in 1960 edn, Unwin, London (first publication 1935).

6   See Colin Alves in Ninian Smart and Donald Horder, eds., *New Movements in Religious Education* (London: Temple Smith, 1975), p. 25.

7   (London: SCM Press, 1976 (first British edn, 1966).

8   Epistle of James 1: 27.

9   J. S. Mill, on the other hand, was glad when black slavery ended, and said it was then time to end the slavery of women!

10   "The philosophers have only *interpreted* the world, in various ways; the point is to *change* it" (Marx's own italics). See *Karl Marx, Early Writings* (Harmondsworth: Penguin, 1975), p. 423. (These theses on Feuerbach were written in 1845).

11   *The Destiny of Man* (London: Bles, 1954), p. 62 (first published 1937).

12   Nietzsche, *Thus Spake Zarathustra*, Part I, Section 1; English translation by Walter Kaufmann in *The Portable Nietzsche* (New York: Viking Press, 1954), p. 137.

13   Rider: an imprint of Random House, 1992.

CHAPTER ELEVEN   **Religion and Science**

1   1919; Eng. tr. by C.K. Ogden, 1924.

2   Karl Popper (1959), *The Logic of Scientific Discovery* (Hutchinson; 11th impression 1982), (original publication as *Logik der Forschung*, Springer, 1934).

3   S. W. Hawking, *A Brief History of Time* (London, New York: Bantam Press, 1988, 1990 reprint), p. 10.

4   Paul Tillich, *The Shaking of the Foundations* (London: SCM Press, 1957), p. 181.

5   Corrected Edition, edited by Griffin & Sherburne (Free Press, 1985).

6   Richard Dawkins, *A Devil's Chaplain* (London: Phoenix, an imprint of Orion Books Ltd., 2003, paperback edn 2004), p. 31.

7   See his *Interpretations of Poetry and Religion* (New York: Charles Scribner's Sons, 1900).

8   See above, pp. 000–000.

9   Quoted in *Hutchinson's Dictionary of Science*, ed. by Peter Lafferty and Julian Rower (Oxford: Helicon, 1993, paperback edn. 1997), p. 582.

CHAPTER TWELVE   **The 'Problem' of Evil; Providence**

1   A. Turner, *Just Capital* (London: Pan Books, 2002), p. 376 (original publication 2001).

2   Ibid., p. 377.

3   D. Rowe, *Depression*, 2nd. edition (London and New York: Routledge, 1996), p. 13 (first published 1983).

4   Quoted by Marcus Chown in his article, *'It's all down to a roll of the dice'*, in the 6 October 2007 issue of *New Scientist*.

5   In an essay to be found on <www.templeton.org/purpose>.

6   See the Chown article – referred to above – in *New Scientist*.

7   Ibid.

8   R. W. Emerson, *Essays* (Oxford: Oxford University Press, 1901), p. 153 (original publication in two parts, 1841 and 1844).

9   Sogyal, *The Tibetan Book of Living and Dying* (London: Rider, 1992), p. 104.

10   Ibid., p. 105.

11   Ibid., p. 105.

12   Ibid., p. 316.

13   In the *Saga* magazine, February 1998 issue.

14   Sogyal, *The Tibetan Book of Living and Dying*, p. 363.

15   Dionysius the pseudo-Areopagite (*c.* 500 CE), a mystical theologian, quoted in Kenneth Clark, *Civilisation* (London: BBC Books and John Murray, 1987), p. 60 (original publication 1969). Clark – but not Dionysius – had Chartres Cathedral in mind.

16   Exodus 20: 5.

17   B. Long, B., *Only Fear Dies* (London: Barry Long Books, 1994), p. 120 (original publication 1984).

18   B. Long, *Only Fear Dies*

CHAPTER THIRTEEN   **Death – and Beyond?**

1   A. N. Whitehead, *Process and Reality* (New York: Free Press, 1985), p. 187 (original publication 1978), p. 104 (Gifford Lectures 1927–28)

2   B. Long, *Only Fear Dies* (London: Barry Long Books, 1994), p. 45 (originally published 1984).

3   See Richard Dawkins, *A Devil's Chaplain* (London: Phoenix, 2004), p. 203. (first published 2003).

4   A. N. Whitehead, *Process and Reality* (New York: Free Press, 1985), p. 187 (original publication 1978).

5   H. Vasari, *The Lives of the Artists*, translated by George Bull (Harmondsworth: Penguin Books, 1971), p. 425. (originally published, 1965).

6   Bhagavadgita 2: 18.

7   N. Berdyaev, N., *The Beginning and the End*, translated from the Russian by R. M. French (London: Geoffrey Bles, 1952), p. 44.

8   Mark 12: 25 (and parallels in Luke and Matthew)

9   B. Long, *Only Fear Dies* (London: Barry Long Books, 1994), p. 127 (originally published 1984).

10   Ibid., p. 130. (The belief that one's spiritual body is accessible at the moment before falling asleep is found in Chinese philosophy).

11   William Wordsworth (1807), *Ode: Intimations of Immortality*, 5 : 65–9. Wordsworth had already begun the writing of it in March 1802: see J. Barker, *Wordsworth: a Life* (London: Viking, Penguin Group, 2000), p. 315.

12   Among the many books that deal with the spirit world, one of the best is that by O'Sullivan, T. & N., *Soul Rescuers* (London: Thorsons/HarperCollins, 2000), (original publication 1999).

13   On this see B. Long, B. (1994), pp. 136 ff. The quotations that follow are from pp. 138 ff.

14 Jung (1951), *Aion*, p. 261, *Collected Works*, vol. 9: 2. Quoted in F. Capra (1983), *The Turning Point* (London: Flamingo imprint of HarperCollins, 1983), pp. 396–7 (original publication 1982).

15 J. Renard, *The Handy Religion Answer Book* (Detroit: Visible Art Press, 2002), p. 264.

16 Sogyal (1992), *The Tibetan Book of Living and Dying* (London: Rider, imprint of Random House UK Ltd., 1992), pp. 344–5.

17 Barry Long, ibid., p. 126.

18 B. Long, (1994), p. 126.

19 Translated by Frederick C. Grant in C. G. Grant, *Hellenistic Religions* (New York, 1953), pp. 157–8.

20 H. Frankfort, *Ancient Egyptian Religion* (New York: Harper Torchbooks, 1961), p. 92 (original publication 1948).

21 Ibid., p. 89.

22 Sogyal, Rinpoche (= 'Reverend') (1992), *The Tibetan Book of Living and Dying*, edited by Patrick Gaffney and Andrew Harvey (London: Rider/Random House, 1992), p. 106.

23 Ibid., p. 105.

24 Ibid., p. 226.

25 Lord Martin Rees, on BBC Radio 3, April 2006.

26 P. Davies, *Superforce* (London: Penguin Books, 1995), p. 132 (original publication 1984).

27 See D. L. Edwards, *After Death?* (London and New York: Continuum, 2001), p. 34 (first published 1999).

28 J. Barker, *Wordsworth: a Life* (London: Viking, Penguin Group, 2000), p. 315.

29 Horace, Roman poet (65–68 BCE).

Select Bibliography

Altizer, Thomas J. J. & Hamilton, William (1968) [1966], *Radical Theology & the Death of God*, Penguin, London.

Anderson, M. (2007) article, *Don't stop till you get to the Fluff* in *New Scientist*, vol. 06.01.2007.

Anderson, W. (1998), *Green Man*, Compass Books, Fakenham, England.

Berdyaev, Nicolas (1927), *Der Sinn des Schaffens (The Meaning of Creativity)* German tr., J. C. B. Mohr (Paul Siebeck) Tübingen. (Russian original 1911).

—— (1954) [1937], *The Destiny of Man*, Geoffrey Bles, London.

—— (1949) [1944], *The Divine & the Human*, Geoffrey Bles, London.

—— (1983) [1952], *The Beginning and the End*, Geoffrey Bles, London.

Bettenson, Henry (1946) [1943] ed., *Documents of the Christian Church*, Oxford University Press, London.

Blake, William (1996), *Complete Writings*, ed. G. Keynes, Oxford University Press, USA.

Buber, Martin (1937) [1923], *I and Thou*, Scribner, London.

Campbell, Joseph (1991), *The Masks of God*, 4 vols. (original publication 1959–68), Penguin Books, London & New York.

Capra, Fritjof (1983), *The Turning Point: science, society and the rising culture*, Flamingo (Harper-Collins), London.

Coates, A. J. (1997), *The Ethics of War*, Manchester University Press; particularly for jihad, Christian crusades, & the Falklands War (for which see index).

Davies, Paul (1995) [1984], *Superforce*, Penguin, London.

Dawkins, Richard (1991), *The Blind Watchmaker*, Penguin, London.

Edwards, D. L. (2001) [1991], *After Death?*, Continuum, London & New York.

Eliade, Mircea (1959), *The Sacred & the Profane*, Harcourt, Brace & World Inc., New York.

Ferris, Timothy (1997), *The Whole Shebang*, Weidenfeld & Nicolson, London.

Feuerbach, Ludwig (1855), *The Essence of Christianity*, Blanchard, New York.

Fletcher, Joseph (1976) [1966], *Situation Ethics*, SCM Press, London.

Fox, Matthew (2000), *Sins of the Spirit, Blessings of the Flesh*, Gateway, Dublin.

Frascina, Francis & Harris, Jonathan (1992) eds., *Art in Modern Culture*, Phaidon, London.

Gruen, Lori & Jamieson, Dale (1994) eds., *Reflecting on Nature*, Oxford University Press, Oxford & New York.

Hawking, S. W. (1988), *A Brief History of Time*, Bantam Press, London, New York etc., 1990 reprint, p. 10.

Higgins, Kathleen M. & Solomon, Robert C. (1988) ed., *Reading Nietzsche*, Oxford University Press, USA.

Hobsbawn, Eric (1994), *The Age of Extremes*, Abacus, UK; particularly chs. 1, 6, 7, 12, 13 & 15.

Kaufmann, Walter (1954) ed., *The Portable Nietzsche*, Viking Press, New York.

Latourette, Kenneth Scott (1955), *A History of Christianity*, Eyre & Spottiswoode, London.

Long, Barry (1994), *Only Fear Dies*, Barry Long Books, London.

Masson, Jeffrey Moussaieff & McCarthy, Susan (1994), *When Elephants Weep: The Emotional Lives of Animals*, Jonathan Cape, London.

Myss, Caroline (1997), *Anatomy of the Spirit*, Bantam Books, London.

Nietzsche, Friedrich (1974) [1882], *The Joyful Science [Die fröhliche Wissenschaft]*, Vintage, New York.

—— (1969) [1884, 1891], *Thus Spake Zarathustra, [Also sprach Zarathustra]*, tr. R. J. Hollingdale, Penguin, London.

—— (1968) [1888], *The Twilight of the Gods [Die Götzendämmerung]*, tr. R. J. Hollingdale, Penguin, London.

Otto, Rudolf (1959) [1917], *The Idea of the Holy*, Penguin, London.

Popper, Karl (1959) [1934], *The Logic of Scientific Discovery*, Hutchinson, [Logik der Forschung, Springer 1934].

Robinson, J. A. T. (1963) [1988], *Honest To God*, SCM Press, London.

de Rosa, Peter (1993) [1988], *Vicars of Christ*, Corgi Books, London.

Sartre, Jean-Paul (1975), *Existentialism & Humanism*, Eyre Methuen, London.

Schweitzer, Albert (2005) [1906], *The Quest of the Historical Jesus*, Dover Publications, USA. [Original publication as *Von Reimarus zu Wrede*].

Sogyal, Rinpoche (1992), *The Tibetan Book of Living and Dying*, Rider, London.

Spong, James (1998), *Why Christianity must Change or Die*, HarperCollins, New York.

Teilhard de Chardin, Pierre (1965), *The Phenomenon of Man*, Fontana, London; revised edition, *The Human Phenomenon*, translated by Sarah Appleton-Weber, Portland and Brighton, Sussex Academic Press, 1990.

Thompson, Thomas L. (2000), *The Bible in History*, Pimlico, London.

Thornton, L. S. (1950) [1942], *The Common Life in the Body of Christ*, Dacre Press (A. & C. Black), London.

Tillich, Paul (1948), *The Shaking of the Foundations*, Charles Scribner's Sons, New York.

—— (1951–63), *Systematic Theology*, 3 vols., Nisbet, London.

—— (1964), *Christianity and the Encounter of the World Religions*, Columbia University Press, New York, pp. 88 – 9 (First published 1963).

—— (1997) [1952], *The Courage to Be*, Collins, Glasgow.

Tipler, Frank (1996), *The Physics of Immortality*, paperback edn., Pan Books, London.

Turner, Adair (2002), *Just Capital*, Pan Books, London.

Underhill, Evelyn (1942) [1911], *Mysticism*, Bracken Books, London.

Wand, J. W. C. (1953) [1937], *A History of the Early Church*, Methuen, London.

Whitehead, Alfred North (1927), *Religion in the Making*, Cambridge University Press, UK.

—— (1985) [1929], *Process & Reality*, The Free Press, New York.

Index